GENEALOGY
QuickSteps®

About the Author

Marty Matthews has been a programmer, system analyst, manager, executive, and entrepreneur in the software business for many years. For over 25 years he has authored, co-authored, or managed the writing and production of over 100 books. For even more time he has been interested in his family history and genealogy in general, being at best a nuisance to his relatives. His recent books include *Computing for Seniors Quicksteps*, *Windows 7 for Seniors QuickSteps*, and *Facebook for Seniors QuickSteps*. He lives on an island in Puget Sound in Washington State.

Bobbi Sandberg has long been involved with computers, accounting, and writing. She is a retired accountant currently filling her time as a trainer, technical writer, and small-business consultant. She teaches at several venues, offering step-by-step instruction in a variety of computer applications. Her extensive background, coupled with her ability to explain complex concepts in plain language, has made her a popular instructor, consultant, and speaker. Since her teen years, she has been poring through old papers and family photos to learn more of her family's history, which led to her interest in genealogy. She has authored and co-authored more than a dozen computer books, including *Quicken 2012: The Official Guide* and *Computing for Seniors QuickSteps*. She lives near the site where her maternal great-grandmother was born.

GENEALOGY
QuickSteps®

MARTY MATTHEWS
BOBBI SANDBERG

New York Chicago San Francisco
Lisbon London Madrid Mexico City
Milan New Delhi San Juan
Seoul Singapore Sydney Toronto

The McGraw·Hill Companies

Library of Congress Cataloging-in-Publication Data

Matthews, Martin S.
 Genealogy quicksteps / Marty Matthews, Bobbi Sandberg.
  p. cm.
 ISBN 978-0-07-178420-7 (alk. paper)
 1. Genealogy—Computer network resources—Handbooks,
manuals, etc. 2. Genealogy—Data processing—Handbooks,
manuals, etc. 3. Internet searching—Handbooks, manuals, etc.
4. United States—Genealogy—Handbooks, manuals, etc.
I. Sandberg, Bobbi. II. Title.
CS21.5.M37   2012
929.1072'073—dc23   2012015873

GENEALOGY QUICKSTEPS®

1234567890   QDB QDB   1098765432

ISBN   978-0-07-178420-7
MHID   0-07-178420-9

SPONSORING EDITOR / Roger Stewart

EDITORIAL SUPERVISOR / Patty Mon

PROJECT MANAGER / Vastavikta Sharma, Cenveo Publisher Services

ACQUISITIONS COORDINATOR / Ryan Willard

COPY EDITOR / Lisa McCoy

PROOFREADER / Claire Splan

INDEXER / Valerie Perry

PRODUCTION SUPERVISOR / George Anderson

COMPOSITION / Cenveo Publisher Services

ILLUSTRATION / Cenveo Publisher Services

ART DIRECTOR, COVER / Jeff Weeks

COVER DESIGNER / Pattie Lee

SERIES CREATORS / Marty and Carole Matthews

SERIES DESIGN / Bailey Cunningham

To our ancestors, without whom we wouldn't be here!
May we understand and learn from your lives.

Contents at a Glance

Contents

4   Chapter 4   **Identifying Web Resources** 75

5   Chapter 5   **Entering and Using Online Sites** 101

9   Chapter 9   **Getting Around Roadblocks** **211**

10   Chapter 10   **Pulling It All Together** **235**

Acknowledgments

This book is greatly enhanced by the real-life genealogy stories that are included in each chapter. We are therefore very indebted to the people who spent time with us and added their stories to ours. Our heartfelt thanks to Jenanne Murphy, Trevor Arnold, Tom Beard, Pam Brager, Becky Foote, Peter Wolf, Anne Colligan, and Harriett DeWolfe, whose stories are included here, and to Daniel Mulhaney and Mark Williams whose stories could not be included due to page and time constraints.

We are, as always, indebted to the editing, layout, proofreading, indexing, and project management expertise of a number of people, only some of whom we know. We thank all of them and in particular acknowledge:

- **Roger Stewart**, editorial director and sponsoring editor of this book and the QuickSteps series
- **Patty Mon**, editorial supervisor
- **George Anderson**, production supervisor
- **Vastavikta Sharma**, project manager
- **Ryan Willard**, acquisitions coordinator
- **Valerie Perry**, indexer
- **Lisa McCoy,** copy editor
- **Claire Splan,** proofreader
- **Cenveo Publisher Services**, layout and production

—Bobbi and Marty

Introduction

Interest in genealogy is probably as old as mankind. We have always wanted to know where we came from. Today, answering that is easier than ever with the huge amount of genealogy information that is immediately available online. The purpose of this book is to make finding and using that information easier, and maybe even fun.

QuickSteps® books are recipe books for computer users. They answer the question "How do I…" by providing a quick set of steps to accomplish the most common tasks for a particular situation.

The sets of steps are the central focus of the book. QuickSteps sidebars show how to quickly perform many small functions or tasks that support the primary functions. QuickFacts sidebars supply information that you need to know about a subject. Notes, Tips, and Cautions augment the steps and are presented in a separate column so they do not interrupt the flow of the steps. The introductions are minimal rather than narrative, and numerous illustrations and figures, many with callouts, support the steps.

Genealogy QuickSteps describes some of the most common ways people are using computers and the Internet to search for and use their own ancestral information. It not only covers core Internet sites and programs, such as Ancestry.com, FamilySearch.org, Family Tree Maker, and Legacy, but also how to go beyond the technology and use libraries, cemeteries, genealogy societies, and professional genealogists to find the answers that are sought.

Explore QuickSteps books on QuickStepsBooks.com and follow us (QuickSteps Books) on ▪ Facebook and ➤ Twitter.

Conventions Used in This Book

Genealogy QuickSteps uses several conventions designed to make the book easier for you to follow:

- A 🔍 in the How To list in each chapter references a QuickSteps sidebar in the chapter; a 🌀 references a QuickFacts sidebar.

- **Bold type** is used for words or objects on the screen that you are to do something with—for example, "click **Start** and click **Computer**."

- *Italic type* is used for a word or phrase that is being defined or otherwise deserves special emphasis.

- <u>Underlined type</u> is used for text that you are to type from the keyboard.

- SMALL CAPITAL LETTERS are used for keys on the keyboard, such as **ENTER** and **SHIFT**.

- When you are expected to enter a command, you are told to press the key(s). If you are to enter text or numbers, you are told to type them.

Chapter 1
Stepping into Genealogy

So just what is genealogy? The word itself stems from the Greek words for generation and knowledge, therefore the study of previous generations or your ancestry. Today, professional genealogists help others document their ancestry and provide scholarly proof of relationships. Documents and records are verified and cited, in much the same way as academic researchers prove their work. However, many other people become involved in tracking their "family history," a phrase that may sound more understandable and interesting than a scientific analysis of who married whom and when. So what is the fascination of finding out that your great-great-great-grandfather's brother went on a Crusade for the king? And, why do so many people spend time viewing tombstones when it isn't Halloween? The answer for each person is as unique as the family they want to research, and there are as many ways of discovering this information. Personal computers and the Internet have expanded by at least a thousand times what the individual family historian can do, the ease with which she can do it, and the degree of collaboration possible. Through this book you will find out how to make the best use of these tools, as well as ideas on where to begin, how to continue, and what to do when you reach the inevitable roadblocks.

Explore Genealogy

At the very beginning of your genealogical journey, you may have a specific goal in mind—say, discovering who was the first person in your family who graduated from high school (or in more modern times, college), or from whom the tendency for red hair comes. Each family is different and has its own set of legends, tall tales (and tall-tale tellers), and good old-fashioned yarns that get us excited about wanting to find the real story, which often is more interesting than the tall tale—if for no other reason than the evidence points to it being true.

Consider What Can You Do with It

So, if you put a lot of your time into genealogy, and maybe some money, what do you get back?

SATISFY YOUR CURIOSITY

Perhaps the most common reason for starting your genealogy research is to discover something. For example, Bobbi was told that one of her ancestors was the first non-native child born on the island on which she now resides. That got her curiosity aroused—just who *was* that person and when did it happen? Is there a family story that you've heard that you'd like to prove? For example, Bobbi's family talks about an ancestor that fought on both sides during the Civil War. So far, that's not been verified, but what a fascinating tale!

QUICK**FACTS**

FINDING U.S. MILITARY INFORMATION

Many genealogy sites offer access to military records for a small membership fee. The best of these for finding U.S. military data may be Fold3.com, which emphasizes military information. You can also find information online at Ancestry.com and Archives.com.

If you know the serial number of the person who served, you can write to the National Archives Records Administration in Washington, D.C., to request the appropriate form and its cost. The National Personnel Records Center, Military Personnel Records Office in St. Louis, Missouri, is another option. Again, you must request a form, which may cost a small fee.

Serial numbers were used by all of the branches of the service through 1969. The Army and Air Force replaced the serial number with the service member's Social Security number starting then. In 1972, the Navy and Marine Corps followed suit, and the Coast Guard started using Social Security numbers as identifiers instead of serial numbers in 1974.

You may also find serial number information on his or her discharge papers, from your county offices, or even the Military Affairs Department in the state where the service member resided. Be persistent and you should be able to find the necessary information.

Just where were your grandparents born? Do you have ancestors that arrived at Ellis Island? If so, you can find information about the landing if you know the names and approximate dates. Is there a U.S. military hero in your background? Check the military records on many of the Internet sites to find out. There are records dating back to the American Revolution, as well as the War of 1812; the Civil War; and in more modern times, the Spanish-American War, World War I, and World War II.

ANSWER QUESTIONS

Another reason for beginning your quest is to answer questions. Bobbi was always curious about her maternal grandfather's surname and found that it dates back to the Bible. Other questions can range from "Who did Grandmother Smith marry after Grandfather Smith died" to "Who was first named Absalom?" Often towns were named after the people who settled there. There is a town in Skagit County, Washington, named LaConner after an L.A. Conner, one of the first settlers in the area.

RESOLVE DISPUTES

If there are lingering questions about just where the well was on grandfather's property, or how Aunt Nell wore her hair on her wedding day, you can often do some quick research through family pictures or letters to find the answers. If you want to find information farther back, you may need to go to county or parish records, census data, and so on. We'll be discussing how to work with all of these sources throughout the book.

LEAVE INFORMATION TO YOUR HEIRS

One of the most-mentioned reasons for creating a family history is to let future generations know what their ancestors did. By creating a written and visual record of your unique and wonderful family, you can give your children, grandchildren, and great-grandchildren roots and a look at their heritage. Consider your aunt's recipe for those wonderful baked beans—perhaps you could video her as she's preparing them for your great-granddaughter to reproduce in 60 years.

Bobbi's grandfather kept journals nearly all of his life, as seen in Figure 1-1. He would note the weather and then make some comments about what happened that day.

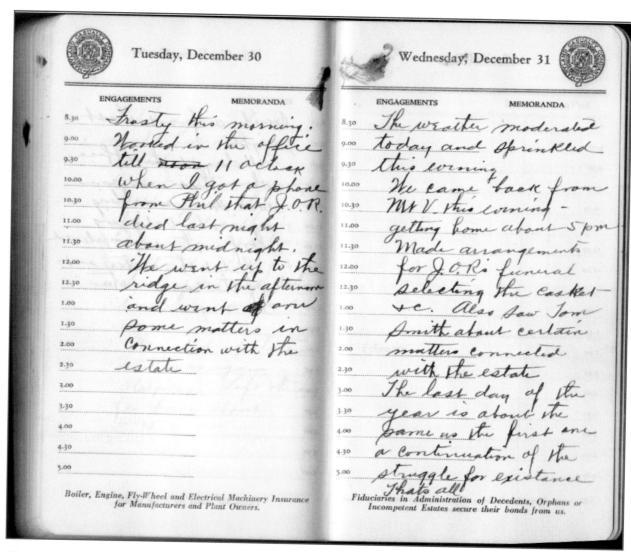

Figure 1-1: **In this journal entry from 1930, A.E. Cornelius noted the passing of his stepfather.**

1. LEANDER WALLACE.
Submitted by Gary Reese

(Bonney, William P. "The Murder of Leander Wallace," History of Pierce County, Washington. Chicago: Pioneer Historical Publishing Company, 1927 p. 54-61.

The act creating Oregon Territory constituted the governor ex-officio superintendent of Indian Affairs, and in that capacity Governor Joseph Lane at once inaugurated an Indian policy. He started on a trip which was intended to take him to the eastern portions of the (Oregon) territory, but when he reached The Dalles, word reached him which caused him to abandon, for a time, his contemplated journey.

This advise was to the effect that Leander C. Wallace, an American citizen, had been murdered on May 1, 1849, by Snoqualmie Indians in an attack upon Fort Nisqually.

An account of the whole affair was recorded in the Journal of Fort Nisqually, kept by Walter Ross, clerk, and is as follows:

"About noon a large party of Snoqualmies and Skewahamish arrived and took up their position before the water gate where they had an affray with our people, in which an American, (Leander) Wallace, was killed and Lewis was slightly wounded. One of the enemy was killed and another wounded.

"The cause and commencement of the difficulty are as follows: As the horn blew for dinner, a large party of Skewhamish and Snoqualmies were reported to have arrived. Our working and other Indians immediately commenced running into the fort and bringing with them their movables.

"When dinner was over, a large party of Snoqualmies, to the number of about one hundred were observed advancing across the plains on the northwest side of the fort; part went to Lahalet's (the Squally chief's) lodge and the others gathered around the water-gate, where they were soon after rejoined by others.

"On being asked the reason for making such a warlike demonstration, they replied that young Lahalet, married to a daughter of one of their petty chiefs, was treating his wife brutally, and they had come to see about it, and did not come with the intention of harming the whites.

"The Chief, Patkanim, was then invited into the fort; to the others was given tobacco to smoke the pipe of peace, for which they retired to one of the deserted lodges. We took the precaution of placing two armed men (Thibeault and Gohome) at the gate, with orders to let none of them in. I also took my gun and went about among our Indians, who were sweeping the fort.

"I had just taken a turn around them when I heard a shot. I repaired to the gate, four or five of the worst Snoqualmies came rushing to the gate. One of their number, Cussass, rudely pushed Gohome into the fort. I demanded why he did that, and told him to keep quiet. He answered only with insolence.

"I then put him out, upon which he cock his gun, and drew his dagger, making two or three thrusts at me. Wren, standing a piece off, was called in. I then directed that the gate be closed; but, finding Wren shut out, it was again opened.

Figure 1-2: **The murder of Leander Wallace, coming within 18 months of the Whitman Massacre, prompted the first murder trial in Pierce County.**

WRITE A BOOK

Some of the most interesting books are biographies—a little bit of "inside" information about the person or persons we might not otherwise know. Some incidents may affect more than just your immediate family. Bobbi's great-great-great-uncle was murdered in 1849, prompting the first murder trial in what is now Pierce County, Washington. (At the time, the area was part of the Oregon Territory.) See Figure 1-2 for a copy of the article about the murder. Many historical books begin with a family history, and with some time put into research, you can write your own.

A distant relative has written two books about two of Bobbi's ancestors, both pioneers in the area. The lives of this mother and daughter spanned the period from before the Civil War to the middle of the Great Depression. From the mother's cross-country journey in a covered wagon in the 1840s to the daughter's passing in 1935, through widowhood and financial hardships, their story is a fascinating tale of the times when water had to be carried from the creek, food was grown "on the place," and a woman could go for months without talking to another woman.

CREATE A WEBSITE

With the advent of the Internet, there are many family websites so everyone in the family can access information, review and edit entries, and add new items. It costs little to create such a website, and by adding pictures, audio and video recordings, and copies of old documents, every member of the family can see the documents, download the items they want to keep, and perhaps listen one more time to the recording of their favorite uncle telling the story about the time he walked across a river on the backs of all the fish that were coming upriver to spawn.

See What Others Have Done

Family research results vary as much as the people doing them. Nearly every family name can be found on at least one website, and usually on more than one. Using various sites on the Internet such as Ancestry.com, USGenWeb.com, CyndisList.com, and RootsWeb.com, many family historians are building their own family trees. Other historians are going to cemeteries, courthouses, and libraries throughout the country (and even the world) to find their family's history. Try typing one of your family surnames into any search engine just to see what will appear.

The process can be time-consuming, but mesmerizing. The "leaf" you may have seen advertised on the Ancestry.com commercials comes up, and it is always fun to see where the latest hint leads you. In many cases, the hint will lead you to another generation's information, or perhaps the maiden name of a great-great-great-great-great-aunt's mother.

INTRODUCE THE STORIES OF OTHERS

In each chapter of this book, we feature a different family historian's story. They will be sharing how they started, what resources they have used, how they have unearthed new information, and many useful tips. Most share how to overcome the inevitable stumbling blocks, such as various spellings of names, name changes, duplicate names, and so on. For example, many families name their children after grandmothers, grandfathers, or other family members, so it is often difficult to ascertain who was the father and who was the son until you verify the birth dates. Many historians have told the tale of finally finding the

CAUTION

Be careful about accepting the information shown in hints. Do your own research and verify information before including it in your family tree!

wife of an ancestor only to discover that the "groom" was actually one of that woman's children.

This leads us to the need to document our findings. While many family historians are not as dedicated about "verifying" a relationship as a professional genealogist, it is important that you verify each of your entries as much as possible. If both a family Bible entry and a copy of a marriage certificate give the same data, the information about the bride and groom is apt to be accurate.

Since many records (including the entire U.S. Census from 1890) have been lost because of fire or other disasters, you can usually find alternative sources of information. Church records, town meeting minutes, newspaper reports, or voters records are a great place to begin.

CONSIDER WHAT OTHERS HAVE ACCOMPLISHED

Family historians and genealogists have discovered both surprising and varied bits of data. For example, one of the storytellers about whom you will read in a later chapter found a relative in Palestine in 1410 through the GenWeb website. Another found that he is descended from royalty. One of Bobbi's ancestors supposedly fought, or at least visited, with both the Union and Confederate sides during the Civil War. You'll also read about one storyteller's family website in which the family is traced back to a castle in England, complete with pictures of the castle!

No matter how far back you can trace your history, you will find interesting anecdotes, family legends, and perhaps the answer to the origin of that traditional family name. By using land claim records, wedding certificates, church records, land grant titles, census data, and county tax rolls, seekers gain volumes of information. As an example, Bobbi's great-great-grandfather and his brother-in-law took advantage of the Donation Land Claim Bill of 1850 to homestead 640 acres each, as Bobbi found on the county tax website shown in Figure 1-3. By the way, the Donation Land Claim Bill was the first law in the United States that allowed married women to hold property in their own name. By law, if a married couple homesteaded under this bill, half of the homestead

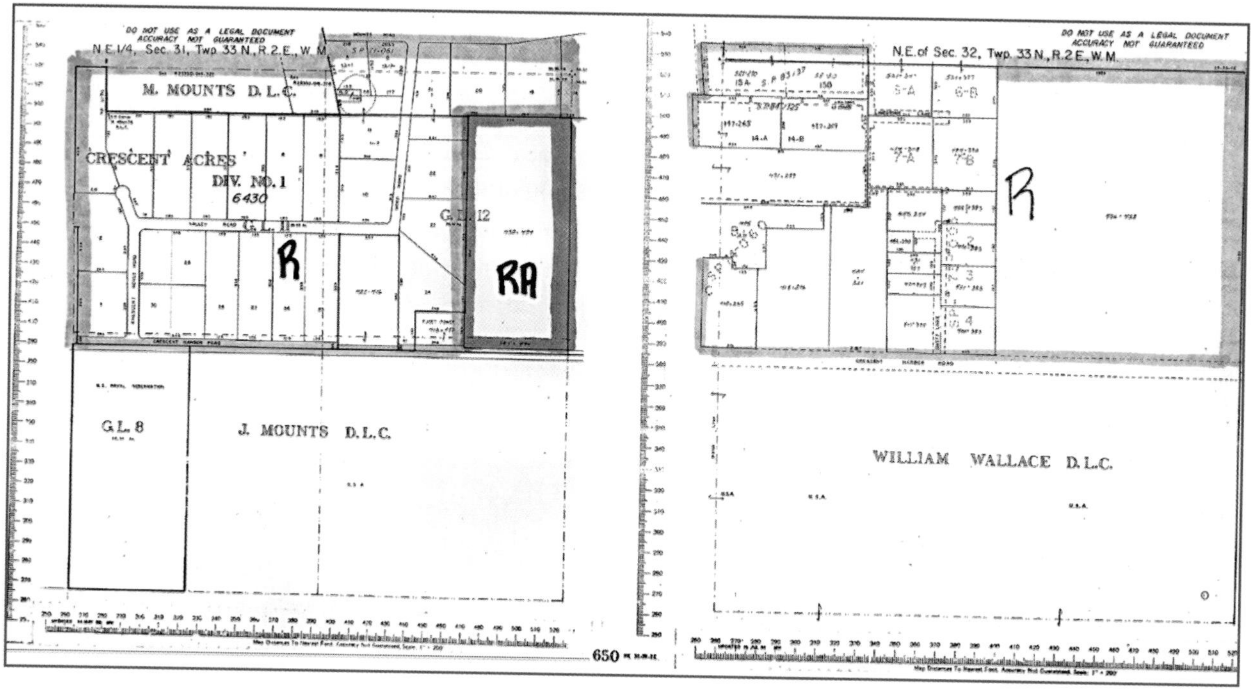

*Figure 1-3: **William Wallace and his wife Ruthinda and Ruthinda's brother, James Mounts, both filed Donation Land Claims (D.L.C.) in what is now Island County, Washington.***

was deemed to be owned by the wife in her own name. This was 70 years before women could legally vote in the United States!

Set Your Objectives

One of the first goals is to decide what you want and just why you are going to start hunting for your ancestral past. Do you want to create a pictorial family tree? Are you trying to find out if an ancestor was a member of a royal family? (If you truly do have royal ancestry, your search will be much easier, as most royal lineage is tracked by the country in which the royals resided.) Is there a medical concern? If so, try to locate death certificates. They may have information that will help in your search, such as a hospital name or cause of death. Obituaries will sometimes show the cause of death. Even if there is no cause of death noted, if donations are suggested to a charity, that might also be a clue.

Do you want to have audio recordings included in your collection? If so, talk to your relatives about sharing their stories in their own voice. A digital recorder is inexpensive and can record memories about earlier times as well as grandparents reading a child's favorite storybook. If you can remember sitting on a grandparent's knee while they were reading to you, think about what a recording could mean to one of your children or grandchildren.

Review the Steps to Get Started

Think about the stories you heard from relatives as a child. Contact cousins, aunts, uncles, anyone in the family and ask about more stories. Even close neighbors can have great information about your family history.

Begin by writing the names and birthplaces of your parents, their siblings, your grandparents (on both sides), and the names of your aunts and uncles. Then start including dates: birth, marriage, and death. If the person was alive in 1935 in the United States but has since passed on, chances are good that information about them will appear in the Social Security Death Index, which is free to use.

Then, start going through old family pictures—hopefully, there will be names and dates, but if not, you can often place the time period by the picture itself. For example, the mode of dress of the picture's subject can place the time. Look in the background; are there wires indicating electricity or telephone connections? Is the subject in uniform? Remember as well that when photography was new, many people posed looking serious to convey the importance of the occasion. So in pictures from the late 1800s until the early 1900s, you will seldom see a smile on anyone's face, as it was considered improper to show emotion. An example of this is shown in Figure 1-4.

Figure 1-4: **Bobbi's grandfather, A.E. Cornelius, as he graduated from college in 1889.**

Discover Your Reasons

Why do you want to learn more about your family? Think about the information you want to learn and how you are going to gather it. Talk to your immediate family members and ask them to help. Once you start gathering information, the pictures, documents, books, and other memorabilia can take up a lot of room. Discuss the project with other, distant family members and start asking for information.

Many historians start with wanting to know which ancestors helped make their Irish, Dutch, Scots, English, Swedish, Cherokee, or Italian heritage. Others start because they want to learn more about history and "what it was like to live back then."

Other reasons can be legal. What happened to the nine acres owned by Uncle John when he passed on without a will? They might find an old stock certificate in their grandfather's papers and need to find if that certificate is worth anything today.

Some families find that past disagreements can be forgotten when they are united in the common cause of locating the great-great grand-uncle that sailed around the Cape of Good Hope. Other researchers are trying to find birth families or what happened to the great-uncle who disappeared just before the turn of the century.

Others start their research in order to join an organization such as the Daughters of the American Revolution or the United Daughters of the Confederacy. Still others want to find out more about the parent who died when they were very young, or to establish a feeling of "family" by finding cousins when they have no siblings. There are many reasons for starting the quest. One common theme among those who have been researching for some time is that the more information they find, the more they want to know.

Determine the Effort You Want to Exert

After you have decided what got you started and why you want to do this, consider that it may cost some money and it will certainly cost you time. Are you willing to travel to other states or even other countries to do your research? Will your family agree to a vacation in Salt Lake City so you can pore over the records The Church of Jesus Christ of Latter Day Saints (LDS) Family History Library makes available? Many researchers plan their vacations so they can visit old graveyards to find information about one more elusive relation. Many spend hours reviewing microfiche records in libraries and county offices to verify something they have found online.

Are you going to use the Internet as a resource? If so, you'll need a good computer with an Internet connection. While some resources can be accessed on a smart phone, a large screen and a printer with a scanner are the most useful for reviewing old records and preserving them for your files.

Most genealogy groups today sponsor a website. Use a search engine to find groups in your area and consider joining. You may even find someone who is researching a common ancestor. If you are unable to visit another location in the United States, look for genealogy societies in that area. If you contact a distant group, you may find help when searching for the birthplace of your great-grandfather who came from that area.

Do consider the time and effort you are willing to expend to find information. And be prepared if the actual time is double or triple what you anticipated. While we don't go as far as calling the hunt an "addiction," it is not uncommon for family historians to become upset if they are interrupted just as they are about to verify another relation.

Explore Available Resources

What type of resources do you have available for your research? A few are mentioned here, but each suggestion may spark additional ideas, and many of these resources are discussed further in this book.

Review Your Memory and Documents

Start with what you already have in your possession. Make notes about the family stories you remember so that you can verify them. Be prepared for the probability that others in the family will not remember the stories in

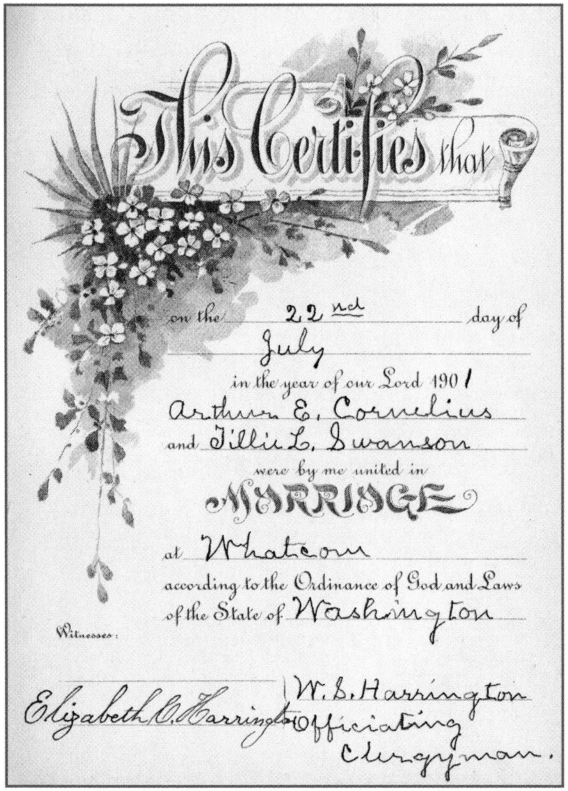
This Certifies that
on the 22nd day of
July
in the year of our Lord 1901
Arthur E. Cornelius
and Tillie L. Swanson
were by me united in
MARRIAGE
at Whatcom
according to the Ordinance of God and Laws
of the State of Washington
Witnesses:
Elizabeth C. Harrington
W. S. Harrington
Officiating
Clergyman.

Figure 1-5: ***This marriage certificate for Bobbi's maternal grandparents was in a wedding book from 1901.***

the same way or may even dispute your memory. Keep all of the notes, written stories, and pictures about that story in one place.

Then, find all of the documents you may have. Did someone leave you a family Bible? Do you have a copy of your grandparents' wedding picture? Do you have birth and death certificates for both your family and your spouse's family? Organize them in groups so you can easily add information and documentation. Bobbi found information about her maternal grandparents' marriage date in a box full of old photographs as seen in Figure 1-5.

Go through your old papers and books to see if notes or other documents have been included. A friend once found her old dollhouse in her mother's attic. Hidden in the dollhouse were several pictures of her grandmother playing with her and the dollhouse during a visit.

Once you have identified a photo subject or established the year of the photo, use an acid-free pen to note the information on the back. Even better, scan the photos into your computer. Create a word-processing document noting the pertinent information about the picture and any story you may know. Save the entire group in a single file with a name that makes the file easily identifiable.

Query Your Relatives

After you have started collecting data, written down any stories you remember, and organized your collection, start talking with relatives. Ask them to write down what they remember, or even better, talk with them and record their memories on a digital recorder. Don't forget to talk to all of the living generations. Ask them for any documents they may have to add to your organized collections. Make copies if they want to keep the originals. Document how they came to have the items so you can double-check with other sources if need be.

Be prepared to hear different perspectives on stories you thought you knew by heart. You and your siblings may have different points of view when recalling an incident from your common past or from a family story. It may not be worthwhile to argue with their perception at this point. The difference of viewpoint may just give you more to investigate!

Search Library Collections

Many libraries have genealogy sections. The LDS Family History Library in Salt Lake City has the most extensive genealogy document collection in the world. There are also LDS Family History Centers throughout the country that can order information from the Family History Library.

Nationally, there are a number of library resources available, including the Library of Congress and the National Archives. Nearly every local library has its own genealogy department, usually containing information focusing on the early settlers in their local area.

The Newberry Library in Chicago and the New England Historic Genealogical Society Lending Library in Boston have extensive collections for genealogists and family historians.

Look at Cemetery Records and Headstones

When paper records do not exist, you can often locate information by spending some time reading headstones in the cemeteries of the area where your ancestors lived. Headstones may contain both birth and death dates, the person's complete name, and even some nicknames. Often the name of his or her spouse is included, and many headstones include the maiden name of a wife. There may be inscriptions such as Our Son or Dear Mother as well as the religious affiliation of the deceased.

Some headstones contain military information, including rank and branch of service. How wealthy the family was at the time of the death can be determined by both the type of headstone and its size.

Watch for abbreviations and symbols. Many small children have butterflies or birds on their headstones, and the headstones themselves are often smaller. Children were often buried close to their parents.

Most cemeteries keep a record of the names of the people buried there. While these are often secondary records, if there are no other governmental records,

History of Pleasant Ridge Cemetery

John A. Cornelius and his wife, Bessie, settled near the north end of Pleasant Ridge in 1868. Cornelius had previously lived on Whidbey Island and was a government surveyor. It was on land owned by Cornelius that Pleasant Ridge Cemetery was established in 1875 when his young son, Charles, died of diphtheria. David Culver, a teacher from La Conner, and Samuel Summers, a farmer from Fir Island, were buried there soon after.

Nothing was easily accomplished in those days before roads and bridges. When Samuel Summers died in 1876 his neighbors sent a boy of fifteen to fetch Reverend B.N.L. Davis from up the Skagit River near Burlington. Another party was dispatched by rowboat to La Conner to register his death at the territorial courthouse and purchase a casket. Still others dug the grave in the new cemetery. The burial party arrived by boat, up Sullivan Slough, carrying the casket a quarter mile up the steep hill to Mr. Summers' final resting place.

John A. Cornelius died on February 15, 1880, leaving his wife, Bessie, and three children. He was fortyyears old. Joseph O. Rudene had come to Pleasant Ridge from Iowa in May 1876 at age 26. Rudene and Cornelius were friends and when Cornelius died, leaving his wife and children without support, Rudene married Bessie in 1882. Rudene then owned the cemetery land and sold 40' x 40' plots which were maintained by individual families.

Skagit County pioneers buried at Pleasant Ridge Cemetery include John S. Conner and Louisa A. Conner who founded the town of La Conner in 1869. La Conner soon became the outlet for the produce of the Skagit delta and the market center where goods and services from the rest of the world could be obtained.

Other pioneers buried at the cemetery include three Civil War veterans, Joseph Franklin Dwelley, Richard H. Ball, and Samuel Thomas Valentine. The families of George and James Gaches who operated a mercantile store and crop brokerage in La Conner from 1873, are also buried there.

In 1956 the citizens of Skagit County formed cemetery districts with Pleasant Ridge named as District 1. Arthur Olson of Pleasant Ridge was named as the first caretaker. Currently maintenance of all types is contracted.

History of the Community of Pleasant Ridge

Pleasant Ridge offered home sites out of the danger of flooding to the single men and families who came to the Skagit and Swinomish flats to build dikes and clear the land for farming. It is thought that Samuel Calhoun who came from the sawmill at Utsalady on Camano Island by Indian canoe, and Michael Sullivan from Nova Scotia, were the first to begin the arduous diking project, perhaps as early as 1863.

Early settlers on Pleasant Ridge include: John and Bessie Cornelius from Whidbey Island, 1868; Harvey Wallace and his wife in 1871; James Williamson; Mrs. David Leamer and sons Albert and Milton, 1868; Isaac Dunlap from California in 1871; Charles Elde from Sweden; Charles Chilberg from Sweden; John H. Chilberg from Sweden; Nels Christianson from Denmark; Charles Nelson; Joseph Sharfenberg from Iowa in 1875; James O'Laughlin in 1872; Samuel T. Valentine from Indiana in 1882.

Figure 1-6: *Cemetery records can sometimes give additional clues about your relatives.*

these burial registers and cemetery records are very valuable. For example, Bobbi's great-grandfather's homestead has now become a pioneer cemetery, as shown in Figure 1-6.

Review Government Information

The federal, state, county, parish, city, and town governments are full of treasures for the family historian to find. Possibly the most useful as you are beginning your research are census records, both federal and state. For example, Bobbi found her grandfather's occupation shown on the 1900 Census (see Figure 1-7). Many states have conducted a census independent of the federal census that is done every ten years. Contact your state's capitol or go to the state website to see what census records exist.

Land grants, tax rolls, voter registration, property tax assessments, and even court documents can be reviewed by any member of the public in most jurisdictions, as all of these things are a matter of public record. You can review court documents to see evidence of divorce, civil litigation, wills, trust agreements, and even traffic tickets. While some jurisdictions provide the information online, in many localities, you must physically examine the documents.

Look at Online Sites, Blogs, Forums, and Communities

The most convenient way of obtaining information is online. All one needs is an Internet connection and a device by which you can access that connection. There are a wide variety of websites, such as Archives.com, Ancestry.com, and many others.

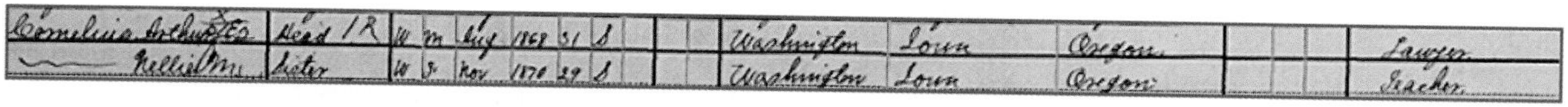

| Cornelius Arthur Es | Head | R | W | M | Aug | 1868 | 31 | S | | | Washington | Iowa | Oregon | | | Lawyer |
| Nellie M. | Sister | | W | F | Nov | 1870 | 29 | S | | | Washington | Iowa | Oregon | | | Teacher |

Figure 1-7: **The 1900 Census included information on the location, month, and year of birth, as well as occupation.**

In addition, many sites and even individual families have started weblogs, or *blogs*, where they post information, requests for connections, family stories, and many other bits of information. Online forums are similar to blogs, but usually anyone can post and contribute to the site. Online communities are similar to forums, but are usually created for a specific purpose by people separated by distance. All of these resources can be used to further your genealogy research.

Bobbi Sandberg, 70, Whidbey Island, WA

OVERVIEW

On my mother's side I can trace her paternal line with some certainty to the mid-1600s in Scotland. However, her maternal line currently dead-ends in Sweden after three generations due to the common names of her mother's parents. I have my great-grandmother's Bible and have been trying, so far unsuccessfully, to determine the region in Sweden from which she came. My father's maternal line has been in what is now the United States since the early 1600s. Unfortunately, I cannot yet document the ancestors from Wales and Scotland prior to that time. Since my father's paternal line has many spelling variations, I'm currently concentrating on my mother's side and hope to verify some additional Scots ancestors.

STORY

I love stories and have been romanticizing my family lore since I was a little girl. The thought that we might be related to Scots royalty, both William Wallace and Robert Bruce, was fed to me along with peanut butter sandwiches when I was young. My mother's only complaint was, "The only bad thing is that the Wallace plaid is not as pretty as many others." Since I've grown, I find I do *not* agree with her assessment. However, there is a modern (since 1842) version of the plaid and it is a bit brighter than the ancient version, both of which are seen next (the original Wallace plaid is on the left).

 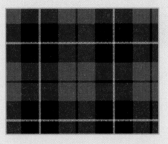

GETTING STARTED

I started with my maternal grandfather's drawing of the Skagit County, Washington, Pioneer Cemetery, seen in Figure 1-8, which is on the land originally homesteaded by his parents and later merged with land owned by his stepfather. He also wrote a three- or four-page summary of what he could

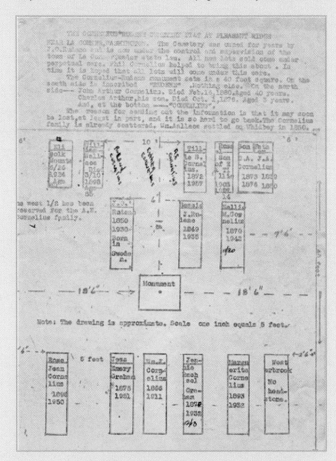

Figure 1-8: **The Rudene-Cornelius section of the Skagit County Pioneer Cemetery in LaConner, Washington.**

remember of the tales told by his mother and grandmother of the early days in what is now the state of Washington.

I also have a copy of a book published by my grandfather about my great-great-uncle, Eli Mounts. The book, entitled *Islands in the Ocean of Memory,* recounts Uncle Eli's adventures at sea, including his time spent on a whaling boat. According to one family biographer, Uncle Eli later earned his way by speaking about these adventures to any audience that would pay him. His picture is shown in Figure 1-9, holding his whale gun and showing bones he collected.

Figure 1-9: **Uncle Eli Polk Mounts told stories that fascinated my grandfather and many others.**

CHALLENGES

Thus far, my biggest challenges have been trying to verify names when there are several generations that have named their children after fathers and grandfathers. I found an exciting headstone image at Ancestry.com that confirmed that my great-great-great maternal grandfather was indeed born in Scotland and that the "Sarah" to whom he was married was also called "Sally."

Also, from my mother's line, I hope to find my great-great-grandparents who were born in Sweden. The Spenserian script in my grandmother's old Bible is difficult to read, even when it is fresh, and considering this Bible is now more than 150 years old, it simply makes the problem harder to solve.

OBJECTIVES

By continuing to research, I am creating a family tree, including the Wallace plaid and crest, and as many pictures as possible. At some point I hope to verify

the connection to Brave Heart, Sir William Wallace of Scotland, and verify that there is an additional connection to Robert The Bruce as well (the Scottish king, Robert I).

Wallace

One of the most fascinating bits of information is how looks carry across generations. Figures 1-10a and b show a picture of the Cornelius children about 1909 on the left, and a picture of the Cornelius daughter's great-great-granddaughter nearly 100 years later on the right.

By using multimedia, each child and grandchild will have a copy of my grandfather's journals, pictures of relatives, stories from as many sources as I can locate, and a feel for how it might have been to live when the only "connection" was a walk or horseback ride to someone's house several miles away. Even now, my grandchildren cannot believe that my maternal grandparents

A

B

Figure 1-10: **The children of Tillie and Arthur Cornelius are running in the field near their home in 1909 and the young girl's great-great-granddaughter nearly 100 years later.**

had no telephone until early in the 1900s and my paternal grandparents had
none until the 1950s.

I keep an Ancestry.com family tree, part of which, my mother's line, is shown in
Figure 1-11, and at least one of my children and one grandchild are fascinated
by what we've discovered there. I'm hoping that some far-flung relative will see
a common ancestor and fill in the Cornelius and Wallace Scotland connections.

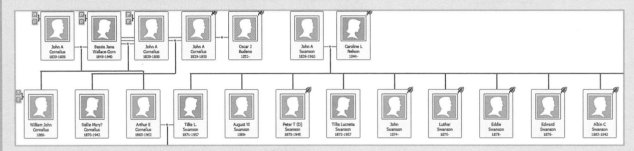

Figure 1-11: *My mother's family is from Scotland and Sweden.*

Chapter 2

Gathering Information

Where to start? There are, of course, many ways and whichever way you choose is right for you. Our recommendation is to gather and sort through the information that is already available to you before diving into the computer tools, whether online or in your computer. The reason for this is that the information you already have may give you a number of important tips on where to start looking with a computer and who to look for.

Document Your Personal Story

A good place to begin is by dumping what you have in your mind because you probably have a number of ancestral facts from things you have been told over your life. While these may be fragmentary with many questions, they represent a foundation from which you can work and both confirm or refute and fill in with your ancestral research.

NOTE

In documenting your personal story, it is *not* important that you be perfectly accurate. Document what you remember. Later you can come back when you are on the Internet or talking to other relatives and correct any errors and fill in any gaps. At this stage it is fine to list "Aunt Betty" even though you know that was a nickname and you can't remember her last name. You'll have lots of opportunity to make needed corrections and additions.

```
09/21/86        SHALLCROSS FAMILY CHRONOLOGICAL LISTING          Page 1

1 Edward Shallcross  born ???  in ???
     died ???  married on Mar 15, 1838
  to Sarah Packer  born ???  died ???
     and had the following children:
       Rebecca Ann Shallcross Watkins  born  Dec 17, 1838
       Aaron F. Shallcross  born  Oct 01, 1840
       George W. Shallcross  born  Dec 17, 1844
       John William Shallcross  born Nov 15, 1847
     NOTES:
       Edward lived on a farm near Steubenville, Ohio. He remarried
       Margret Brewer on Sep 25, 1862. He & Sarah also had a son,
       Isaac Shallcross on Sep 04, 1842. Also a daughter, Hannah,
       (date unknown) married a physician named Wilson in Phil.

2 John William Shallcross  born Nov 15, 1847  in Belmont County, Ohio  (??)
     died ???  married on ???
  to Amelia Bada (Martin)  born ???  died 1877  (??)
     and had the following children:
       (Frank Martin)  born  ???
       William John Shallcross  born  Dec 23, 1873
       Anna Shallcross Hogue  born  Oct ??, 1875
       Flora Warnke  (??)  born  ??? ??, 1877
     NOTES:
       John was English whose ancestors came to Amercia as Quakers.
       Amelia came to Amer. at 12 from Berlin Germany. She married
       (??) Martin who died in the Civil war.  John was a hotel and
       store keeper.  Amelia's mother remarried becomming Warnke.

3 Luther B. Smith  born ???  in ???
     died ???  married on ???
  to Mary E. Lyon  born ???  died ???
     and had the following children:
       Waldo Edward Smith  born  ???
       Frances (Frankie) Smith  born  ???
       Roberta (Bertie) Smith Redding  born  ???
       Agnes Gertrude Smith Shallcross  born Apr 12, 1875
     NOTES:
       Mary Lyon was the daughter of Waldo Edward Lyon who founded
       Lyons Nebr. Waldo Lyon came to Nebr. from Minn. in a covered
       wagon.  Luther and Mary had a fifth child named Guy Smith.

4 William John Shallcross  born Dec 23, 1873  in Glenwood, Mills county, Io
     died Jul 06, 1970  married on Dec 25, 1900
  to Agnes Gertrude Smith  born Apr 12, 1875  died Dec 28,1956
     and had the following children:
       Waldo Edward Shallcross  born  Jul 01, 1902
       Maida Lucille Shal. Trout  born  Aug 29, 1904
       Ruth Enalda Shal. Maynard  born  Sep 28, 1906
       Winifred Agnes Shal. Bloom  born  Mar 08, 1913
     NOTES:
       William was an author, poet, minister, farmer, & realtor. He
       wrote songs, books and poems: loved to travel, dance and eat
       strawberries; was interested in history, Bellevue Nebr, and
       other people.
```

Figure 2-1: One of Marty's earliest genealogy efforts was to list everyone he knew about or had information about in his family. This is the beginning of his mother's side, which continued to the most recent grandchild. You can see he had a lot of questions.

List Your Important Milestones

You say, "Why my milestones? I want to document my ancestry, not me." First, because you are the beginning of your ancestral exploration, and second because most people plan on leaving their genealogy work to their descendants, who will be as interested in you as you are in your ancestors.

List all the important events thus far in your life, the dates when and the places where they occurred, and the important people who were involved. Include the following:

- The date and place of your birth
- The locations to which you moved and the address of each location
- The important religious events in your life, such as your baptism, first communion, confirmation, bat or bar mitzvah, and so on, with the organization with which they took place
- The important educational events in your life, such as the start and graduation from each school you attended, including the names of the schools, the fields of study, and the degrees you received
- The important personal events in your life, such as marriages; divorces; births of children; and deaths of parents, siblings, children, and spouses
- The major jobs you've had and the organizations they were with, including elected offices
- Major property acquisitions you have made
- Major achievements, including writings, inventions, artistic works, companies or organizations started, and awards received

List Your Relatives and Ancestors

Create a list from your mind and easily available information of your relatives and ancestors that you know about and to whom you are closely related (see Figure 2-1). Once again, it is not important that you be precise at this point; the important element is to get down everyone who is in your head. Include the following, if possible, but don't worry if you don't have all the information:

- Parents, grandparents, great-grandparents, siblings, aunts and uncles, cousins, and any other extended family members

- Dates of birth, death, and marriage
- Places where they lived and the approximate dates they lived there
- Occupations, elections, achievements, organizational or honorary positions, and awards and the approximate dates
- Stories that you remember about the people, with dates and places if possible

Collect, Organize, and Review Documents and Photos

If you are like most people, you have probably collected a lot of photos and documents relating to your ancestors. These almost always contain excellent and needed starting places for further research. Figures 2-2 through 2-7 and 2-9 show various documents Marty has collected about his family.

Collect Documents

Collect in one place all the documents and photos you have about your ancestry and relatives, both official documents and narrative writings. These provide important names, dates, places, and relationships that are clues for your genealogy research. Include the following:

- Birth certificates, death certificates, wedding licenses, divorce decrees, immigration and naturalization papers, passports, and drivers licenses
- Wills, titles, licenses
- Baptismal, christening, confirmation, and bat and bar mitzvah certificates
- High school and college diplomas and professional licenses
- Newspaper clippings, magazine articles, yearbooks, organizational bulletins, and newsletters

*Figure 2-2: **Birth certificates provide not only important dates, but also locations and parentage. (Ruth Inglis is Marty's stepmother.)***

- Bible ancestry pages, scrapbooks, baby books, journals, diaries
- Letters, invitations, Christmas cards
- Photos, drawings, and paintings of individuals and events in your family and ancestry

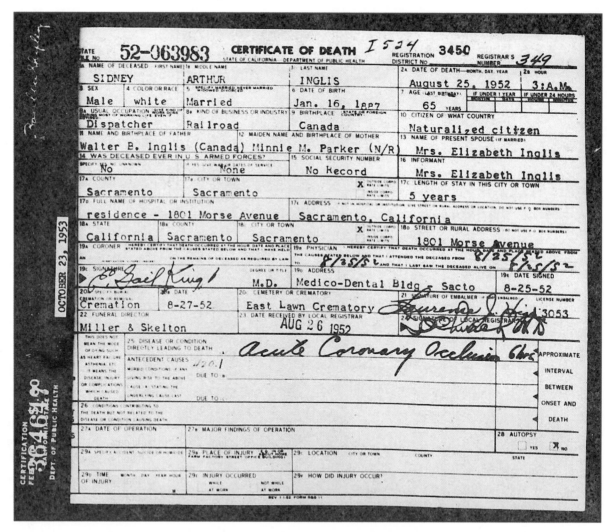

Figure 2-3: Death certificates provide an important date and sometimes a lot more information, such as the date of birth, parents' name, occupation, and spouse's name, as shown here. (Sydney Inglis was Marty's stepmother's father.)

QUICKSTEPS

ANALYZING YOUR DOCUMENTS

Look carefully at each document as you organize your files. Note any information that has been written on either the front or back. Think about the story the document is telling you and how it might help you find out more about your ancestry. Not only do documents give you information, they can also indicate information that you are missing, both by the absence of information and by stray pieces of information that may be new to you or that doesn't fit the picture you have been developing for your family—for example, two people, maybe a father and son, of the same name, or a woman who may have been married to two brothers at different times.

Make a separate list of information and documentation that is missing for your ancestors that are important to your genealogy. You can then use this list when you talk to your living relatives, as discussed later in this chapter, and as you begin searching the Internet genealogy sites, as discussed later in this book.

TIP

Chapter 3 discusses what you need on a computer and how to set it up to work with genealogy, as well as performing certain tasks such as setting up a spreadsheet and scanning documents.

Organize Documents

As you collect documents, you will want to organize them so that they can be easily used in your research and as both source documentation and illustrations of your results. The steps Marty has followed are:

1. Sort the documents by the person(s) they refer to.

2. For each person with a number of documents, create a file folder and put the corresponding documents in it. You may want to combine some related people, like husband and wife, if they individually do not have very many documents.

3. Within each folder, sort the documents by date.

4. Create a list or index of the documents by person, and by date within each person, so you can easily see what you have without going through the documents. If you do this on a computer, use a spreadsheet program, such as Excel, and put first name, last name, date, city, county, state, country, and document type (birth certificate, death certificate, wedding license, and so on) in separate columns so you can sort by each column (called *fields* in Excel).

5. Scan your documents (see Chapter 3) into your computer, where you can store them in a folder system similar to the paper folder system you developed to store the originals.

Figure 2-4: Marriage licenses or certificates provide names, date, and location at a minimum. Sometimes they also provide a list of witnesses and other information. This is the marriage certificate of Marty's grandfather's sister.

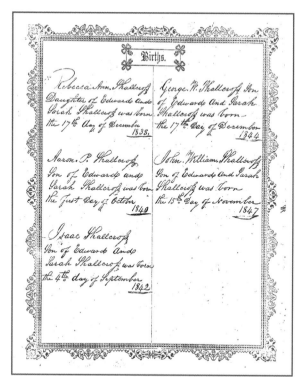

Figure 2-5: *The genealogy pages of old family Bibles can be a treasure trove of genealogy information. Here is the Births page from a Bible belonging to the Edward Shallcross family. Edward was Marty's great-great-grandfather.*

Survey Your Relatives

There are probably others in your extended family who have done or are doing genealogy research, and it may be helpful to your own research to see and get copies of what they have done. This can be useful to confirm or refute your work, as well as add significant links, extensions, and ancillary information.

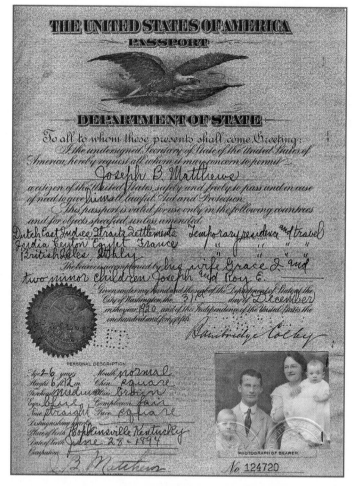

Figure 2-6: *Passports, especially older ones, can not only provide names, dates, and locations, but also dates and places of travel. Here is Marty's father's passport from 1920.*

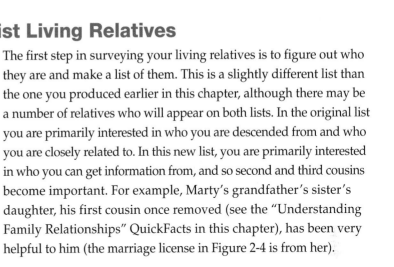

52 Days Until. . . ?

Died July 6th in the morning

BELLEVUE

The Home of SAC Museum

THIS WEEK'S CIRCULATION
14,506

VOLUME 5 PUBLISHED EVERY WEDNESDAY AT 2217 FRANKLIN STREET, BELLEVUE, NEBRASKA

'Mr. Bellevue'

W. Shallcross

Dies at Age 96

The "First Citizen of Belle-vue," William J. Shallcross, died Monday in an Omaha hospital at the age of 96. He took ill the morning of July 4 at the Belle-vue home of his son, Waldo, 1711 Shallcross Lane.

Funeral services will be today at 2:00 p.m. at the First United Presbyterian Church.

Mr. Shallcross, perhaps the best known of Bellevue residents, was a poet, author, songwriter and historian. He had long had extensive real estate interests in Bellevue.

He was born in Glenwood, Ia., on December 23, 1873. He at-tended old Bellevue College in the late 1890s, graduating in 1900. While at college he met Agnes Smith. They were mar-ried in December, 1900. She died in 1956.

Mr. Shallcross and his wife bought property in Bellevue and moved here in 1912. He left just long enough to play a leading role in the Armenian Children's Relief about the time of World War I. He visited Russia and other countries, but returned to Bellevue to make his home.

Although he always expressed a deep love for his adopted com-munity, he traveled extensively, visiting all 50 states, and spent his winters in southern Calif.

WILLIAM "BILL" SHALLCROSS

Figure 2-7: Newspapers, especially obituaries, can be a treasure trove of information, but they are not always 100 percent accurate. Here is an obituary for Marty's grandfather from the Bellevue – Guide newspaper of July 8, 1970.

List Living Relatives

The first step in surveying your living relatives is to figure out who they are and make a list of them. This is a slightly different list than the one you produced earlier in this chapter, although there may be a number of relatives who will appear on both lists. In the original list you are primarily interested in who you are descended from and who you are closely related to. In this new list, you are primarily interested in who you can get information from, and so second and third cousins become important. For example, Marty's grandfather's sister's daughter, his first cousin once removed (see the "Understanding Family Relationships" QuickFacts in this chapter), has been very helpful to him (the marriage license in Figure 2-4 is from her).

The objective, then, is to spread out to include as many relatives as possible, although you may have to go up several generations to find a common ancestor, to find a relative who has researched their genealogy. The hard part may be finding out how to contact them. It may be that you have information about these relatives, but it is many years old and in most cases, the existing contact information is no longer valid. First contact the relatives you know how to get a hold of and see if they know how to contact any of the others. If that fails, try searching the Internet, such as Intelius.com. You can actually start by putting in the person's name and last known city and state in Google or Bing and then follow the links.

Get Ancestral Information

Once you have a list of living relatives, you need to contact them by mail, email, phone, or in person. Your objective is to find out about them and their ancestry, if you don't already know it, what genealogy information they have, either in the form of documents and photos they have received from others, or from research they have done.

UNDERSTANDING FAMILY RELATIONSHIPS

In an extended family it is easy to get mixed up on what the correct names are for the relationships between individual members over several generations. Considering a family over four generations, as shown in Figure 2-8, here are some of the possible relationships:

- **Siblings**   Same parents: Bill and Sue, Bob and Sally, Brian and Janet

- **Cousins**   Same grandparents: Sally and Tom, Bob and Don, Janet and Lynn

- **Second cousins**   Same great-grandparents: Bev and Lynn, Janet and Jane

- **Third cousins**   Same great-great-grandparents: Roy and Amy, Gene and Teri

- **First cousins once removed**   A generation apart: Janet and Gene, Lynn and Roy

- **First cousins twice removed**   Two generations apart: Bob and Amy, Sally and Teri

- **Second cousins once removed**   Lynn and Amy, Brian and Rex

- **Uncles and aunts**   Janet is Roy's aunt, Bob is Lynn's uncle, Sue is Sally's aunt

- **Nephews and nieces**   Bev is Tom's niece, Brian is Sally's nephew, Don is Bill's nephew

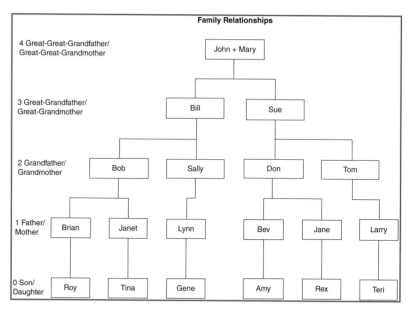

Figure 2-8: *The relationship between any two people in a family depends on the number of generations between them and who their common ancestor is.*

If they are willing, here is a list of questions, some of which you might ask them to answer, depending on what you already know:

1. What is your name and age?

2. Where were you born?

3. Where and when were your parents and grandparents born?

4. What got you started exploring your ancestry?

5. What were your objectives when you started?

6. What were the first steps you took in researching your ancestry?

7. What information did you already have and where did you get it?

8. Could we copy any historical documents or photos of relatives you have?

9. What genealogy Internet sites have you used?

10. What information did you get off of various sites?

11. Do you participate in online genealogy forums and, if so, what have you gotten off them?

12. What genealogy software do you use?

13. How have you used census data and what information did you get from it?

14. What roadblocks did you encounter in your quest?

15. How did you work around the roadblocks, if you did?

16. What libraries and cemeteries have you visited and what did you get from those sources?

17. Have you done any travel to ancestral locations and, if so, what information did you find?

18. What genealogy organizations, clubs, and/or societies do you belong to and what do you get from them?

19. How far back, in terms of generations and birth year, have you been able to trace your ancestry?

20. How many of your ancestral lines have you traced back prior to their coming to the United States? Prior to the founding of the United States?

21. How sure are you of all the links in your genealogy? Do you have multiple sources and do you feel they are pretty accurate"

22. What have you done with the information you collected?

23. What plans do you have for further research and with publishing your results?

24. How are you going to transfer what you collected to others?

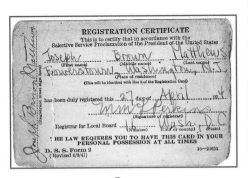

A

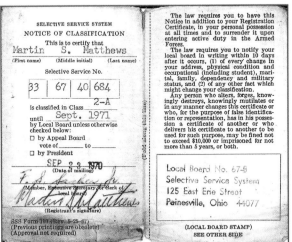

B

C

Figure 2-9: Military records and documents can provide information valuable to your ancestry research. Here you see Selective Service documents from Marty's grandfather for World War I, his father for World War II, and for him during the Vietnam War.

COLLECTING PHOTOGRAPHS

Photographs help bring your ancestors to life (see Figure 2-10). Having pictures or paintings of them helps you picture them and keep them in your mind as you are working on your ancestry. You can also use the pictures as you document your ancestry, both in print and on a website. Finally you can use photos of individual ancestors on your family tree on Ancestry.com.

Gather photos as you gather other documents about your ancestry. When you talk to other family members, always ask them if you can copy any photographs they have (if you get a new printer, get one with a flatbed scanner, called all-in-one printers, so you can easily copy documents and photos—see Chapter 3). Copy anything that is written on the back of the photo. If possible, store electronic (.jpg) images of your photos on your computer so you can easily move them to documents, a webpage, and a family tree, as well as send them to other family members.

As you gather photos, organize them as you have other documents by ancestor and date, and keep paper photos in protective envelopes. It is good to note on the back of photos who is in it and the date it was taken, but be careful what you use to write on photos so you don't damage them. A soft felt-tip pen or a soft pencil works best.

*Figure 2-10: **Photographs are an important addition to your genealogy documents. Here are three photos of Marty's ancestors: his great-great-grandfather Waldo Lyon, taken around 1875 and obtained from the website for the city of Lyons, Nebraska, which he co-founded; his grandmother (in the center) and her two sisters, taken around 1885; and his grandfather, taken around 1900.***

25. What have you accomplished of your original genealogy objectives and what are your future objectives for that?

As you collect this information and the documents and photos that will come with it, organize it by family, ancestor, and date, as you did your own information, and then integrate it with your information. Compare this new information to what you already have and ask these questions:

- Does it substantiate or refute the other information you have?
- Is it based on better and/or more sources than your other information?
- Does it add individuals to your ancestry and are you comfortable with the reliability of those additions?
- Does it cause you to question your previous work and to what degree?
- What do you need to do to increase your confidence in both your previous information and the new information?
- Is your relative, or the person you got the information from, willing to help you work through your questions and improve the confidence you have in the combined information?
- What is your plan for achieving these objectives?

A   B   C

MARTY'S STORY

Marty (Martin S.) Matthews, 70, Whidbey Island, WA

OVERVIEW

It is reasonably certain that my father's maternal line reaches back eight generations to 1678 in Ireland, and then, though less certain, continues back another 17 generations (25 in total) to 1047 in Scotland. My father's paternal line is currently dead-ended with my great-grandfather (three generations) at about 1830. My mother's paternal line reaches back eight generations to about 1680 in England, and her maternal line goes back four generations to the founding of Lyons, Nebraska, in 1884. I have used Ancestry .com, RootsWeb.com, Family Search.com, and Genealogy.com Internet sites, as well as Family Tree Maker and Legacy software.

STORY

I have been interested in genealogy for many years, collecting documents and photos from a number of sources, talking to many people, and doing some of my own research. As the genealogy content on the Internet has grown, I have increasingly used the major Internet sites and genealogy software to enhance my research.

GETTING STARTED

Like many people, I first received information about my family from other family members. My father and his sister had done some amazing genealogy research that I received. Also, my mother's sister did some work on their ancestry. One of the most fascinating items I got was a hand-drawn family tree, shown in Figure 2-11, done by my father's sister. Shown on the bottom are Fannie Brown and Burrel Jones Matthews, my grandparents, and at the top, nine generations removed from me, is a French-Huguenot family named Lemont who left France for Ireland about 1670.

My father also wrote about this legacy in 1938, the first few paragraphs of which are shown in Figure 2-12. He may have used a little editorial license that created a bit of a mystery.

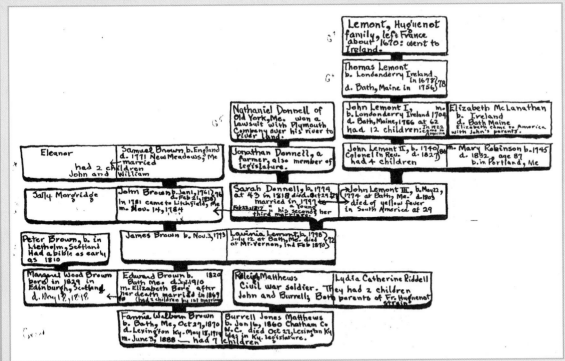

*Figure 2-11: **A hand-drawn family tree, drawn by my aunt, has been an article of fascination for many years.***

Figure 2-12: **The beginning of my father's narrative on his ancestry**

Notice in the hand-drawn family tree, the Lamont at the top has no first name, while my father's writing calls him "Thomas Lemont I." Who's right?

CHALLENGES

My challenges show a typical process of searching, finding blind alleys, and having some breakthroughs, but often ending up with more questions than when I started. My first steps were to find my great-grandfather Riley (my father's name for him, or Raleigh, as my aunt called him) Matthews' ancestry. I began by entering Riley into Ancestry.com along with other known family members. Unfortunately, no hints or other help were available for Riley. I then put a question on Genealogy.com's GenForum asking for any information about Riley and his wife Catherine Riddle. I got back a number of citations, all centered around Catherine. Several of the citations said that her full name was Lidia Catherine Riddle and that she was married to W.R. Matthews, or in another citation to W.R. Mathis (Matthews?). I assume that the "R" is for "Riley." At this point, that is all I have on Riley.

My second challenge was to substantiate the ancestry described by my father and my aunt, leading back to Thomas Lemont. The entire ancestry as described proved to be the same as a number of sources on Ancestry.com, which included a photo of Thomas Lemont's grave stone. Figure 2-13 shows this lineage.

My father and aunt said that Thomas Lemont was descended from French Huguenots (French Protestants) who came to Ireland around 1670. I did find a note in one family tree that suggested French ancestry, but it gave no names, dates, or other information.

However, on Ancestry.com I found a number of other family trees, possibly copying each other, that showed that Thomas Lemont was the son of John Sitlington Lemont of the Scottish Clan Lamont, which was very easy to trace back another 17 generations (beyond the 8 generations between me and Thomas Lemont, for a total of 25) to Hugh Lamont, who was born in 1047. This was a

NOTE

The grave stone of Thomas Lemont is not readable as it is shown here, but is interestingly hand-engraved:

HERE LIES Y̊
BODY OF M.ʳ
THOMAS LEMONT
DIED FEBᴿʸ 15
1 7 5 6
AGED 78 YEARS

The "e" in "Ye" is actually directly above the "Y" and the "r" in "Mr." is above the colon and looks like it was inserted as a correction, as does the "ry" in "FEBᴿʸ."

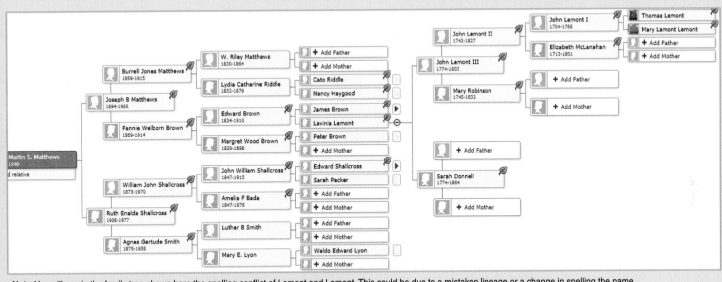

Note: You will see in the family tree shown here the spelling conflict of Lemont and Lamont. This could be due to a mistaken lineage or a change in spelling the name.

*Figure 2-13: **My ancestry back to Thomas Lemont, born in 1678, proved to be strongly supported on Ancestry.com.***

fun line to explore, with photos of castles, coats of arms, and clan crests. Being royalty, this family line is also very well documented, as shown in Figure 2-14, which displays the first 8 of the 17 generations behind Thomas Lemont on top, and then the final 9 on the bottom. But this line is questionable because a source on Ancestry.com and my father and aunt point to an ancestry in France. As a result, I need to explore other sources to validate which ancestry is correct.

LAMONT

OBJECTIVES

My objectives going forward include finding the ancestry of Riley Matthews, possibly using Confederate Civil War records, and whether John Sitlington Lemont is the father of Thomas Lemont or if there a French ancestor. In addition, I would like to work further back on the Brown, Shallcross, and Lyon ancestries.

I would like to create a website, and possibly a blog, with the genealogy information I have collected. I also plan on keeping my information maintained on Ancestry.com as a public family tree. This allows anyone looking for any of the information in my family tree to see it, as you can see in Figure 2-15, where I am looking for information for John Brown and see related information from five other family trees.

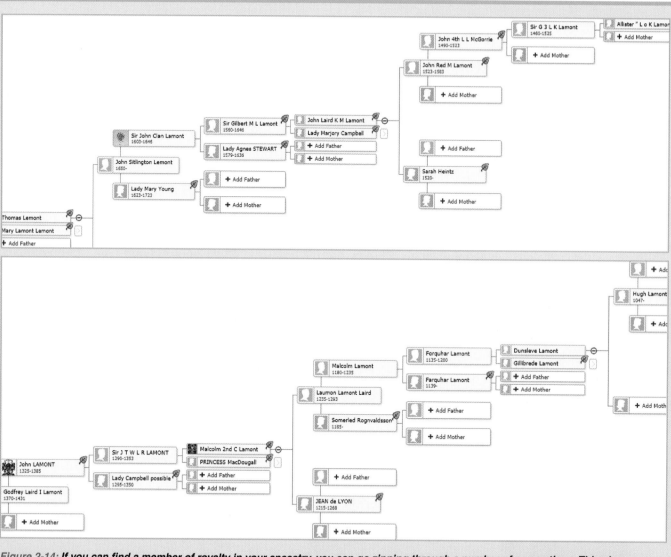

Figure 2-14: *If you can find a member of royalty in your ancestry, you can go zipping through a number of generations. This shows my father's maternal line, first, from Thomas Lemont (b. 1678) to Allister Lamont (b. 1424), and then from Allister's father Godfrey Lamont (b.1370) to Hugh Lamont (b. 1047)*

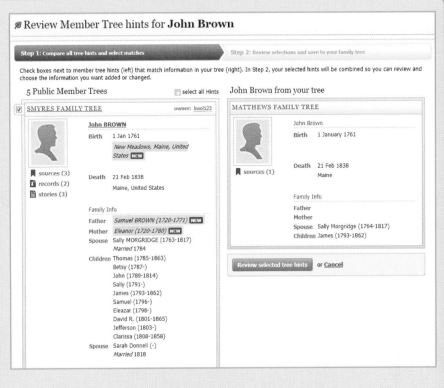

*Figure 2-15: **Other people's family trees can provide a lot of information for your own research, such as place of birth and father and mother, seen here.***

How to...

Chapter 3

Assessing Computer Needs

While people have done genealogy for hundreds, and probably thousands, of years without using computers, computers have made genealogy not only much more accessible and much easier to do, but with the Internet, computers have added a major new dimension to genealogy: online networking. In the past, you could work together on a family or community history only through word of mouth—if you knew or heard about that work. Today, all of the major genealogy websites, including Ancestry, RootsWeb, and Genealogy, provide ways of contacting and querying others who are working on families and communities of interest to you. In the genealogy story by Jenanne Murphy in this chapter, you'll read how she was able to learn about, get significant information from, and join others working on her family lines. She was able to do this with her computer and the Internet.

In this chapter we'll look at what the genealogy requirements are for computer and Internet resources and how to select those resources so they fulfill your genealogy needs. We'll then look at a comparison of genealogy software in general, and then Family Tree Maker and Legacy in particular, and how to get started using those products. Finally, we'll review how to protect yourself on the Internet and protect your data from disappearing.

Review Needed Hardware and Software

The computer hardware and the software that you need depend on what you want to do, so your first step is to determine that. Based on what you come up with, you can determine what you need, compare that to what you have, and then consider what you want to get.

Look at What You Want to Do

In Chapter 1, and to a lesser extent in Chapter 2, you were introduced to a number of tasks that you can do with a computer while working with genealogy. Among these are:

- Run genealogy software
- Use word processing, spreadsheet, and presentation software
- Store, edit, retrieve, and print documents, including audio and video files
- Access photos on a digital camera
- Scan documents, possibly in color

- Back up information
- Connect to and use the Internet
- Send and receive email
- Exchange documents and information

In this book, when we're talking about "information," we're talking about anything that you can store on a computer, including text, sound, and images. From the standpoint of genealogy, this includes, but is not limited to

- Names of individuals, parents, spouses, and children
- Dates of birth, marriage, immigration, arrival/departure, and death
- Locations born, lived, visited, and died
- Documents such as birth, marriage, immigration, naturalization, and death certificates; as well as photos, video and audio files, stories, military records, census data, and other public records

For our use here, the words "information" and "data" are synonymous (although there are people that will argue that they are different); "documents" generally have a structure that contains information, which can be visual, either still or motion, or auditory.

Consider Hardware

To handle the basic needs of genealogy, almost all computers built since 2005 will do the job, as well as many older computers. Newer ones, though, will generally do it faster and do so with more features and capabilities.

EXAMINE THE REQUIREMENTS

Examine the requirements of the various genealogy tasks that you might want to undertake:

- **Run genealogy software** The various genealogy software packages have minimum requirements for the computer on which they can run, as shown in Table 3-1. In this table the Recommended column is what we would recommend as a minimum if you are buying a new computer.

COMPONENT	LEGACY	FAMILY TREE MAKER	ROOTS MAGIC	RECOMMENDED
Processor (CPU)	Pentium	Pentium II 500 MHz	Pentium	Dual core 2 GHz
Memory (RAM)	256MB	1GB	64MB	2GB
Hard Disk	100MB	500MB	160MB	500GB
Display	VGA	1024 × 768	VGA	1280 × 800
Operating System	Windows XP-7	Windows XP-7	Windows XP-7	Windows 7
CD/DVD ROM	Yes	Yes	Yes	Yes
Mouse	Yes	Yes	Yes	Yes
Internet Connection	Yes	Yes	Yes	Yes
Internet Browser	IE7	IE7	IE7	IE9

Table 3-1: Minimum Requirements for Genealogy Software Packages

TIP

An alternative to having a productivity package on your computer is to use productivity software on the Internet. Microsoft Office Web Apps provides free web versions of Word, Excel, PowerPoint, and OneNote (office.microsoft .com/webapps). Google Docs offers free online programs to create documents, spreadsheets, presentations, drawings, and forms (docs.google.com).

● **Run productivity software**   While productivity software such as Microsoft Word (word processing), Excel (spreadsheets), and PowerPoint (presentations), which are part of Microsoft Office, are not directly tied to genealogy, they are often used and needed to fulfill many genealogy-related tasks. You can see in Table 3-2 that the requirements for Office 2010 are not that different than those for genealogy software, except for the display, and are within our recommended specifications.

COMPONENT	MINIMUM REQUIREMENTS
Processor (CPU)	Pentium III 500 MHz
Memory (RAM)	256MB minimum, 500MB recommended
Display	1024 × 576 resolution
Operating System	Windows XP-7
Hard Disk	3GB
CD/DVD ROM	Yes
Mouse	Yes
Internet Connection	Yes
Internet Browser	IE7

Table 3-2: Minimum Requirements for Microsoft Office 2010

TIP

To learn more about acquiring, setting up, and using a computer and Internet connection see *Windows 7 SP1 QuickSteps,* by Marty Matthews; *Windows 7 for Seniors QuickSteps,* by Marty Matthews; and *Computing for Seniors QuickSteps,* by Marty Matthews, Carole Matthews, Bobbi Sandberg, and Gary Bouton, all of which are published by McGraw-Hill.

QUICK**FACTS**

UNDERSTANDING COMPUTER NOMENCLATURE

Unless you are fairly familiar with computers and their components, it is easy to get mixed up with computer nomenclature—understanding what MB, GB, Mbps, and MHz mean and how they differ.

- KB, MB, GB, and TB deal with memory size, the capacity of a memory component to store information. The "B," which is capitalized, stands for "byte." It is roughly equivalent to a character: alphabetic, numeric, or special. The "K," "M," "G," and "T" stand for "kilo," "mega," "giga," and "tera" and mean, respectively, thousands, millions, billions, and trillions. So "MB" stands for "megabytes," or millions of bytes, and "TB" stands for "terabytes," or trillions of bytes. If you have 2GB of memory, you have two billion bytes (roughly characters) of memory.

Continued . . .

- **Work with documents**   Storing, editing, retrieving, and printing documents are fundamental functions handled by all personal computers with a printer. The speed and quantity that can be handled improve with newer computers and printers. Handling pictures, photographs, and audio and video files is also standard, but they take up a lot more storage space and can use more processing power, so newer devices become important. Computers and printers made in the last five years with Windows XP or later do these tasks well.

- **Connect to a digital camera**   Connecting to a digital camera requires either a memory card reader for the card in your camera or a Universal Serial Bus (USB) connection. Almost all computers made in the last five years have this.

- **Scan documents**   As you get involved in genealogy, you'll find lots of times when you'll want to scan old documents into your computer, both to have digital images you can store either on your computer or on a website like Ancestry, and to preserve the document. To scan documents you need a flatbed scanner, so it can scan both books and delicate documents. While you can buy separate scanners, the easiest and possibly most economical is to buy a printer with a flatbed scanner.

- **Back up information**   Backing up information means to copy it someplace other than on your hard drive so if something happens to your hard drive you have a copy of the information you probably spent a lot of effort putting on your computer. There are a number of ways to do this, both on your computer and on the Internet, as described later in this chapter in "Back Up Your Information." If you do it on your computer, it may mean that you need to get another hard drive, either external or internal. See the later section.

- **Use the Internet**   Using the Internet requires that you have an Internet connection and, in most cases, an account with an Internet service provider (ISP). If you have access to a wireless or wired Internet connection provided by someone else or only use the Internet from an Internet café, then you do not need an account with an ISP and can send and receive email using Google's Gmail or Microsoft's Hotmail free services. Otherwise, you will need an account with an ISP—often your phone company and/or cable TV company will fill this roll. Generally, one or more free email accounts come with the servicing account. Also, in most cases, the ISP will help you connect the service to your computer.

SELECT NEEDED HARDWARE

If you currently have a computer that is not too ancient, less than five or six years old, a printer with a scanner or a separate scanner, and an Internet

UNDERSTANDING COMPUTER NOMENCLATURE *(Continued)*

- Kbps, Mbps, and Gbps deal with the speed of transmission to, from, or within a computer. The "K," "M," and "G" are the same as described for memory capacity. The "b," which is lowercase, stands for "bit." It is a binary digit, a zero or a one. There are eight bits in a byte. The "ps" stands for "per second." So, "Mbps" stands for megabits per second. Your Internet connection is probably between 2 and 20 Mbps. The USB connection on most computers in the last several years is USB 2, which is 480 Mbps. USB 3 is up to 5 Gbps—up to ten times faster than USB 2.

- MHz and GHz deal with the speed of a computer processor—the CPU (central processing unit). The "M" and "G" are the same as described for memory capacity. The "Hz" stands for "Hertz" and is the frequency in cycles per second at which the processor operates. The greater the frequency, the faster the processor. Most processors in current personal computers operate between 1 and 3.5 GHz.

NOTE

Tablet computers such as the iPad and Android equivalents are not alternatives for most genealogy work because they don't run genealogy software, although they can do many of the Internet functions.

connection, you probably have all you need for genealogy work. If you are not totally comfortable with using your computer, see the accompanying note on other books we've written on more general practices of using a computer.

If you do not have a computer or are interested in getting a new one, here are some considerations:

- In choosing among a desktop, laptop, or integrated computer, the pros and cons are as follows:
  - An integrated computer uses a little less desk space, but costs substantially more.
  - A desktop computer provides the most capability, is most comfortable to use, and provides the most features for the money, but it isn't portable.
  - A laptop computer can be carried and used almost anywhere and has most of the capabilities of a desktop, but it costs somewhat more and is not as comfortable to use.
- Any new computer should have at least the recommended features shown in Table 3-1, plus a memory card receptacle, at least two USB ports, preferably USB 3, which are faster, and either or both a 1 Gbps Ethernet port and/or wireless "n" capability to connect to the Internet.
- For a printer, an inkjet model is preferable for economic personal use, and you want one with a flatbed scanner. Hewlett Packard (HP) makes a number of different models. Cannon, Epson, Panasonic, Samsung, Lexmark, and Brother all make other good options.
- You can back up your data in small amounts to CD and DVD writable discs or, for larger amounts, to either online sites or to internal or external hard disk drives (see "Back Up Your Information" later in this chapter). External hard disks holding 500GB to 1TB are easy to install and use and cost between $100 and $200..

Evaluate Genealogy Software

Genealogy software provides a way to store your genealogy information on your computer in an organized way. You can then search and utilize that information in many different ways, including creating reports, charts, to-do lists, timelines, forms, webpages, and even books. You can also transfer your information with other people and other programs using a genealogy file format called GEDCOM (see the "Explaining GEDCOM" QuickFacts).

EXPLAINING GEDCOM

GEDCOM stands for Genealogical Data Communication. It is a file format standard for the exchange of genealogy data used by virtually all genealogy programs and websites, although some programs use proprietary extensions to the standard, while other programs do not use all of the features in the standard. GEDCOM was developed by The Church of Jesus Christ of Latter-day Saints (LDS) and is currently in version 5.5.

While files created with the GEDCOM format are text files that can be opened in a word processor or text editor, they are not meant to be directly read or edited. They are files created by one computer program to be read by another program, and are not very intelligible on their own in a text editor, as you can see here with a small snippet of the Matthews GEDCOM file.

Just because a program can transfer information using a GEDCOM file does not mean that it is always easy to do so. Some programs have a GEDCOM validation feature to identify areas in a GEDCOM file that are not clear. See the discussions later in this chapter on using the Legacy and Family Tree Maker programs, as well as discussions in Chapter 5 on using the various online genealogy sites.

```
0 @P1@ INDI
1 DEAT
2 DATE about 1864
1 BIRT
2 DATE about 1830
2 PLAC North Carolina, USA
2 SEX M
1 NAME W. Riley /Matthews/
1 FAMS @F1@
0 @P2@ INDI
1 BIRT
2 DATE 1/16/1860
2 PLAC Chatham County, North Carolina, USA
2 SOUR @S-1646735420@
3 PAGE Year: 1900; Census Place: Hopkinsville, Christian, Kentucky; Roll: T623_515; Page: 2A;
Enumeration District: 5.
3 NOTE http://trees.ancestry.com/rd?f=sse&db=1900usfedcen&h=53226518&ti=0&indiv=try&gss=pt
3 NOTE
3 DATA
4 TEXT Birth date:  Jan 1860Birth place:  North CarolinaMarriage date:  1888Marriage place:
Residence date:  1900Residence place:  Hopkinsville City (South, East Part), Christian,
Kentucky
3 _APID 1,7602::53226518
1 RESI Chief of Police
2 DATE 1900
2 PLAC Hopkinsville City (South, East Part), Christian, Kentucky
2 SOUR @S-1646735420@
3 PAGE Year: 1900; Census Place: Hopkinsville, Christian, Kentucky; Roll: T623_515; Page: 2A;
Enumeration District: 5.
3 NOTE http://trees.ancestry.com/rd?f=sse&db=1900usfedcen&h=53226518&ti=0&indiv=try&gss=pt
3 NOTE
3 DATA
4 TEXT Birth date:  Jan 1860Birth place:  North CarolinaMarriage date:  1888Marriage place:
Residence date:  1900Residence place:  Hopkinsville City (South, East Part), Christian,
Kentucky
```

REVIEW YOUR NEEDS FOR GENEALOGY SOFTWARE

What you need in genealogy software depends a lot on what you want to accomplish with genealogy. It may be fully possible to accomplish everything you want using only online sites like Ancestry.com and never using a genealogy program. That said, there are a number of reasons why you might want such a program, among them are the following (not all software provides all of these functions):

● Print customizable reports with a number of options based on a family tree

● Create customizable charts with a number of options based on a family tree

● More flexible data entry with customizable options

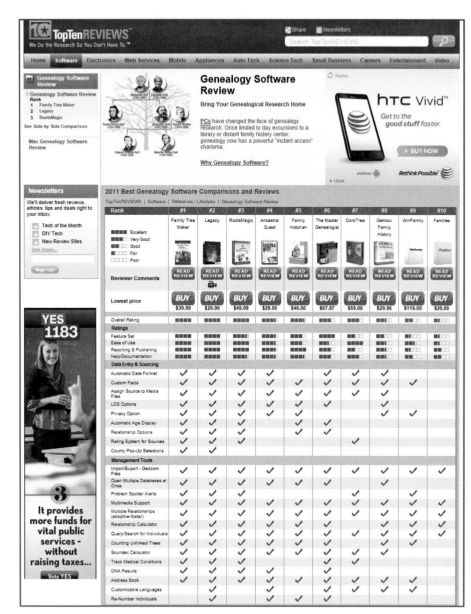

- More flexible and customizable display of the family tree information

- Better tracking of sources along with a source rating system

- Numerous specialized tools, such as problem spotter alerts, relationship calculator, Soundex calculator, and to-do lists

- Directly create webpages, books, and forms

The degree to which these functions are important to you should be the determinate of whether you get genealogy software.

EXAMINE THE ALTERNATIVES

There are a number of genealogy programs and several sources for comparing them. One of the more comprehensive comparisons and ranking is Top Ten Reviews (genealogy-software-review .toptenreviews.com), which takes reviews from several sources and combines them into a single chart, as you can see in Figure 3-1. This chart shows ten genealogy packages with what it considers the best on the left and the least capable on the right. Down the page there is an extensive list of features (only a part of which is shown in Figure 3-1) that show which are included in each package. The result of this comparison is that the top three packages are Family Tree Maker, Legacy Family Tree, and RootsMagic, in that order. It is, of course, just an opinion and can be swayed by any number of factors, not the least of which may be advertising from the products.

Figure 3-1: Top Ten Reviews provides a number of features on which to compare genealogy software and provides a ranking of their result.

	Legacy Family Tree ✕	Brother's Keeper ✕	RootsMagic ✕	Family Historian ✕	The Master Genealogist ✕	Family Tree Maker ✕ (Windows)

COMPARE ALL

Key Details

	Legacy Family Tree	Brother's Keeper	RootsMagic	Family Historian	The Master Genealogist	Family Tree Maker (Windows)
Genealogy Software	Legacy Family Tree	Brother's Keeper	RootsMagic	Family Historian	The Master Genealogist	Family Tree Maker (Windows)
Smart Rating	★★★★★	★★★★★	★★★★★	★★★★½	★★★★☆	★★★☆☆
Price	$30	$45	$30	$46	$34	$40
Upgrade Price	$22	$22		$26	$30	$28
Free Trial	✓	✗	✓	✓	✓	✗
Delivery Method	✓ CD Software ✓ Downloadable Software	✓ CD Software ✓ Downloadable Software	✗ CD Software ✓ Downloadable Software	✓ CD Software ✓ Downloadable Software	✓ CD Software ✓ Downloadable Software	✓ CD Software ✗ Downloadable Software
Platform	✓ Windows	✓ Windows	✓ Windows	✓ Windows	✓ Windows	✓ Windows
Optimized Database	✗ Ancestry.com ✗ Familysearch.org ✓ Kindred Konnections ✗ No Optimized Database* ✗ World Vital Records	✗ Ancestry.com ✗ Familysearch.org ✗ Kindred Konnections ✓ No Optimized Database* ✗ World Vital Records	✗ Ancestry.com ✓ Familysearch.org ✗ Kindred Konnections ✗ No Optimized Database* ✗ World Vital Records	✗ Ancestry.com ✓ Familysearch.org ✗ Kindred Konnections ✗ No Optimized Database* ✓ World Vital Records	✗ Ancestry.com ✗ Familysearch.org ✗ Kindred Konnections ✓ No Optimized Database* ✗ World Vital Records	✓ Ancestry.com ✗ Familysearch.org ✗ Kindred Konnections ✗ No Optimized Database* ✗ World Vital Records
Optimized Database Price	$120 per year		$0 per year	$40 per year		$156 per year
Optimized Database Details	Legacy Family Tree is optimized to work with Kindred Konnections hosted MyTrees.com. It allows you ... More	No optimized database – this means that no one genealogical database is directly optimized to work... More	RootsMagic is highly optimized to work with FamilySearch.org, a free genealogical database curated b... More	"Each boxed copy includes Getting the Most From Family Historian 4 as an online book, plus 30 days a... More	No optimized database – this means that no one genealogical database is directly optimized to work... More	Family Tree Maker is both optimized and produced by Ancestry.com. It allows you to search the Ances... More
Database License Length	12 months			12 months		12 months
Exporting	✗ .JPG ✗ .PDF ✗ CD/DVD ✓ GEDCOM ✓ Print ✓ Text ✓ Web		✓ .JPG ✓ .PDF ✓ CD/DVD ✓ GEDCOM ✓ Print ✓ Text ✓ Web	✗ .JPG ✓ .PDF ✓ CD/DVD ✓ GEDCOM ✗ Print ✓ Text ✓ Web	✗ .JPG ✗ .PDF ✓ CD/DVD ✓ GEDCOM ✓ Print ✓ Text ✓ Web	
Importing	✓ GEDCOM Files ✓ Images ✗ Sound ✓ Text Files ✗ Video		✓ GEDCOM Files ✓ Images ✗ Sound ✓ Text Files ✓ Video	✓ GEDCOM Files ✓ Images ✗ Sound ✓ Text Files ✗ Video	✓ GEDCOM Files ✓ Images ✗ Sound ✓ Text Files ✓ Video	

Figure 3-2: One interesting and unique piece of data on the Find The Best site is the database to which the package is optimized.

Wikipedia, the online encyclopedia (wikipedia.org/wiki/Comparison_of_genealogy_software), provides a comparison of genealogy software. This shows 21 software packages, a number of which are free, and compares them on several features, but not nearly to the extent of TopTen Reviews, and it does not rank the packages.

Another site that ranks genealogy software and provides significant detail about the products is Find The Best (genealogy-software.findthebest.com). It lists 29 packages that you can choose to compare. Figure 3-2 shows such a comparison. This site is newer and has "Beta" in its title, indicating that it is still being developed. Some of the packages seem to be lacking information, notably Family Tree Maker, which also has a low rating in opposition to most other sources. The top three packages on this site are Legacy Family Tree, Brother's Keeper, and RootsMagic. Family Tree Maker is thirteenth on the list. We suspect that Family Tree Maker has not gotten a complete review here. Nevertheless, this site offers a lot of information.

To see additional sites discussing genealogy software, use either Google or Bing and search on "genealogy software comparison." On the sites you look at, try to note their biases. So long as you know what it is, the information can still be valuable.

DECIDE ON THE SOFTWARE FOR YOU

In addition to looking at the comparisons on the Internet, talk to your friends and possibly family members who are doing genealogy and see what software they like. It may be that you will want to work closely with one or more of these people, and it might be handy to use the same software. We agree with Top Ten Reviews that the top three packages are Family Tree Maker, Legacy Family Tree, and RootsMagic. Of these, Bobbi is a fan of Legacy and Marty favors Family Tree Maker. All of them are very good products and will serve you well. Legacy has more features and seems to be preferred by people with more experience and ties to FamilySearch.org, the LDS online database. Family Tree Maker is closely tied to Ancestry.com (and is produced by them), and is substantially easier to use. RootsMagic is also closely tied to FamilySearch.org.

All of these packages cost money, $30 to $40, and so you might want to look at one or more of the free packages. Like most things in life, though, you generally get what you pay for. We believe that is true in this case and that the reasonable price of these packages is well worth paying.

Whichever package you choose, it will be right for you. In this book, though, we will focus on Family Tree Maker and Legacy, both of which are discussed at greater length later in this chapter.

Install and Use Genealogy Software

To get started using a genealogy software package, we will discuss acquiring, installing, and initial usage of both Family Tree Maker and Legacy Family Tree. The discussion of each of these packages could easily generate a book by themselves, so here we will only briefly touch on how they are used. Throughout the remainder of the book, we will occasionally refer to how a particular package will perform some function. This book, though, is not meant as a how-to for using either package.

Set Up and Use Family Tree Maker

Family Tree Maker was created and is sold by Ancestry.com. As a result, it is closely integrated with that online site and database. Family Tree Maker is relatively easy to use and allows you to easily go back and forth between the software package on your computer and the Ancestry.com online site. As a matter of fact, it is not always obvious in which product you are working, provided you have a relatively fast Internet connection.

Figure 3-3: **Family Tree Maker has only one version of the software, but you can get additional products with it.**

PURCHASE AND INSTALL FAMILY TREE MAKER

Family Tree Maker can be downloaded or shipped to you.

1. In your browser, such as Internet Explorer, click in the address box, type familytreemaker.com, and press **ENTER**. The Family Tree Maker site will open.

2. In the upper-right corner, click **Buy Now**. Review the comparison between Family Tree Maker and Family Tree Maker Complete with a printed guide, six electronic books, and photo editing software (see Figure 3-3).

3. For the package you choose, click either **Download** or **Ship It**. If you click **Ship It**:

   a. Enter your postal or ZIP code, any coupon code you may have, and click **Update** to calculate freight and tax.

   b. Review the amount and when ready click **Checkout**. Enter your name, address, and phone number and select the shipping speed you want.

c. Click **Continue**, enter your credit card information, and again click **Continue**. Review and confirm the final shipping and billing information.

d. If all is correct, click **Complete Your Order**. You are told your order is complete and that you will be sent an email receipt.

e. When you receive the package in the mail, put the disc in your CD/DVD drive, click **Run Setup**, click **Yes** you do want to allow Family Tree Maker to make changes to your computer, and click **Next** to begin installing.

If you click **Download**:

a. Enter the quantity you want, either or both of the specials, a discount or promotion code if you have one, and click **Continue**.

b. Enter your email address, your name, mailing address, and click **Continue**.

c. Enter your credit card information or click **PayPal** to enter this information, and click **Place My Order**.

d. Click **Print Your Receipt** to make sure you have a copy of your serial number, which you will have to enter into the software later, and click **Download Now**.

e. Click **Save** to save the software on your hard disk. When it is done downloading, click **Open Folder**. Look at the address bar at the top of the Windows Explorer window that has just opened and write down, if needed, the full address of the folder where Family Tree Maker has been placed (for example, mine is C:\Users\Marty\Downloads) so you can come back in the future and find the program if you need to.

f. Double-click the **Family Tree Maker** application, click **Run**, enter your name, type the serial number you printed out in step d., and click **Next** to begin installing.

4. In either case, click **Next** again to start the InstallAware Wizard, click **I Accept The Terms Of The License Agreement**, and click **Next** a third time.

5. Click **Next** to install the software in the default location, click **Next** to begin configuration, and finally click **Finish** when the installation has completed.

6. If you are asked, click **OK** to update Family Tree Maker, click **Update**, click **Accept All Downloads In The Future**, click **Start**, and click **Yes** to accept all future downloads.

7. Family Tree Maker may automatically start; if not, double-click its icon on the desktop.

8. Click the checkbox to agree to the Terms And Conditions, and click **Register Program**. If you already have an Ancestry.com account, enter your user name and password and click **Login**. If you do not have an account, click **Create Account**, enter the requested information clicking **Continue** as needed, and then enter your user name and password and click **Login**.

9. Accept the default of allowing Family Tree Maker to save your Ancestry.com login information so it can do that automatically, and click **Continue**.

10. Click **Activate Now** to activate your free 14-day membership to Ancestry.com (or 14-day extension to your existing membership), enter your password, click **Sign In**, fill in the needed credit card information if you don't have an existing membership, and click **Place Order**. You are shown your order information, which you can print. Click **Continue** and click **Close**.

11. Family Tree Maker will open, as shown in Figure 3-4, and you are given three choices to begin:

    ● Enter people directly into Family Tree Maker

    ● Import a family tree from an existing file

    ● Download a family tree from Ancestry.com

Figure 3-4: Family Tree Maker provides a direct tie to Ancestry.com.

ENTER PEOPLE INTO FAMILY TREE MAKER

If you are just starting out or want to start a new family tree, begin by typing people's names into Family Tree Maker.

1. Accept the default **Enter What You Know**, click in the **Name** text box, and type a person's name, possibly your own, to begin a tree with you and go back through your ancestry.

2. Click the **Sex** down arrow, and click the sex of the person you entered. Click in the **Birth Date** text box and type a date (it can be in any normal date format; Family Tree Maker will automatically change it to the "day, month, year" genealogy standard).

3. Begin typing the birthplace, and a drop-down list of place names in the genealogy-standard format of "city, county, state, country" will appear. Click the place you want to enter.

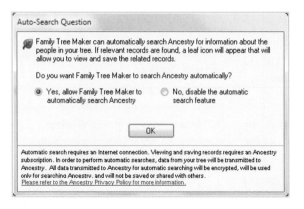

4. Click in the respective text box and enter a father's name (the last name will automatically appear) and then a mother's name.

5. Look at the default family tree name that has been assigned. If you want to change that, click in the text box and type your changes. Note the file location on your hard disk. If you want to change that, click **File Location**, select the folder in which you want to store the file, or create a new folder, and click **OK**.

6. When you are ready, click **Continue**. You are told the Family Tree Maker can automatically search Ancestry.com for information about people in your tree. Accept the default of **Yes** and click **OK**. The People page of Family Tree Maker opens with the person you just entered, as you can see in Figure 3-5.

7. Click each of the pages across the top of the window, entering additional information as desired and uploading to Ancestry.com if you want.

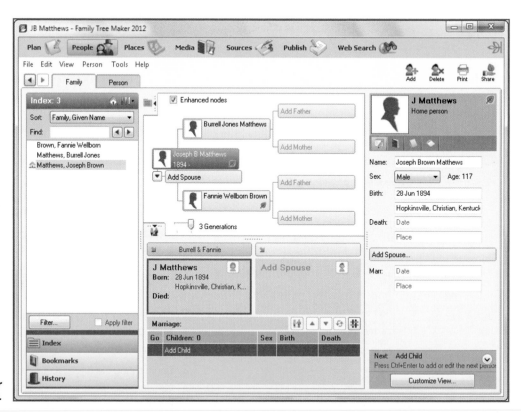

Figure 3-5: The People page of Family Tree Maker provides an excellent view of individuals.

IMPORT FROM AN EXISTING FILE

If you have used a different genealogy program or an online site other than Ancestry in which you have created a family tree, in most circumstances, you can import that tree into Family Tree Maker. (If you want to import from Ancestry.com, jump to the following section.)

1. In the other program or website, export the family tree that you want to import into Family Tree Maker. If asked, select the GEDCOM format.

2. In Family Tree Maker's Getting Started pane for a new family tree, click **Import From An Existing File**. You will see a list of the formats Family Tree Maker can import. The most important one is GEDCOM because almost all genealogy programs and websites can export family tree information in the GEDCOM format. (See the "Explaining GEDCOM" QuickFacts earlier in this chapter and the "Exporting a GEDCOM File from Ancestry.com" QuickSteps later in this chapter.)

3. Click **Browse**, and in the Choose File To Import dialog box (see Figure 3-6), select the folder on the left, click the file on the right that you want to import, and click **Open**.

4. Look at the default family tree name that has been assigned. If you want to change that, click in the text box and type your changes. Note the file location on your hard disk. If you want to change that, click **File Location**, select the folder in which you want to locate the file, or create a new folder, and click **OK**.

5. When you are ready, click **Continue**. You will see a dialog box telling you the progress. When the importing is finished, you will get a message telling you the number of individuals, records, and families that were imported. Click **Close**.

6. Review the People and other pages, looking at what you imported and filling in information as desired.

Figure 3-6: GEDCOM files, with a .ged extension, are almost universally used to exchange files among genealogy programs.

DOWNLOAD FROM ANCESTRY.COM

Since Family Tree Maker is a product of Ancestry.com, it is closely tied to it and you can easily move whole family trees as well as individual pieces of information back and forth between the two products.

1. In Family Tree Maker's Getting Started pane for a new family tree, click **Download From Ancestry**. The Ancestry Login dialog box will appear. If necessary, enter your user name and password, and click **OK**.

2. The family trees that you have on Ancestry.com are displayed, as shown in Figure 3-7. Select the family tree you want to import, and click **Request Download**.

3. The Download From Ancestry dialog box will open. Make any desired changes to the filename that will be used in Family Tree Maker. Choose whether to automatically synchronize the family tree between Ancestry.com and Family Tree Maker, and then click **Continue**.

4. You will see a dialog box showing you the progress of the download. When it has completed, another dialog box will tell you that the tree data has been downloaded, but that media items (photos, documents, audio and video files) will be processed in the background until they have all been downloaded.

5. If you want to go to Ancestry.com and view the family tree, click the **View Online Tree Now** checkbox, and in any case, click **Close**. If you did not go to Ancestry.com, the Family Tree Maker People page will open and display the downloaded data. If you have photos on Ancestry.com, they may not appear in Family Tree Maker for several minutes.

6. Review the People and other pages, looking at what you imported and filling in information as desired.

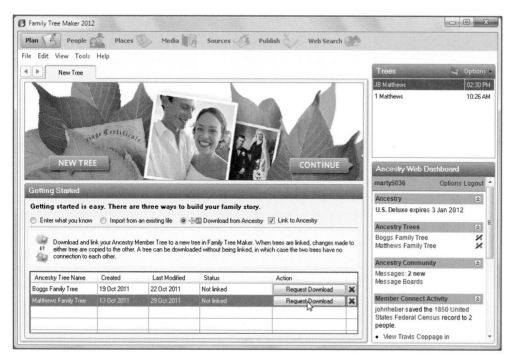

Figure 3-7: The tie between Family Tree Maker and Ancestry.com can be beneficial in working on your genealogy.

![clock icon] QUICKSTEPS

EXPORTING A GEDCOM FILE FROM ANCESTRY.COM

If you have a family tree created on Ancestry.com, you can export it to use on your computer in programs such as Legacy or RootsMagic (Family Tree Maker will automatically download your Ancestry.com family tree).

1. In Ancestry.com, move the mouse pointer over **Family Trees** in the navigation bar, and click the family tree you want to export. The family tree will be displayed.

2. Mouse over the **Tree Pages** drop-down list, and click **Tree Settings**.

3. Click the **Export Tree** button on the right of the page. You'll see a message "Generating a GEDCOM File…" and the percentage complete. This could take a few minutes, depending on the size of your family tree.

> Manage your tree
> Export your family tree data, as a GEDCOM file, to your computer.
> ⬇ Export tree

4. When the GEDCOM file has been generated, the Export Tree button will change to Download Your GEDCOM File. Right-click this button and click **Save Target As** in the options menu that opens. The Save As dialog box will open, as you can see in Figure 3-8.

> Manage your tree
> Export your family tree data, as a GEDCOM file, to your computer.
> ⬇ Download your GEDCOM file
> download tips

Continued . . .

Get Started with Legacy

Legacy Family Tree is a very comprehensive genealogy program containing many ancillary databases such as U.S. counties on a certain date so the program can validate a county existed on a date and you can look up on a map what counties existed. Legacy, as we said earlier, has a close tie with FamilySearch.org, and you can choose to get LDS support if you want it.

PURCHASE AND DOWNLOAD LEGACY

Legacy Family Tree can be purchased in several forms, with or without material that can be shipped to you.

1. In your browser, such as Internet Explorer, click in the address box, type Legacyfamilytree.com, and press **ENTER**. The Legacy Family Tree site will open (see Figure 3-9).

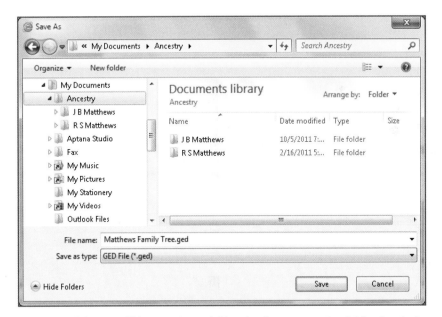

Figure 3-8: It is a good idea to set up a folder structure on your hard drive for storing your genealogy data.

QUICKSTEPS

EXPORTING A GEDCOM FILE FROM ANCESTRY.COM (Continued)

5. Select the folder on the left in which you want to store the file, correct the filename if needed, and click **Save**. You will see a message that the download has been completed.

6. Click **Open Folder** to assure yourself that the file is in the folder where you thought you put it. If the file is someplace other than this, be sure to note the folder it is in so you can locate it in the future.

2. First decide if you want to start out with the free Standard Edition; if so, click **Download** opposite Standard Edition; or take the plunge and buy the Deluxe Edition for (currently) $29.95 to $59.95 and click **Buy Now** opposite those words.

The Matthews Family Tree.ged download has completed.		Open ▾	Open folder	View downloads	×

3. If you clicked Download for the Standard Edition, you are shown a comparison of what's in the Standard Edition and what is in the Deluxe Edition. The first part of the comparison is shown here. We believe that the Deluxe Edition is well worth the modest cost beginning at $29.95.

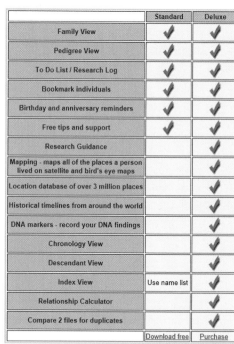

	Standard	Deluxe
Family View	✔	✔
Pedigree View	✔	✔
To Do List / Research Log	✔	✔
Bookmark individuals	✔	✔
Birthday and anniversary reminders	✔	✔
Free tips and support	✔	✔
Research Guidance		✔
Mapping - maps all of the places a person lived on satellite and bird's eye maps		✔
Location database of over 3 million places		✔
Historical timelines from around the world		✔
DNA markers - record your DNA findings		✔
Chronology View		✔
Descendant View		✔
Index View	Use name list	✔
Relationship Calculator		✔
Compare 2 files for duplicates		✔
	Download free	Purchase

*Figure 3-9: **Legacy Family Tree** provides a number of extras you can access, including the webinars and wall charts shown here.*

4. If you clicked Buy Now on the initial page or clicked **Purchase** on the comparison page, you are shown a number of options for purchasing Legacy. For $29.95 you can download all of the software—the full Legacy package. For various additional amounts you can add user's guides, training videos, and CDs with the software.

5. For the package you want to buy, click **Add To Cart**. Enter a coupon code if you have one, confirm the price you will pay, and click **Proceed To Checkout**.

6. Enter your billing information, confirm the shipping information is the same or enter it, select the shipping method, enter your credit card information, and click **Place Order**. You are told that you'll be sent two email messages; one is your invoice, the other is a set of instructions for downloading and installing Legacy.

7. Follow the instructions to download and install the software. Upon completion, the Legacy Guided Startup Wizard will open.

SET UP LEGACY FAMILY TREE

Setting up Legacy is really just an extension of the installation. Once you have completed installation, you are led through the guided setup.

1. In the Legacy Guided Setup Wizard, enter your name and customer number if you purchased the Deluxe Edition. If you are new to Legacy, we recommend that you click **Watch Legacy Tour** to do that, which requires an Internet connection. When you are ready, click **Next Step**.

2. You will be thanked for purchasing the Legacy Deluxe Edition, if you did. Click **OK**. You will be asked if you want to integrate Legacy with FamilySearch, the LDS online site. If you are an LDS member, click **Yes**; otherwise, click **No**. In either case, click **Continue**.

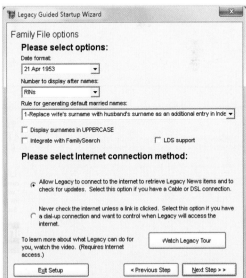

3. Choose the date format you want to use. The genealogy standard is "day month year"—for example, 23 Nov 2011. If you want to share information with other programs and online sites, it is recommended that you use this format.

4. Choose the number to display after a name. The options are

- **RIN**, or Record Identification Number, which is automatically generated in Legacy with each person you enter
- **User ID**, which is any number you enter on your own for each person
- **AFN**, or Ancestral File Number, from the FamilySearch database
- **FamilySearch ID**, which is also assigned by the FamilySearch website

5. Choose whether you want to have the husband's surname automatically added as an additional entry to a wife. Review the other options and make the choices that are correct for you. Putting the surname in all capital letters makes the software scan for a name. Click **Next Step** when you are ready.

6. If you are new to Legacy, it is worthwhile to watch the "Getting Started" video. If you have used Legacy in the past, the "What's New" video is worthwhile.

7. Choose how you want to begin using Legacy:

- If you have never entered any genealogy information in a program or an online site in the past, click, **I'm Just Starting**, click **Next Step**, and jump to the section "Enter People into Legacy" to see how to start a new family file and enter people into it.
- If you have entered some of your ancestors into another program or into an online genealogy site, such as Ancestry.com, click **I Want To Import My Information**, click **Next Step**, and go to the following section, "Import Information into Legacy."

IMPORT INFORMATION INTO LEGACY

In most cases, genealogy information to be transferred between two genealogy programs or between a genealogy program and an online site is in the form of a GEDCOM file. If needed, open the How To Create GEDCOM Files Legacy Help topic. If you want to export a GEDCOM file from Ancestry.com, see "Exporting a GEDCOM File from Ancestry.com" QuickSteps earlier in this chapter.

1. Having completed the second option in the last step of the previous section, choose whether you know where the file you want to import is stored, or whether you want Legacy to search for it, and then click **Next Step**.

2. If you said you didn't know where the file was stored, Legacy will search your hard disk drives for a file. This process is less than perfect. If a file can't be found, you will be

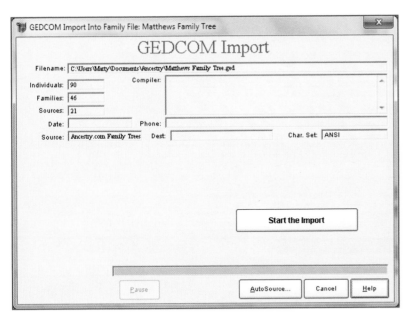

GEDCOM Import Into Family File: Matthews Family Tree

GEDCOM Import

Filename: C:\Users\Marty\Documents\Ancestry\Matthews Family Tree.ged

Individuals: 90 Compiler:

Families: 46

Sources: 21

Date: Phone:

Source: Ancestry.com Family Trees Dest: Char. Set: ANSI

Start the Import

Pause AutoSource... Cancel Help

Figure 3-10: Legacy can utilize all of the information that Ancestry.com puts in a GEDCOM file.

given a message to that effect and sent back to the previous dialog box in step 1. Choose **I Know Where The File Is Stored** and click **Next Step** once more.

3. In the Import GEDCOM File dialog box that opens, select the folder on the left and then the file on the right, and click **Open**. Accept the suggested name or enter a new name for the new family file and click **Open** again.

4. Legacy's GEDCOM Import dialog box will open (see Figure 3-10). Click **Start The Import**.

5. You may be told that a source can be assigned to each individual and marriage as the file is imported. Click **Add Source To All Incoming Fields That Have Information**, and click **Select A Master Source**. Click **Add**, click **No** you don't want to use a template, type your source, such as <u>Ancestry.com</u>, click **Save**, and click **Select**. If needed, click **Start The Import** once again.

6. When the import is complete, you are given a message to that effect. Click **OK** and click the **Pedigree** tab to see the family tree you just imported (see Figure 3-11).

ENTER PEOPLE INTO LEGACY

If you don't have an existing family tree you want to import, or if you want to start a new family tree:

1. If you have gone through the Setup Wizard and are in Legacy itself, click the **File** menu and click **New Family File**; otherwise, jump to step 2. You are asked if you want to use the Setup Wizard. Click **Yes** to open it.

2. In the Setup Wizard, where you are asked how you want to start, click **I'm Just Starting** and click **Next Step**.

3. You are asked if you want Legacy to help you, as shown in Figure 3-12. Accept the default, **Yes, Please**, and enter as much of the information as you know. When you are done, click **Finished**, enter the name of the new family file, and click **Save**. Your entries are shown on the Pedigree page, which you saw earlier in Figure 3-11.

4. To enter another person, click in one of the empty boxes on the Pedigree page, and click **Add An Individual**. The position you clicked is shown. Click **Add A New Person**. The new person's dialog box is opened.

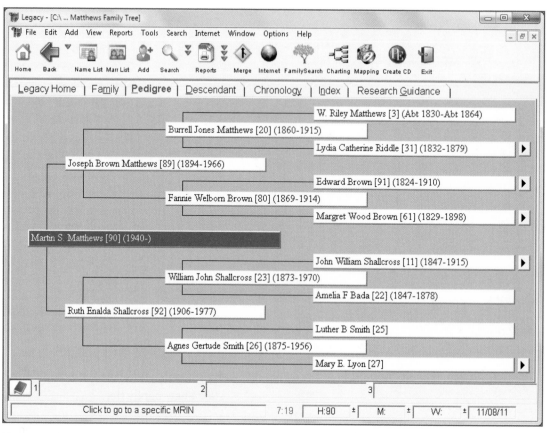

Figure 3-11: *Legacy provides a number of views of your data. Pedigree view is most immediately useful.*

5. Fill in the information as you can (see Figure 3-13). Here are some tips:

- "Title Pre." is the title prefix, such as Doctor or President.
- "Title Shf." is the title suffix, such as Jr. or III.
- "Chr" is for christened.
- For events such as Born and Died, enter dates on the left and location on the right.
- Dates should be entered in the format "day month year," for example: 12 Mar 2012.

Legacy Guided Startup Wizard

My information is not in another genealogy computer program.

Would you like Legacy to help you get started?

○ **No thanks. Please create a new empty family file and I'll do the rest.**

◉ **Yes, please. I'll start by entering what I know below:**

	Given names	Surname
Your Name:		
Your Birth Date:		○ Male ○ Female
Your Birth Place:		

Add Father's Father
Add Father
Add Father's Mother
Add Mother's Father
Add Mother
Add Mother's Mother

Are you married?   ○ Yes   ◉ No   Marriage Date: _____   Marriage Place: _____

	Given names	Surname
Spouse's Name:		
Spouse's Birth Date:		○ Male ○ Female
Spouse's Birth Place:		

Add Father's Father
Add Spouse's Father
Add Father's Mother
Add Mother's Father
Add Spouse's Mother
Add Mother's Mother

| Exit Setup | To learn more about what Legacy can do for you, watch the video. (Requires Internet access.) | Watch Legacy Tour | < Previous Step | Finished |

Figure 3-12: Legacy provides a number of tools to help you enter your ancestors and research your genealogy.

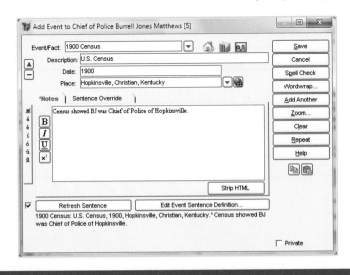

6. To add events, click **Add** on the right to open the Add Event dialog box. Enter the event name, description, date, place, and notes.

7. When you have all the information that you want entered for a person, click **Save**.

8. Repeat steps 4 through 7 as needed to enter as many more people as you want.

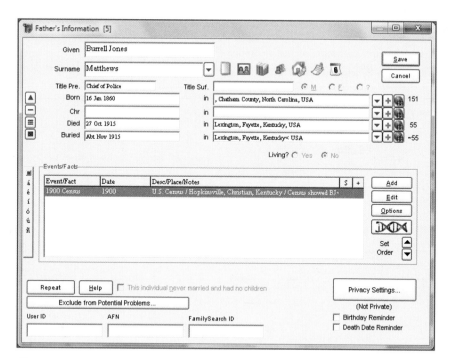

Figure 3-13: *You can enter an unlimited number of events for a person.*

Be Comfortable on the Internet

Genealogy today means that you will be going on the Internet and spending a lot of time there. If you listen to what many people are saying about the Internet, it can be scary. The key is to learn to protect yourself so that you are comfortable using it.

Keep Yourself Safe on the Internet

Your connection through your computer to the Internet is your doorway to the cyberworld. It allows you to communicate with others through email; it allows you to shop for virtually anything without leaving your home; and it provides an enormous resource for gathering genealogy information. It also is a doorway that can let in things that can harm you, your computer, and your data. It is like the front door to your house—you need it to see and interact with other people, but it also has locks on it to keep out the people you don't want to let in. Similarly, there are a number of barriers you can place in the way of people who want to do damage via the Internet.

Understand Internet Threats

As the Internet has gained popularity, so have the threats it harbors. Viruses, worms, spyware, and adware have become part of our vocabulary. Look at each of these threats to understand what each can do and how to guard your computer and data, as described in Table 3-3.

PROBLEM	DEFINITION	SOLUTION
Virus	A program that attaches itself to other files on your computer. There are many forms of viruses, each performing different, usually malevolent, functions on your computer.	Install an antivirus program with a subscription for automatic updates, and make sure it is continually running.
Worm	A type of virus that replicates itself repeatedly through a computer network or security breach in your computer. Because it keeps copying itself, a worm can fill up a hard drive and cause your network to malfunction.	
Trojan horse	A computer program that claims to do one thing, such as play a game, but has hidden parts that can erase files or even your entire hard drive.	
Adware	The banners and pop-up ads that come with programs you download from the Internet. Often, these programs are free, and to support them, the program owner sells space for ads to display on your computer every time you use the program.	Install an anti-adware program.
Spyware	A computer program that downloads with another program from the Internet. Spyware can monitor what you do, keep track of your keystrokes, discern credit card and other personally identifying numbers, and pass that information back to its author.	Install an antispyware program.

Table 3-3: Security Issues Associated with the Internet and How to Control Them

Use an Antivirus or Security Program

To counter the various Internet threats, you need to install an antivirus or security program. A number of such programs are available, both free and at a cost. You can buy these in computer stores and on the Internet. There is a lot of variability in the pricing, and the opinion of which is the best also varies widely. Table 3-4 shows a few of these programs with which we have had direct experience. The best thing for you to do is go on the Internet and do a search of "Internet Security Suites reviews." Look for the toptenreviews.com site—it gives you a quick comparison, but also look at several other sites and read the reviews, because there is considerable difference of opinion. When you have decided on the program you want, determine the version to get. Most companies have a basic antivirus program, an Internet security program, and an overall security program (see Figure 3-14). Our opinion is that the Internet security programs are a good middle ground. Finally, do some price hunting,

NOTE

AVG's free edition provides very basic antivirus protection. Microsoft's Security Essentials is more robust, but still less than the Internet Security offerings, although it could be argued that it provides what the majority of users need.

NAME	WEBSITE	LIST PRICE (AS OF 3/2012)
AVG Antivirus Free Edition	free.avg.com	Free
AVG Internet Security	avg.com	$54.99 for three PCs, one year
BitDefender Internet Security	bitdefender.com	$69.95 for three PCs, one year
Kaspersky Internet Security	Kaspersky.com	$69.95 for three PCs, one year
Microsoft Security Essentials	microsoft.com/ security_essentials	Free
Norton Internet Security	Symantec.com	$64.99 for three PCs, one year

Table 3-4: 2012 Antivirus and Internet Security Programs

making sure you are looking at the version you want. At the time this was written (3/2012), Amazon.com was offering the following 2012 Internet Security packages for three PCs and one year for these prices: BitDefender $29.98, Kaspersky $28.53, and Norton $29.85. There have been mail-in rebate deals that allow you to get the program for the price of shipping after the rebate.

Figure 3-14: There are often three levels of security protection you can buy.

NOTE

Protected Mode—which you can turn on or off at the bottom of the Security tab (the notice for which you'll see at the bottom of Internet Explorer)—is what produces the messages that tell you a program is trying to run in Internet Explorer or that software is trying install itself on your computer. In most cases, you can click in a bar at the top of the Internet Explorer window if you want to run the program or install the software. You can also double-click the notice at the bottom of Internet Explorer to open the Security tab and turn off Protected Mode (clear the **Enable Protected Mode** checkbox).

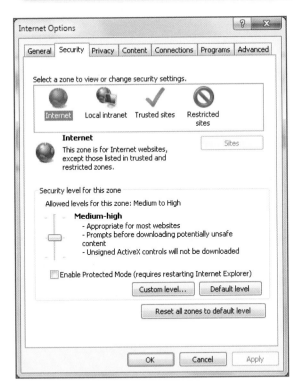

Figure 3-15: Internet Explorer allows you to categorize websites into zones and determine what can be done within those zones.

Control Internet Security

Internet Explorer allows you to control three aspects of Internet security. You can categorize sites by the degree to which you trust them, determine how you want to handle cookies placed on your computer by websites, and set and use ratings to control the content of websites that can be viewed. These controls are found in the Internet Options dialog box.

In Internet Explorer, click **Tools** on the tab row, and click **Internet Options**.

CATEGORIZE WEBSITES

Internet Explorer allows you to categorize websites into zones: Internet (sites that are not classified in one of the other ways), Local Intranet, Trusted Sites, and Restricted Sites (as shown in Figure 3-15). From the Internet Options dialog box:

1. Click the **Security** tab. Click the **Internet** zone. Note its definition.

2. Click **Custom Level**. Select the elements in this zone that you want to disable, enable, or prompt you before using. Alternatively, select a level of security you want for this zone, and click **Reset**. Click **OK** when you are finished.

3. Click each of the other zones, where you can identify either groups or individual sites you want in that zone.

HANDLE COOKIES

Cookies are small pieces of data that websites store on your computer so that they can remind themselves of who you are. These can save you from having to constantly enter your name and ID. Cookies can also be dangerous, however, letting people into your computer where they can potentially do damage.

Internet Explorer lets you determine the types and sources of cookies you will allow and what those cookies can do on your computer. From the Internet Options dialog box:

1. Click the **Privacy** tab. Select a privacy setting by dragging the slider up or down.

2. Click **Advanced** to open the Advanced Privacy Settings dialog box. If you wish, click **Override Automatic Cookie Handling**, and select the settings you want to use.

3. Click **OK** to return to the Internet Options dialog box.

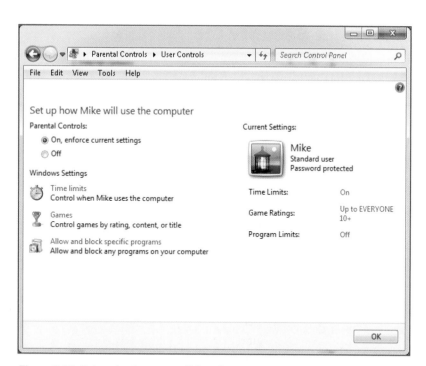

Figure 3-16: *Determine how you will handle cookies that websites want to leave on your computer.*

4. In the middle of the Privacy tab, you can turn off the pop-up blocker, which is on by default (it is recommended that you leave it on). If you have a site that you frequently use that needs pop-ups, click **Settings**, enter the site address (URL), click **Add**, and click **Close**.

5. At the bottom of the Privacy tab, you can determine how to handle InPrivate Filtering and Browsing. See the Note on InPrivate later in this chapter.

CONTROL CONTENT

You can control the content that Internet Explorer displays. From the Internet Options dialog box:

1. Click the **Content** tab. Click **Parental Controls**. Click the user you want to control to open the User Controls window, shown in Figure 3-16. Click **On** to turn on parental controls, and configure any other settings you want to use. Click **OK** when you are done, and then close the Parental Controls window.

2. Click **Enable** to open the Content Advisor dialog box. Individually select each of the categories, and drag the slider to the level you want to allow. Detailed descriptions of each area are shown in the lower half of the dialog box.

3. Click **OK** to close the Content Advisor dialog box.

4. When you are done, click **OK** to close the Internet Options dialog box.

Back Up Your Information

After a bit of time exploring genealogy, you will accumulate a sizable amount of information, documents, and pictures about your ancestry that you do not want to lose. You therefore need to protect it by backing it up off your computer.

Computers are a great asset, but like any machine, they are prone to failures of many kinds. Once you have started using your computer regularly, it becomes important to make a copy of your information and store it in another location should your hard drive fail or something else happen to your computer.

There are several solutions to copying and saving your information. The term normally used for this is *backup* (or to back up—the verb form). This means storing a copy of your information in a location other than on your computer. You can back up both to CDs/DVDs or another hard drive on or connected to your computer, and by copying your files to a site on the Internet.

Back Up on Your Computer

Within your computer, you can back up your information to a CD or DVD, to another drive that is connected to your computer (including an external hard drive and a USB flash or thumb drive), or to a hard drive on another computer.

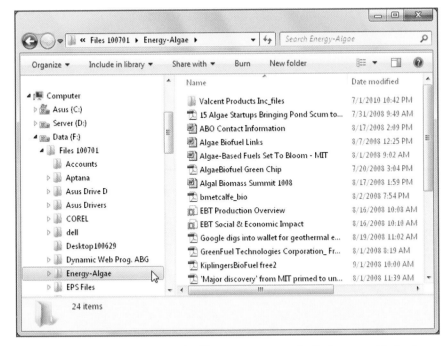

Figure 3-17: *You must first locate the files on your computer that you want to back up.*

You may want to perform backups to a couple of these items on a periodic basis, and a couple of times a year, back up your data to a CD and put it in your bank safety deposit box.

Windows 7 has a backup program, but without a lot of setup, it backs up things you don't really care about, like programs you already have on CDs or DVDs. A simpler way to do a backup is to simply copy your files from the hard disk in your computer to an external device, like a CD, DVD, USB flash drive, or external hard drive. Here's how to copy some files to a writable (or "burnable") CD:

1. Click **Start**, click **Computer**, and open (click the triangle on the left) the drive and folders in the left column needed to display the files you want to back up in the right column, as you see in Figure 3-17.

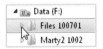

NOTE

Your AutoPlay dialog box may look different from the one shown here, depending on the options that have been selected in the past.

2. Open your CD/DVD drive, insert a blank writable disc, and close the drive. An AutoPlay dialog box will open offering you several options.

3. Click **Burn Files To Disc** to open the Burn To Disc dialog box. Type a title, click **Like A USB Flash Drive**, and click **Next**. You will see a message that the disc is being formatted, and then another AutoPlay dialog box will appear.

4. Click **Open Folder To View Files** to open another window with a blank right pane with the message "Drag Files To This Folder To Add Them To The Disc."

5. In your original folder, similar to the one shown in Figure 3-17, select the files you want to back up by clicking the first file, pressing and holding **SHIFT** while clicking the last file if the files are contiguous, or pressing and holding **CTRL** while individually clicking the other files if they are not contiguous.

6. When all the necessary files in a folder are selected, drag them (point on the selected files, press and hold the left mouse button, and move the mouse) to the right pane of the new folder for the CD or DVD, as you can see in Figure 3-18, and release the mouse button.

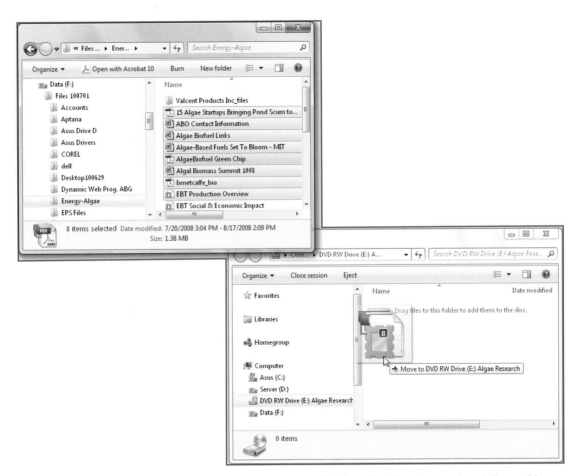

Figure 3-18: An easy way to back up files is to drag them to an external disc or drive.

7. You can open other folders and drives and drag other files to the CD/DVD folder. Periodically look at how much space on the CD/DVD has been used by right-clicking the drive in the left pane of its window and clicking **Properties** in the context menu. In the Properties dialog box, look at how much free space you have left, and then click **OK**.

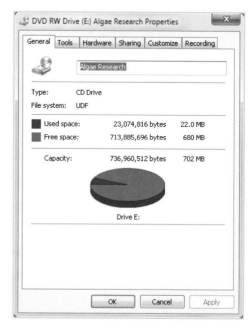

8. When you have all the files you want to back up in the CD/DVD, click **Close Session**. You'll see a message that the disc is being closed. When that is done, you'll see a message that the disc is ready. Click **Eject**, remove the disc, label it with a soft felt-tip pen, and store it with a paper or plastic sleeve in a safe place, preferably away from your computer and in a fireproof container.

ⓘ Disc Ready
Your disc is now ready to be used on other computers.

Back Up Over the Internet

Recently, many people are choosing to save their information to the *cloud*, meaning that they back up the data on their computer to a location (a server) accessed through the Internet. This method makes it easy to access your data from any location, as well as your new computer, should your old computer fail. These services are reasonable in cost, or even free, and are easy to set up.

NOTE

A disc created with the Like A USB Flash Drive option can be put into the CD/DVD disc drive again and have files deleted and added to it, as well as edited and restored to the disc.

Some programs, once you have subscribed to them, install a small software program on your computer. These programs work behind the scenes, copying new photos, data files, or letters to a secure, encrypted location. Should your old computer break down, you can restore your files and data to your new computer.

An example of a currently free cloud service is Microsoft's SkyDrive. Microsoft gives you 25GB of storage. You'll need to set up an account with a user ID and a password.

1. Click the **Internet Explorer** icon on the taskbar to open it. In the address bar, type skydrive.live.com and press **ENTER**. Windows Live will open, and if you are not already signed up as a Windows Live or Hotmail client, you will be asked to do that. Click **Sign Up**, fill out the form that opens, and click **I Accept**. Your SkyDrive page will open, where you can use existing folders or set up your own, as you can see in Figure 3-19.

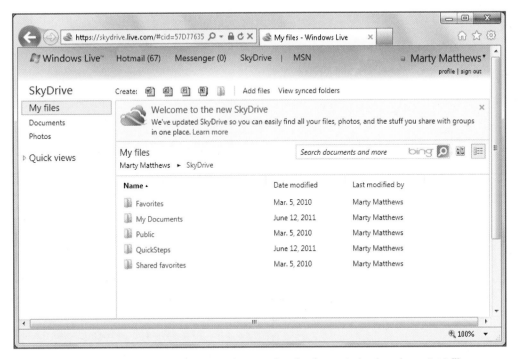

Figure 3-19: Online, "cloud" Internet storage is a good and safe way to back up important files.

QUICKSTEPS

LOCKING A COMPUTER

By default, when your screen saver comes on and you return to use your system, you must go through the logon screen. If you have added a password to your account, you have to enter it to get back into the system, which is a means of preventing unauthorized access when you are away from your running computer. If you don't want to wait for your screen saver to come on, you can click **Start**, click the **Shut Down** right arrow, and click **Lock**; or you can press 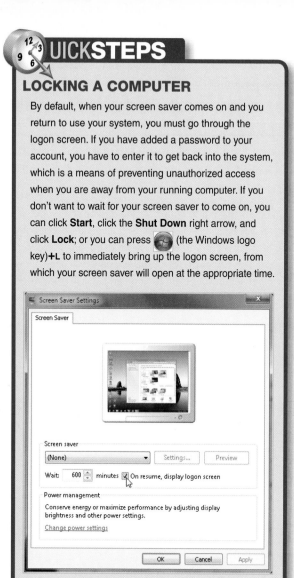 (the Windows logo key)**+L** to immediately bring up the logon screen, from which your screen saver will open at the appropriate time.

Continued . . .

2. Click a folder you want to use to open it, and then click **Add Files**; or click **Create Folder** (the folder icon in the Create list), enter a name for the folder, and click **Next**. In either case, a window will open inviting you to drop documents there or select documents from your computer.

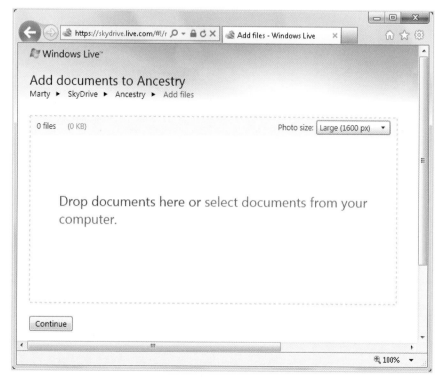

3. You can use steps 1, 5, and 6 under "Back Up on Your Computer" and drag the files to the window shown in the previous step; or you can click **Select Documents From Your Computer**, select the files as in step 5 in "Back Up on Your Computer," and click **Open**.

4. You'll see the files being added. When the files have been added, you can remove individual files by clicking the X after the file size of each file. You can add files using either method in step 3.

5. When you have added all the files you want, click **Continue**. A list will appear of the files you have added. You can select a particular file and share, move, copy, rename,

QUICKSTEPS

LOCKING A COMPUTER (Continued)

Depending on your environment, having to go through the logon screen every time you come out of the screen saver may or may not be beneficial. To turn off the screen saver protection or turn it back on:

1. Right-click the desktop and click **Personalize**. Click **Screen Saver**.

2. Select or deselect **On Resume, Display Logon Screen**, depending on whether you want to display the logon screen upon returning to your system (see Figure 3-20).

3. Click **OK** to close the Screen Saver Settings dialog box, and close the Personalization window.

and delete it. If the file is for Microsoft Word, Excel, or PowerPoint, you can edit it directly in your browser (Internet Explorer) using the Microsoft Office Web Apps.

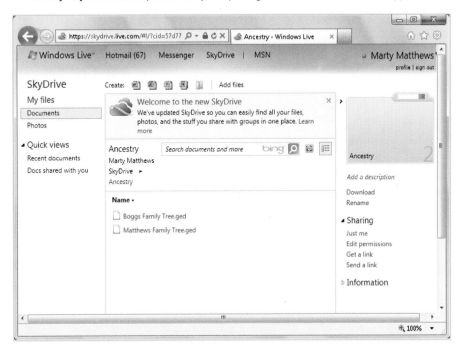

6. When you are done, click **Sign Out** in the upper-right corner and, if desired, close Internet Explorer.

Other cloud sites work similarly.

Figure 3-20: *You can password-protect your system when you leave it unattended by having the logon screen appear when you return after using the screen saver.*

Jenanne Murphy, 56, Whidbey Island, WA

OVERVIEW

Through visits to Ireland and West Virginia, plus several very helpful relatives and census data, I have traced my father's paternal line back four generations to my ancestors immigrating to the United States. My father's maternal line had been researched previously and was already well documented. I have been able to communicate via the Internet with other family members who are also doing genealogy research, and their willingness to share the information they have gathered has been invaluable in my research. I have used both Ancestry.com and RootsWeb.com Internet sites, and Family Tree Maker 2006.

STORY

My father and I were returning from a family reunion in October 2004 when he commented that we know a lot of history about his mother's side of the family, but very little about his father's side. His maternal Sayre line had already been extensively researched, tracing the family back to an early ancestor who came to America from England in 1638, and further back to 1564 in Bedfordshire, England. We wanted to know more about the Murphy side of the family.

GETTING STARTED

Within two weeks of starting our research, my dad was able to obtain from a cousin a copy of an old letter (see part of the first page in Figure 3-21) written by his great-grandfather's brother, John W. Murphy, to his great-grandfather Michael Murphy. This letter has been a guiding document ever since, not just for me but also for others researching the Murphy family. It was the first time any of us knew that there were at least three brothers and one sister of my great-great-grandfather who came over from Ireland, and that their parents came over as well. We also learned

that Deeshart, County Cork, Ireland, was an important place for them. This was ultimately confirmed when another relative found John's naturalization papers, which showed he was born in Deeshart (see Figure 3-22).

My second big break came in response to queries I posted on Ancestry.com message boards asking for any information on my great-great-grandfather Michael W. Murphy. I received a reply from a woman who is researching the

Figure 3-21: A letter from 1868 provided a number of clues that got my dad and I started in our research.

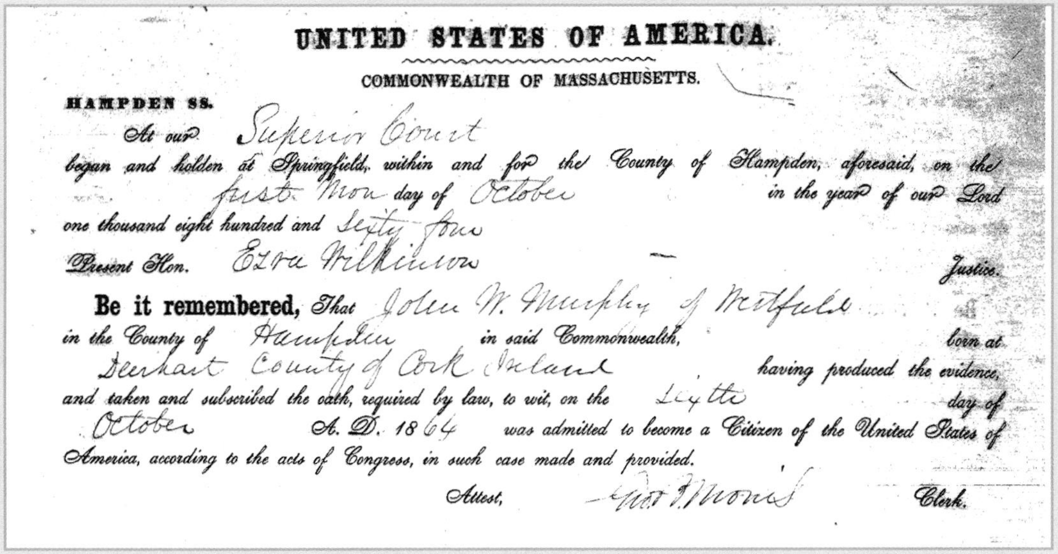

UNITED STATES OF AMERICA.
COMMONWEALTH OF MASSACHUSETTS.

HAMPDEN SS.

At our *Superior Court* began and holden at *Springfield*, within and for the County of Hampden, aforesaid, on the *first Mon* day of *October* in the year of our Lord one thousand eight hundred and *Sixty four* Present Hon. *Ezra Wilkinson* Justice.

Be it remembered, That *John W. Murphy of Westfield* in the County of *Hampden* in said Commonwealth, born at *Deeshart County of Cork Ireland* having produced the evidence, and taken and subscribed the oath, required by law, to wit, on the *Sixth* day of *October* A. D. 18 *64* was admitted to become a Citizen of the United States of America, according to the acts of Congress, in such case made and provided.

Attest, *Geo. ___* Clerk.

Figure 3-22: The naturalization for Michael Murphy's brother provided proof that the family originated in Deeshart, Ireland.

Figure 3-23: This charcoal drawing of my great-great-grandparents, Michael and Barbara Murphy, is treasured by a number of Murphy relatives.

family of Michael's wife, Barbara Baldwin. She sent me a photo of my great-grandfather and more information about the Baldwin family. A second reply came from another woman who is a descendant of Michael Murphy through his oldest son Jeremiah. She sent me an image of a wonderful charcoal drawing of my great-great-grandparents (see Figure 3-23), as well as an invitation to join her in a network of Murphy descendants sharing their research on Ancestry.com.

CHALLENGES

After our initial successes, we knew that we had ancestors from Ireland and West Virginia, but we also had many questions. To try to answer those questions my father and I took trips to West Virginia and to County Cork, Ireland. The trip to West Virginia was very successful. I had done some research using census data and had found that my ancestors had lived in Nicholas County in an area known as "the Wilderness." During our visit we went to the cemetery in Summersville, West Virginia, and found the graves for my great- and great-great-grandparents and many other family members (see Figure 3-24). At the Nicholas County Courthouse, we found records of Michael Murphy's land purchases and learned that he had been a surveyor of roads in the Wilderness District for many years. We also visited the original homestead in Runa, West Virginia, which is still owned by one of the Murphy cousins.

The trip to Ireland was wonderful in terms of learning about our ancestral homeland, but was not as productive learning about our ancestry. We contacted the Mallow Heritage Center in County Cork, where Deeshart is located, and provided them with the names and dates. They provided a list of possible ancestors, but the information did not correlate well with what we already know about the family. We visited the Cobh Heritage Center in County Cork, which provided a lot of historical information about various waves of immigration. We also looked at gravestones in an old church cemetery (see Figure 3-25), but we did not find any that might be our ancestors. For now, the story goes only back to the *Brig Garland*, which carried the Murphy family to Boston from Galway in May 1850.

A   B

Figure 3-24: *The grave sites we found in West Virginia provided solid evidence of our ancestry.*

Figure 3-25: *My father looking at graves in Ireland.*

OBJECTIVES

Thus far, we have been able to trace Dad's ancestors back four generations to the point where the immigration from Ireland took place (see Figure 3-26). We have found records of my great-great-grandfather, as well as the names of his mother and father. I would like to continue this research to see whether we can ultimately find records from Ireland that correlate with this family. I would like to meet some of the other descendants of Michael Murphy, who are also researching the family genealogy and do more with my mother's line.

Descendants of Michael W Murphy

1 Michael W Murphy 1826 - 1907
.. +Barbara Ann Baldwin 1838 - 1917
.... 2 Jeremiah Martin Murphy 1855 - 1935
.... +Margaret Jane Curran 1861 - 1956
.... 3 Annie Agnes Murphy 1879 - 1961
.... 3 Mary Francis Murphy 1880 - 1963
.... 3 Patrick Leo Murphy 1883 - 1924
.... 3 Nellie Bierne Murphy 1885 - 1969
.... 3 Charles Michael Murphy 1886 - 1939
.... 3 Betty Belle Murphy 1889 - 1985
.... 3 Edward Paul Murphy 1892 - 1951
.... 3 William Cornelius Murphy 1893 - 1922
.... 3 Verna Margaret Murphy 1896 - 1978
.... 3 Jesse John Murphy 1899 - 1931
.... 3 Donald Murphy 1901 - 1974
.... 3 Agnes Dell Murphy 1904 - 1997
.... 3 Lucille Adeline Murphy 1904 - 1980
.... 2 John William Murphy 1856 - 1932
.... +Sarah Francis Reynolds 1858 - 1942
.... 3 Anna Laura Murphy 1884 - 1962
.... 3 Frank Guthrey Murphy 1885 - 1978
.... 3 Hattie Marie Murphy 1889 - 1980
.... 3 Margaret Vera Murphy 1891 - 1978
.... 3 Robert John Murphy 1893 - 1957
.... 3 Carl C Murphy 1895 - 1968
.... 3 Rose Murphy 1896 - 1995
.... 3 Ernest Murphy 1899 - 1981
.... 3 James Ralph Murphy 1902 - 1980
.... 2 Mary Jane Murphy 1866 - 1918
.... +Charles John Beirne 1852 - 1895
.... 3 Annie Beirne 1885 - 1958
.... 3 Pat Beirne 1886 - 1977
.... 3 Betty Beirne 1888 - 1915
.... 3 John Cornelius Beirne 1891 - 1942
.... 3 Margaret Beirne 1894 -
.... 3 Charles Robert Beirne 1896 - 1922
.... *2nd Husband of Mary Jane Murphy:
.... +Charles Patrick Sweeny 1872 - 1951
.... 3 James Bernard Sweeny 1901 - 1978
.... 3 Gladys E Sweeny 1903 - 1987
.... 3 Ruth Marie Sweeny 1905 - 1978
.... 3 Michael Andrew Sweeny 1907 - 1907
.... 2 Michael William Murphy 1864 - 1954
.... +Ada Isenhower 1865 - 1894
.... 3 William Murphy 1891 - 1892
.... *2nd Wife of Michael William Murphy:
.... +Ida M Dingess

.... *3rd Wife of Michael William Murphy:
.... +Mary Alice Scherer 1876 - 1939
.... 3 Vincent Matthew Murphy 1900 - 1974
.... 3 Edward Philip Murphy 1903 - 1984
.... 3 Veronica Wanda Murphy 1906 - 1974
.... 3 Mary Cecilia Murphy 1908 - 1974
.... 3 Michael Andrew Murphy 1910 - 1979
.... 3 Rita Jane Murphy 1915 - 2005
.... 3 Barbara Ann Murphy 1921 -
.... +Paul S. Jackson 1916 - 2004
.... 2 Cornelius C. Murphy 1865 - 1952
.... +Ada J Jenkins 1873 - 1946
.... 3 Dana Cornelius Murphy 1897 - 1961
.... +Margaret Walker 1903 - 1990
.... 2 James Andrew Murphy 1872 - 1928
.... +Lucy McClung 1874 - 1946
.... 3 Michael Jennings Murphy 1895 - 1972
.... +Dorothy Sayre 1895 -
.... 3 Sarah Pearl Murphy 1896 - 1977
.... +John Abney Trent 1886 -
.... 3 James Andrew Murphy 1899 - 1992
.... +Marian Downs
.... 3 Minnie Ethel Murphy 1901 - 1987
.... +Emil G. Huffman 1904 - 1996
.... 3 John D Murphy 1902 - 1905
.... 3 Alice Mahone Murphy 1908 - 1999
.... +Reginald T. McCutcheon
.... 3 Greely Sheridan Murphy 1910 - 1947
.... 3 Kyle McClung Murphy 1912 - 1967
.... +Edna Wanita Postlethwait 1918 - 1993
.... 3 Mary Sybil Murphy 1915 - 2011
.... +Eugene C Tinnel 1917 -
.... 2 Joseph Daniel Murphy 1874 - 1962
.... +Florence Viola Burdett 1875 - 1965
.... 2 Elizabeth Adeline Murphy 1877 - 1935
.... +Wesley Franklin Thomas 1880 - 1905
.... 3 Arthur Ray Thomas 1905 - 1977
.... +Mary Frances "Kitty" Holmes
.... *2nd Husband of Elizabeth Adeline Murphy:
.... +Arnold Patrick Neylon 1877 - 1923
.... 3 William Arnold Neylon 1912 - 1994
.... +Freda Magdalene Wade 1914 - 1981
.... *2nd Wife of William Arnold Neylon:
.... +Orie Madden Allen 1903 - 2002

*Figure 3-26: **Michael and Barbara Murphy's descendants created an extensive family tree in only two generations.***

Chapter 4

Identifying Web Resources

So now what? You've gotten your computer running, you're connected to the Internet, and you're ready to go. But go where? Many think that the best way to begin is to go directly to a known genealogy site, while others just type in their mother's maiden name into a general search engine and hope for the best. This chapter introduces you to the wide variety of resources for your genealogy research available on the Internet and explains a bit about each type of resource. See Chapter 5 for how to enter your information and analyze what you see, and then Chapter 6 for how to search once you are on the sites.

USING SPECIAL SEARCH TERMS

With nearly all search engines you can use special terms, called *Boolean* terms, to help you narrow your searches. While not all search engines allow you to designate which terms to use, most will use some variation of the following terms:

- AND

  For example, if you wanted to look up information about the Baltimore Orioles, you could enter "Baltimore AND Orioles" and the resulting list of "hits" would contain both words. When using altavista.com we entered "Baltimore Orioles" and received 14,400,000 results. When we "asked" the search engine to only return sites with both words (Baltimore AND Orioles), the results were narrowed down to only 9,300,000.

- NOT

  When we used the term "orioles NOT Baltimore" at the same search engine, our results were "only" 2,200,000.

- OR

  By entering "orioles OR Baltimore" we received 153,000,000 possible sites that contained either the word "orioles" OR the word "Baltimore."

- WITH

  In some search engines, if you enter the search term "Baltimore WITH Orioles" the results will contain only those sites that contain the terms "Baltimore" and "Orioles" next to each other. Other search engines assume "closeness" if the words are in the same paragraph or sentence.

Continued . . .

Review Web Search Sites

Web search sites, or *search engines,* can help you with your genealogy searches. Several types of search engines are available, and the results you see from their searches will depend on how that search engine looks for information.

Use General Search Sites

The most common search engine looks for information on the keyword(s) that you have entered. Google and Bing are both examples of this type of search engine. You type in a word, such as <u>genealogy</u> and an automated searcher (called a "web bot," "web crawler," "spider," or just "bot") is activated to search through all of the pages the search engine recognizes on the Web. Some search engines search every word on each page, while other search engines store parts of webpages so that a search is faster. Many webpages include hidden "meta tags," or keywords that summarize what is included on that page. These tags are often noted by the bot and help make the search results faster.

Other search engines that base their results on indexes or directories often use human-based searches or some variation to include websites in their database. Most of today's general search engines use a combination of the human and the keyword search, most notably Bing.

Meta-search engines search several other search engines to speed up your search process. Some examples of meta-search engines are zuula.com, dogpile.com, and mamma .com. As seen here, dogpile.com searches Google, Yahoo!, and Bing for you.

Locate Specialized Genealogy Sites

There are literally thousands of websites designed specifically for genealogy. We discuss several in this and succeeding chapters, and you may find others as you continue your genealogy searches. Most sites have the following in common:

- Links to other genealogy websites
- A location where you can enter your own information or start a family tree
- Links to databases such as census or Social Security death records in the United States
- Forums or other utilities by which you can leave messages for others on the site to help with your search

Utilize Governmental Sites

In addition to the sites maintained by national agencies that are discussed throughout this book, consider looking for county or state records that maintain an online database for property ownership, tax assessments, and the like. Many states store information about birth and death records as well as marriage licenses and divorce decrees. While you may not be able to access the records themselves, by accessing the state website you can usually find at least the address to which you can write.

If the state doesn't maintain the records, consider looking for county seat records, parish tax rolls, or voting records. Nearly every county and parish in the United States now has a website, with most of them publishing addresses, email addresses, and telephone numbers by which you can contact the county.

Find Other Sites

There are many other sites from which you can obtain information. Genealogy societies or groups usually maintain their own websites, as do churches, newspapers, and cemeteries. For example, nativeweb.org maintains a website that offers help, links, and suggestions for researching your Native American ancestors.

Use General Search Sites

General search engines are just that: general. While you can find information by beginning with a popular search engine, such as Google or Bing, you may find that general search engines return too much information to be useful or that the name or item for which you are searching is taken out of context.

Draw on Google and Bing

Google, the most popular search engine, is often the place where new family-history seekers begin. While in no way a true genealogy search site, it does offer some help for the beginner.

GOOGLE HINTS

Google does not recognize uppercase letters, so you need only create a search in lowercase letters. And while Google does recognize Boolean operators, the easiest way to enter more specific terms when doing a Google search is to use their Advanced Search function. To access this function:

1. From the Google home page, click the small gear icon to the right of the Sign In link at the upper-right corner of the webpage as seen here.

2. From the drop-down menu that appears, click **Advanced Search**.

3. The Advanced Search dialog box appears as seen in Figure 4-1. From this dialog box you can tell Google to find webpages

   a. With all the words in your search term, which is similar to the Boolean operator AND

   b. With the exact wording of your search term, as with the Boolean operator WITH

   c. With one or more words you enter, as you would do with the Boolean operator OR

   d. With the words that you do *not* want to include

From this same dialog box you can also choose the reading level, the results per page, and the language of pages to display, and set the type of file you want to have Google display. As you can see in Figure 4-1, you can also set date, location, keywords, and other criteria for your search.

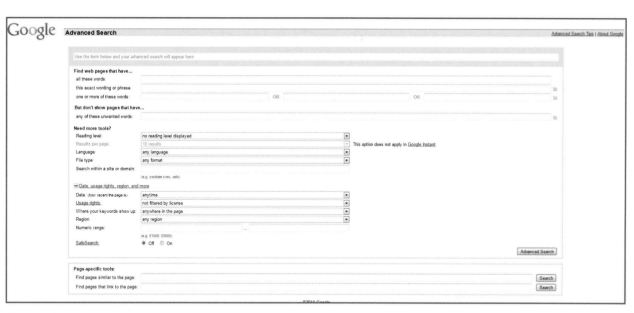

Google Advanced Search

Figure 4-1: Like many general search engines, Google gives you the opportunity to customize a search.

BING TIPS

In the same way that Google provides advanced options, Bing offers Advanced Search capabilities. After you have entered your search term, click **Advanced** at the upper part of your window to open the Advanced Search options as seen in Figure 4-2.

Also in Bing, you can use keywords and other items to narrow your search. For example, if you want census records from the United Kingdom you would enter census loc:UK in the search box.

Or, if you are packing for a genealogy trip to Sicily, you could enter the search term Sicily weather forecast 10 day to find out what to pack. If you are entering this search term from a computer in the United States, the results will return in Fahrenheit numbers; however, if you add the word Celsius to your search term, the results display in Celsius as seen here.

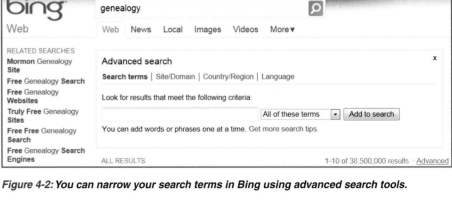

Figure 4-2: *You can narrow your search terms in Bing using advanced search tools.*

QUICKSTEPS

USING WEB DIRECTORIES

Some sites, known as web or search directories, organize websites by subject. These sites are often maintained, at least in part, by humans and are often smaller than the databases used by search engines. To use a web directory, such as the Yahoo! Directory:

1. In the address bar of a browser, type dir.yahoo.com.

2. Choose a directory from the sections on the left side of your window, as seen in the next illustration. For example, in the Yahoo! Directory, genealogy is found under the main Social Science section.

YAHOO! DIRECTORY

Search: ○ the Web | ● the Directory

[Search]

Yahoo! Directory

Arts & Humanities
Photography, History, Literature...

Business & Economy
B2B, Finance, Shopping, Jobs...

Computers & Internet
Hardware, Software, Web, Games...

Education
Colleges, K-12, Distance Learning...

Entertainment
Movies, TV Shows, Music, Humor...

The Spark: Current and Upcoming Events
By Adrienne DelRossi
Tue, November 8, 2011, 11:46 am PST

Yahoo! Directory categories for current and upcoming events:

Sports in Season:

National Football League (NFL)
Fantasy Football (NFL)
College Football
National Hockey League

Continued . . .

Discover Search Techniques

While there are as many techniques for searching the Web as there are searchers, here are some general suggestions when you perform a search:

- Be as specific as possible.
- Use the search engine's advanced options when needed to narrow down the results.
- Use capital letters to narrow down a search—for example, webpage titles often include capital letters, and some search engines might not recognize the term if you've used all lowercase.
- Use quotation marks around a search term to specify a phrase.
  - Use more than one search engine. All search engines do not return the same results.
  - Use the links that appear on the left of your search results to filter your search further.

Explore Genealogy Sites

There are so many genealogy sites available today that we cannot cover them all. We have included a brief overview of the more well-known sites, as well as a few useful sites that are not as well known. Remember you can always use the general search sites to search for genealogy sites.

QUICKSTEPS

USING WEB DIRECTORIES *(Continued)*

3. Choose a category to narrow your search as seen here. Many category lists have subcategories to further focus your search.

CATEGORIES (What's This?)

- **Beginners' Guides** (7)
- **Chats and Forums** (6)
- **GEDCOM** (4)
- **Heraldry** (14)
- **Lineages and Surnames** (1115)
- **Magazines** (7)
- **Organizations** (81)

- **PAF** (2)
- **Reference** (32)
- **Regional and Ethnic Resources** (94)
- **Royal Genealogies** (6)
- **Shopping and Services**@
- **Tombstone Rubbing**@
- **Web Directories** (21)

4. Choose to search a category, the entire directory, or the entire Web.

5. Press **ENTER** or click **Search** to see the results.

See Chapter 6 for additional information about search engines and directories.

While most sites offer some free services and others are totally without cost to you, many genealogy websites require you pay some type of membership or subscription for continuing access. This fee usually helps defray the costs of maintaining the page and adding new information.

Many sites offer free or low-cost genealogy software you can download to create records on your own computer. The sites we have included are in no particular order (other than Ancestry.com), but are simply sites we have used and like.

Here are some tips to remember when dealing with genealogy websites:

- Understand where the site obtains its records. Are the records confirmable and reputable?

- "Free" offers may only be for a short time or for limited information. Do not submit a credit card to any site before you understand the rules for that site.

- Ensure there is a valid contact phone number or physical address by which you can contact the owner of a site.

- Do an Internet search for complaints or concerns about the website.

- Consider submitting a question to the site before giving them any money. If a human does not respond within a reasonable amount of time (24 to 48 hours), you might want to reconsider your purchase.

- Look at genealogy message boards or other forums to see if anyone has experienced issues with this website.

- Do not submit records for living persons to a site you have not investigated.

Examine Genealogy Websites

The most compelling reason to search for your ancestors on a genealogy website is the convenience. Since many websites offer free software and built-in family tree forms, you can easily enter information that you know that may lead to other data. You do not have to drive to a county seat to research birth records. Instead, many of the records have been entered into a database from which you can pick the appropriate record.

Consider the following when choosing to use one or more genealogy websites:

- What are its sources? The database(s) maintained by the website are its most important asset. Ensure the database stems from appropriate sources and that these sources can be independently verified.

- How easy is it to use the site's tools? If you can create a family tree, how many records can be entered at no cost?

- Can you download the information you create on the site to a complete file on your own computer? If the information can only be stored online, consider the stability of the website *and* the protections the website owners take to ensure your privacy.

- How extensive is the database? Does it include information from just the United States or from all over the world? How much effort (if any) is put forth by the website to ensure the information is accurate?

- What kind of support does it offer *you*, the researcher? Is the support in a frequently asked question (FAQ) forum or from real live people?

ANCESTRY.COM

The largest and most well-known site, Ancestry.com is owned by a publicly traded, for-profit company and is traded on the NASDAQ exchange. Ancestry.com currently has the largest number of records, a number that increases every day with new members' adding information to the database.

You may use parts of Ancestry.com in an introductory free trial for (currently) 14 days; however, to continue you must subscribe to their service. There are different prices based on the information you choose to include. For example, someone seeking information from locations other than the United States would pay about $300.00 for an annual membership. Their website states new information is added weekly from across the world.

ANCESTRY.COM FEATURES

Once subscribed, you have access to the various types of records included in the Ancestry.com database. These include but are not limited to

- Census and voting records
- Birth, marriage, and death records (note that Ancestry.com does *not* include divorce records)
- Emigration and immigration records
- Court records, such as probate and land transfers
- Military records

Ancestry.com also has an extensive set of education tools, offers message boards and public family trees, and even maintains a DNA database that you can join for (currently) $149, as seen next.

The site also offers products that help you publish your genealogy results as books, posters, calendars, and more.

ANCESTRY.COM GENERAL COMMENTS

As with all genealogy research, the need to confirm and verify information is always present. Since there are many instances of duplicate names, similar surnames, and so on throughout genealogy record-keeping, it is extremely important to verify each connection. Contrary to popular television advertising, a "leaf" showing on an ancestor's name is only a "hint," as clearly stated on the Ancestry.com website. It is not a verified connection to your ancestor!

If you choose to subscribe to Ancestry.com, as with all Internet purchases, be sure to read all of the information on each webpage before you submit your credit card information. Also, ensure you keep copies of any receipts, confirming emails, or other correspondence should there be an issue later. There have been a number of complaints from users who had difficulties cancelling their subscriptions.

TIP

Since many banks use your mother's maiden name as an identifier, ensure that your family tree is protected from unauthorized users. Consider making your family tree a private rather than a public record, or change your bank identifier.

OTHER ANCESTRY.COM SITES

Ancestry.com has additional sites, such as www.ancestry.com.au and www .ancestry.com.uk. Currently, your login information for your current subscription will also let you access records on those sites.

ROOTSWEB.COM

RootsWeb.com is a free site, supported by Ancestry.com. It states that its primary purpose is to "connect people so that they can help each other and share genealogical research." The site offers connections to mailing lists and message boards, and offers users the chance to create their own free website.

The World Connect Project was started by RootsWeb in 1999 and today has more than 662 million names contained in its database. It is simply a group (a very large group) of family trees that have been combined to form a searchable database available online.

GENEALOGY.COM

This site, a partner of Ancestry.com, offers primarily information from U.S. sources. It is a subscription-based site that many find easy to use. Many people have used this online site, as it partners with the Family Tree Maker software.

This site's Learning Center offers a wide array of free lessons to get you started in your genealogy search, as seen in Figure 4-3. The center offers both beginning and intermediate-level courses as well as several sets of lessons on tracing immigrant origins and sources. Since not every immigrant came through Ellis Island, this set of lessons is particularly useful.

FAMILYSEARCH.ORG

This site, owned and maintained by the Church of Jesus Christ of Latter-day Saints (LDS), is a free site; however, you do have to register to use its features. This site covers more countries than any other genealogy site, including countries from nearly every continent. As with many other genealogy sites, you can access professional genealogists for assistance in addition to its fine online help.

TIP

During much of your genealogy research, you'll encounter the name "GEDCOM." This is a file format created by the LDS Church Family History Department to provide a uniform way of exchanging genealogy data among websites and programs. You'll see the file extension .ged at the end of a file formatted in this manner. For example, your information might be entitled *JonesFamily.ged* when it is converted to this format. Most genealogy software can both import and export files in this format. See Chapter 3 for more information about GEDCOM.

TIP

To protect your privacy, names of living people in your database can be hidden from public view in the World Connect Project database.

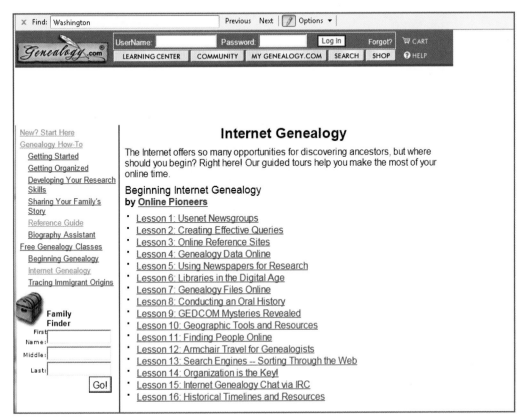

Its online help chat lines are available 24/7. It maintains its database from birth, marriage, death, census, and court records. It also has information from both immigration and emigration records as well as military records.

From the site, you can access instructional videos, as seen in Figure 4-4, search tips, and download free genealogy software. There is a useful blog maintained on the site that includes articles by users offering tips and information. There is even a research wiki maintained by site users that offers additional information. The discussion forums are equally useful.

While some users say it is not as easy to use as other sites, notably Ancestry.com and Archives.com, its worldwide databases, solid user support, and its many other features available at no cost to the user make it very highly ranked among genealogy researchers.

Figure 4-3: *The free online lessons found at the Genealogy.com website are useful for both beginning and intermediate researchers.*

MYHERITAGE.COM

Based in Israel, this family-focused site is geared to helping you create a family tree. It covers the entire world and offers an interface in multiple languages. This fee-based site offers searches based on images as well as searches of multiple spellings of a name. It includes a face recognition feature, which purports to help you identify people in your family photographs.

Figure 4-4: From the Learning Center at FamilySearch.org you can access dozens of useful video lessons.

The photograph must be in digital format for this feature to work. You can easily share photos as well as videos by uploading them to the site, as seen next.

Different from Ancestry.com and Archives.com, MyHeritage.com performs an aggregate search of online databases, which can yield different information than other sites. The site offers instructional videos, forums, and a blog. While you can email the site, to physically correspond with the site, you must send a letter via regular mail to the United Kingdom even though the site states it is based in Israel.

From the site you can download a free genealogy program called Family Tree Builder to help you build your family tree, which can, if you choose, be published to the Internet using the services provided on the MyHeritage.com website.

FAMILYTREESEARCHER.COM

FamilyTreeSearcher.com has become one of our favorite sites. First, it's our favorite price—free. But more importantly it gives free advice, offers information about many of the other genealogy sites and how to work with them, and includes definitions of terms used on genealogy sites, as seen in Figure 4-5.

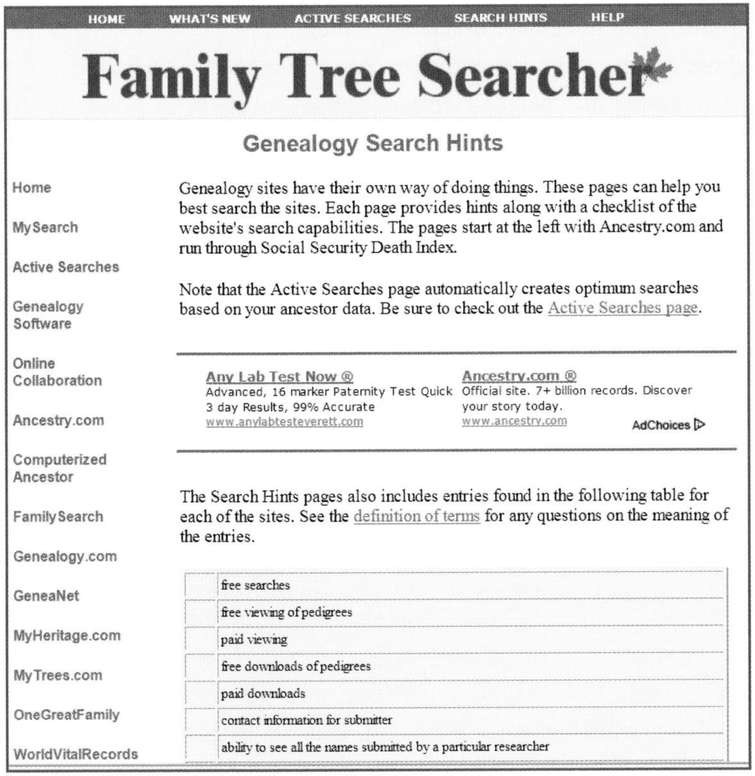

Genealogy's answer to a meta-search engine, the site searches nine major genealogy sites at the same time. Using its Active Search section, the user can save up to ten ancestors at a time. This Active Searches section ensures that the latest information for our current searches is always up to date.

MORE FREE GENEALOGY WEBSITES

This list is by no means comprehensive. It simply includes several free sites that may be useful:

- **kindredtrails.com** This site offers lots of free resources and links to a number of useful databases.

- **genealogytoday.com** A great site from which to get started, it contains lots of useful information and hints on beginning your research.

- **cyndislist.com** This site, one of the most comprehensive online, has been around for more than 15 years. While it takes some time to understand how it is arranged, the data is comprehensive. Other than mentioning "donations are always welcome," there is no charge for the voluminous resource.

Figure 4-5: There are many hints and links as well as advice you can find at the FamilyTreeSearcher.com site.

Assess Government Information

When one is researching information, much of it is found at "government" pages. Whether these pages contain census records for the nation or a state, land grant information for a county, or local voting records, they are valuable resources. While many entities provide the information at no cost, others require a subscription or a deposit to research the data.

Decipher Census Records

Many researchers use census records as their "go-to" resources. Census records can be very useful *if* you remember that most of them were handwritten by volunteers whose penmanship makes the process sometimes questionable. Abbreviations and other misspellings are common, as are errors in the ages and other data shown on each line.

That being said, they are a valuable resource for any genealogy researcher. Since 1790, the United States has taken a census every ten years. By congressional decree, the detail records are not available to the public for 72 years. The 1940 census became available in April 2012.

Currently, the U.S. Census records are on file at the National Archives and are kept on microfilm. There are copies in other locations, such as the Family History Centers run by the Mormon Church, and many state and local libraries or genealogy societies. One can even rent copies for a nominal rate from the National Archives Census Microfilm Rental Program at P.O. Box 30, Annapolis Junction, MD, 20701-0030.

There is currently no online comprehensive database for the entire existing census records of the U.S. Census. The USGenWeb Census Project is currently transcribing the records state by state, line by line, with the idea that eventually all of the data will be available online at no cost. This is a tremendously time-consuming project. You can access what has been completed to date at us-census.org. An example of what you might see is shown in Figure 4-6.

```
===============================================================================================================
LN  HN  FN  LAST NAME    FIRST NAME     AGE SEX RACE OCCUP.          REAL VAL. PERS VAL.  BIRTHPLACE      MRD. SCH. R/W DDB
===============================================================================================================
1   23  23  Alexander    F.              40  F         Boarding House 3,000    1,000       Canada
2   23  23  Alexander    John            22  M         Miner                               Canada
3   23  23  Alexander    Joseph          10  M                                             Ill                      X
4   23  23  Alexander    Abraham          8  M                                             W. Territory             X
5   24  24  Brum         R.              30  M         Merchant       1,000     500         Germany
            REMARKS:  surname actually Brunn
6   24  24  Brum         Margarett       19  F                                             Sidney N.S.W.
            REMARKS:  surname actually Brunn
7   24  24  Robertson    John            21  M         Merchant                 3,000       Md.
8   25  25  Libby        Saml            46  M         Farmer         1,000     50          Maine
            REMARKS:  surname actually Libbey
9   25  25  Libby        Sarah           45  F                                             Maine
            REMARKS:  surname actually Libbey
10  25  25  Libby        George B        14  M                                             Maine                    X
            REMARKS:  surname actually Libbey
11  25  25  Libby        Joseph B        12  M                                             Maine                    X
            REMARKS:  surname actually Libbey
12  26  26  Holbrook     R.B.            34  M         Farmer         2,000     100         Mass
13  27  27  Howe         S.D.            31  M         Farmer         2,000     1,600       Kty
14  27  27  Turner       I. T.           33  M         Farm Laborer                         Md.
15  27  27  Madox        J.L.            22  M         Farm Laborer                         Michigan
16  27  27  Swift        J.H.            45  M         Farmer         4,000                 Mass.
17  28  28  Sullivan     J.              37  M         Farmer         300       300         Ireland
18  28  28  Night        G.P.            28  M         Farmer                               Kty.
19  29  29  Bozarth      U. E.           40  M         Farmer         1,000     100         Kty.
20  29  29  Bozarth      Mary            43  F                                             Ohio
21  29  29  Bozarth      Thomas          20  M         Farmer                               Ohio
22  29  29  De Lorium    F.              47  M         Farm Laborer                         France
23  30  30  Dickson      Thos            25  M         Farm Laborer                         Ill
24  30  30  Morse        G.W.            30  M         Ship Carpenter                       Maine
25  30  30  Underwood    A.              28  M         Farmer                               Tenn
26  31  31  Mount        M.L.            33  M         Farmer         1,200     100         Ohio
            REMARKS:  surname actually Mounts
27  31  31  Mount        J.H.            31  M         Farmer         2,000                 Ohio
            REMARKS:  surname actually Mounts
28  32  32  Bigby        James           42  M         Farmer         3,500     500         N.J.
29  32  32  Bigby        Margarett       41  F                                             N.Y.
30  32  32  Bigby        Isaac W.        15  M                                             Ohio
31  32  32  Bigby        Sarah R         13  F                                             Ohio                     X
32  32  32  Wimouth      O.              26  M         Farm Laborer                         Maine
33  32  32  Wimouth      Jane            23  F                                             Maine
34  32  32  Wimouth      Sarah           16  F         Teacher Pub.School                   Maine
35  33  33  N.S.         John M          28  M         Farmer         1,200     200         Scotland
            REMARKS:  surname left blank
36  33  33  N.S.         Nancy           23  F                                             Ill
            REMARKS:  surname left blank
37  33  33  N.S.         George           1  M                                             W.T.
            REMARKS:  surname left blank
38  33  33  Walker       N.              32  M                        25                    Germany
39  34  34  Wallace      W.              49  M         Farmer         8,000     1,000       Vermont
40  34  34  Wallace      Ruthda          38  F                                             Ohio
            REMARKS:  No White Males 30, No White Females 10  $30225  $8,250
```

Figure 4-6: *This is an example of a transcription taken from the 1860 Census in what is now the state of Washington.*

NOTE

The 1890 U.S. Census was destroyed in 1921 by a fire in the Commerce Department building.

While many genealogy sites offer access to some census records, and even offer images from the microfilm records, the information is usually only available with a paid subscription to the site.

Investigate Other Federal Sites

While many historians use the census records to start their genealogy research, there are other United States sites that can help in your investigation.

NATIONAL ARCHIVES

One of the most detailed resources available to researchers in the United States is the National Archives. This website at archives.gov/research/genealogy/ gives tips on starting research; offers free online research tools; and includes information about census, immigration, and military records, as seen in Figure 4-7.

LIBRARY OF CONGRESS

The Library of Congress has more than 2,500 useful resources for research. While most items are not available online, the library houses newspaper collections back to the 1830s as well as photographs, maps, and books. The books date back to 1815 when the entire collection of Thomas Jefferson was purchased for the library.

One of the features on the Library of Congress website is a list (all of which are links) to libraries, archives, and other resources available online, as seen in Figure 4-8. This resource can be found at loc.gov/rr/genealogy/other.html.

BUREAU OF LAND MANAGEMENT

With some items dating back to 1810, the Bureau of Land Management's records can provide information about land ownership and survey information. This site is located at glorecords.blm.gov.

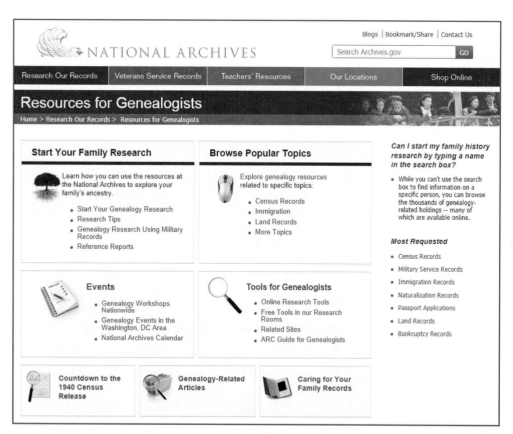

Figure 4-7: The National Archives offers many helpful tools for genealogy research.

SEARCHING FOR MILITARY RECORDS

Some U.S. military records are available online. For example, the enlistment records for World War II are available from the National Archives Access to Archival Data at aad.archives.gov. Information pertaining to veterans who were discharged more than 62 years ago is considered archival information and is available to the public at this National Archives website.

Records prior to 1917 are stored at the Textual Archives Services Division in Washington, D.C. Military records from 1917 to the present are housed in the National Military Personnel Records Center in St. Louis, Missouri. To order copies, go to the National Archives site at archives.gov and enter Veterans Service Records in the search box.

The Department of Veterans Affairs maintains a national gravesite locator for veterans who have been buried on U.S. soil. The link is gravelocator.cem.va.gov

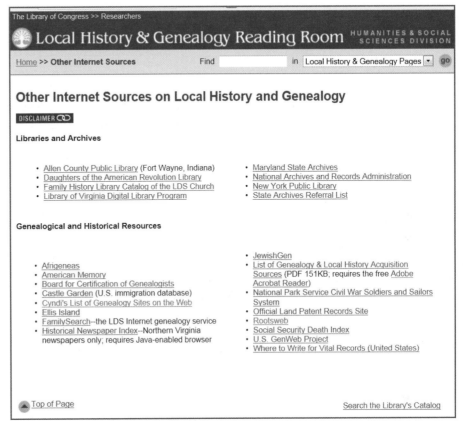

Figure 4-8: The Library of Congress lists several useful links for research.

If you think an ancestor was given a land grant, or *patent*, and you have some of the information, you can search for that information at the Bureau of Land Management site.

1. To access the information, open the U.S. Department of the Interior Bureau of Land Management site (glorecord.blm.gov).

2. Select the type of information you want to research. We chose Land Patents to open the window shown in Figure 4-9.

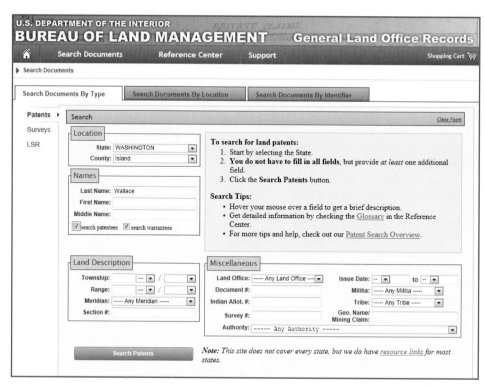

Figure 4-9: The Bureau of Land Management website has thousands of records pertaining to land ownership in the United States.

3. Click the appropriate link. In our example, we've chosen Search Documents By Type.

4. Enter the information you have. You need only fill in one of the fields.

5. Click the **Search Patents** button.

Locate State and Local Government Sites

Every state in the United States has its own website, as do most counties, townships, and parishes. From the Cook County, Illinois, genealogy site found at cookcountygenealogy.com, to the Washington State Digital Archives site at digitalarchives.wa.gov, many local sites are leading the way for genealogy research.

Some sites even include audio and video files as well as photographs, copies of public records, and so on.

To find what resources are available in your state, use a general search engine to find your state's website. From your state's site, review all of the resources available, or type <u>genealogy</u> in a search box. Here is an example of a "mortality census" from 1880 in the territory of Washington.

Look at Other Sites

There are still many more sites that you can access to aid you in your research. Churches, cemeteries, libraries, universities, newspapers, and genealogy groups may all maintain a web presence. Consider, too, looking up a family surname to see if there are any family websites created by a distant cousin.

Discover Church and Cemetery Sites

Many churches today have their own websites. If you know the religious denomination of your ancestor, you might be able to locate the church they attended by using one of the online search sites. It is often an easy task to type in the denomination name in a search engine and find the denomination's website. Once on the main website for any denomination, you can find local church websites. On the local church's website, you will usually find contact information and other resources.

The genealogy page at About.com offers an extensive list of links to various archives and church records. You can find that list here at genealogy.about.com/od/church_records/Church_Parish_Religious_Records.htm. When you find the church, you may also find that the church maintains a cemetery. Gravestones are a very useful tool for the genealogy researcher, as they often show dates of birth and death, as well as the reason the person died. You may also find information about children, spouses, and other family members in a cemetery. There are even websites that contain databases of cemetery records.

Work with Libraries

There are a number of specialized genealogy libraries in the United States. A partial list may be found at gwest.org/gen_libs.htm. While many of the libraries found at that location do not have website links, all have physical addresses to which you can write. Some of the libraries may even have started websites for which there is not yet a link.

Most public libraries have genealogy sections, and many give their library card holders access to genealogy resources at no cost to the library card holder. Contact your local library and ask for historical or genealogy collections, and you may well find a treasure-trove of information.

Find University Special Collections and Archives

Many universities maintain archival information for their graduates. If one of your ancestors graduated from a college or university, chances are good that someone

there will have information about that student. Look up the school's website and find links to their Archives, Special Collections, or other such department. An example of this is shown here from the Wesleyan University website.

Use Newspaper Resources

Old newspapers can yield a wide variety of information. From death and marriage notices to society news, your ancestors' activities may have appeared in the local newspaper. Even church announcements, classified advertisements, and legal notices can give you much information.

In many cases, you will need to borrow microfilm to view information; however, some public libraries will arrange for interlibrary loans so that you need not travel long distances to see the information contained on the microfilm. Also, many papers are digitizing their records and placing them online and available to subscribers or others for a small fee.

There is even a national program that is cataloging old newspapers on microfilm to preserve them. Learn about this project at neh.gov/projects/usnp.html. ProQuest, which is available through most college and many public libraries, has digitized many newspapers (reportedly over 16 million), and has made them available.

When you use a newspaper as a resource, consider the limitations of the time. The information may not be complete or the reporting may be biased. Record all information that you include in your research completely as to the paper's name, date of publication, page number, and so on. If possible, obtain a photo of the paper for your files, as shown in the following example.

1) [Arthur E. Cornelius; Seattle; Mrs. H. S. Taylor]

Date: May 21, 1922
Location: Washington
Paper: Morning Olympian
Article type: News Article

.rd | day.
.lr. |
he | Arthur E. Cornelius and family of
|ss | Seattle will visit Mr. and Mrs. H. S.
rs. | Taylor and family at their home 221

Find Magazine Articles

Popular magazines may not provide direct information about your ancestors, but the articles found within can provide great detail about the time in which your ancestors lived. From magazines found in the archives of your local library to current magazines that discuss historical events, it can be useful to learn about battles, epidemics, natural disasters, and so on to learn more about the geography and everyday life of the people you are researching.

Even the advertisements can provide a peek into the culture of the day. Think about the *Saturday Evening Post, Colliers,* and *Life* magazine and how those publications captured the spirit of their times.

Utilize Genealogy Groups/Communities

Many genealogy societies and groups today have their own websites. The National Genealogical Society's site offers some basic tutorials to help you with research. They also offer other learning opportunities at no charge to members, as well as a home-study course one can purchase. Membership in the national society is $60 per year.

To see websites for local groups, in a general search engine type genealogy society websites and the location in which you are searching. Once you have located a group, there will be contact information to connect with it. Many even post local historical information on the group's site. Figure 4-10 shows an example from the state of Maine.

Investigate Family Sites

Many genealogy websites offer the chance to create your own family site. In addition, try simply typing your family name into the search box of a general search engine and see what happens. You may find long-lost cousins!

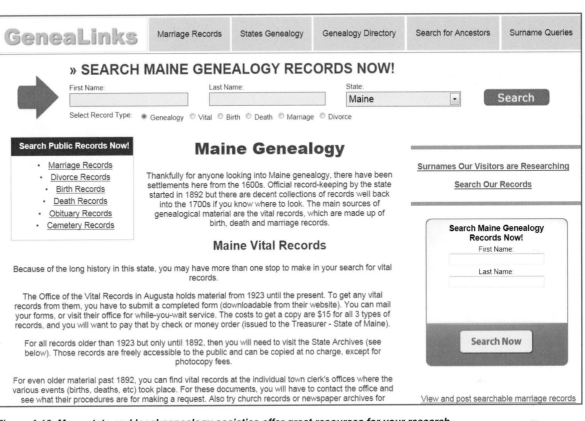

Figure 4-10: *Many state and local genealogy societies offer great resources for your research.*

Trevor Arnold, 75, Whidbey Island, WA

OVERVIEW

My mother often commented on "how strange your father's family was!" There was no contact with his family, as they were mostly "prisoners" on the island of Newfoundland, a great distance away from Winnipeg, Manitoba, Canada, where I grew up. Both of my parents were born in Canada—my mother in Nova Scotia and my father in Heart's Content, Newfoundland. The name "Heart's Content" always fascinated me, especially after I learned that both of my father's parents had also been born in Heart's Content. Inhabited since the 1600s, it was also the site of the first successful landing of the transatlantic cable in 1866.

STORY

I was born Patricia Anne Legge in Brooklyn, New York, but grew up in Winnipeg. During the 1970s, while working in outside sales through the United States, I found that the business card with my name "Patricia" somehow never made it past the reception desk wastebasket, so I changed my name to Trevor. The strategy worked, and my sales "increased mightily" when my card actually arrived at the desk of the business owner with my new "unisex" name.

After my mother passed on, while going through her things I found photographs, papers, and a number of newspaper clippings, including some of her as a young dancer with the Paul Whitman Follies in New York. I started trying to make sense of all of the memorabilia and found she had done some genealogy work on her mother's side (the Laing family) that dated back to about 1750. Figure 4-11 is a picture of her parents taken in the 1890s.

Her research and my curiosity were the beginnings of my consuming interest in genealogy. I wanted to learn as much as possible about all of my ancestors, but especially more information about my father's family. From my mother's records, I found that my father had 16 siblings, none of whom I ever met. Somewhere I learned that one of his brothers had been an artist in New York. I was later able to verify this through a copy of his death certificate, which I obtained after I found his information using the Social Security Death Index on Ancestry.com.

Figure 4-11: Eugene Phineas Iler and Jenny Laing were my mother's parents.

The three sons who were old enough to serve were in the military at the same time as my grandfather. My uncles James, Ralph, and Richard served until the end of the war in 1918. The illustration at right is the official military picture of my Uncle Jim from 1917. Figure 4-14 is a picture of my uncle, Ralph A. Iler, in his kilt.

During 1979, my son was an exchange student to Madely, England, and that year my two daughters and I were able to create a "Christmas surprise" by visiting him there. While I was there, I searched current city directories and found a large

GETTING STARTED

A lot of my mother's clippings were society pages, baby announcements, and marriage and death notices, which helped me start my family tree. I found that her father (my maternal grandfather), Eugene Phineas Iler, joined the Canadian Army during World War I. He served as a baker and a bass drummer and is shown in Figures 4-12 and 4-13. He's the one holding the eggs at the far right of the first row of Figure 4-12 and is in the front with his hand on the bass drum in Figure 4-13. Grandpa Iler died of "noncombat" wounds in 1917. I've not yet been able to ascertain exactly how he died.

Figure 4-12: My grandfather, Eugene Phineas Iler, with his cooks company during World War I.

Figure 4-13: Grandfather Iler's two jobs in the army always intrigued me.

number of Legges (my father's family) listed, but was unable to contact anyone during our short stay. However, with the advent of the Internet, through GenUKI, I contacted the Devonshire registrar and found Legge information dating back to the 1700s.

Then, during a trip to the Family History Library in Salt Lake City, I was able to find copies of the records deposited by the Earl of Dartmouth from the County Record Office in Stafford, England, with information about the Staffordshire and Buckingham estates as far back as 1644. Among them was a series of papers, seen in Figure 4-15, which describe how George Legge, the 1st Baron of Dartmouth, was named Admiral of the Fleet and was sent to Tangier by order of the king to assist in the evacuation of the Tangier garrison during 1683 and 1684. Figure 4-15 is a copy of the "Dartmouth papers" I obtained at the library. However, evidently George's conduct in Tangier was not to the king's liking, and he was imprisoned in the Tower of London and killed in 1691. His son, William, was named Earl of Dartmouth in 1711 and served as Secretary of State for the Colonies from 1772 to 1775.

Through military information located on Ancestry.com, I learned that my paternal grandfather was deemed too old at 56 to join the Canadian Armed Forces during World War II. Even so, he opted to join the Newfoundland Forestry unit and was sent to Scotland to prepare lumber for shipment to England. During the time he was there, he was killed in a pub brawl and died on December 7, 1941. Because he was considered to be on active service, his family received death benefits. The record shows he was buried in a military cemetery in Ireland. The following image shows the data I found in the Ancestry.com database.

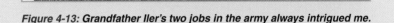

Military

Military Information

Date

1939 to 1941

example: 12 Apr 1945

Location

Laggan Parish, Inverness-shire, Ireland

City, County, State, Country

Description

Newfoundland Overseas Forest Unit, Register No.3201 None action death on 7 December 1941. Was placed on Honour Roll

Figure 4-14: Proud of his Scots heritage, Ralph A. Iler posed in his uniform kilt.

CHALLENGES

My biggest challenge has been finding and verifying immigration dates and places, especially the immigrants to Newfoundland and Nova Scotia. While the Legge family can be traced to 1348, I cannot verify when and where my father's ancestors arrived in Canada. I plan on traveling to Newfoundland and perhaps Nova Scotia in 2012 for further research. I also plan another trip to the Family History Center in Salt Lake City, Utah, to complete my maternal research.

OBJECTIVES

As I continue to research my ancestors, my eventual goal is to create a journal about my life as well as a family history book for my children and grandchildren to keep.

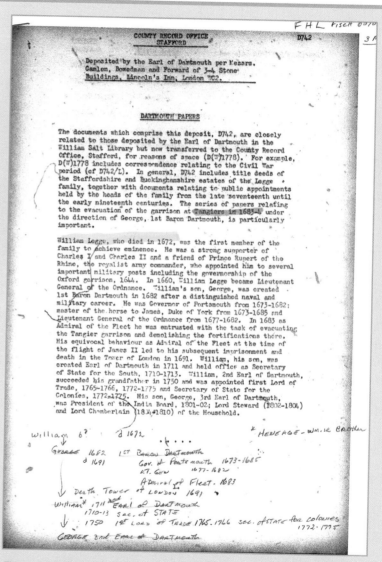

Figure 4-15: These are copies of the "Dartmouth papers" detailing George Legge's royal command to evacuate the garrison at Tangiers.

Chapter 5

Entering and Using Online Sites

From previous chapters you understand that the Internet is a major resource for genealogy, but questions remain: what sites do you use, how do you use them, and what do you do on them? This chapter will answer those questions. In particular, we'll take a look at using Ancestry.com and FamilySearch.org. The genealogy story in this chapter looks at how Tom Beard made extensive use of online genealogy sites to both find his ancestors and connect with and get help from others researching the Beard family.

Decide Where to Start

As you begin building your family tree, you have two possible paths: enter and verify the information you have, or begin searching for information you want to know more about, but where to start? There probably isn't one correct answer, but some considerations are as follows:

- Has a lot of work already been done on one or more of your ancestral lines? You may want to enter and verify this to get you started, or since so much is already known, you may want to ignore this line and start on another.

- What are your personal interests? Maybe stories about your great-grandfather have always fascinated you and you want to learn more about him and his family line.

- What are the interests of your family? Maybe several family members are interested in pursuing a particular family line together, or maybe there has been a lot of discussion about whether a particular pedigree went one way or another.

- Where are the big question marks in your genealogy where nothing is known? Trying to solve a mystery can often be intriguing.

In Tom Beard's story in this chapter, a lot of work had been done, including a whole book written on his mother's line, so Tom's choice was to begin researching his father's side, where he knew very little before his grandfather. In Marty's story in Chapter 2 he has both a total unknown as to his ancestry prior to his Matthews great-grandfather and a lot of family discussion about whether his father's maternal line came from France or Scotland, causing him to pursue both of these areas.

Wherever you want to start, have at least two generations, such as your father and grandfather, with their birth and death (if applicable) dates and places. You can also include yourself if you wish to further anchor the line, but some people are concerned about putting their birth date online.

Collect Family Information

In Chapter 3 you saw how to enter people into a family tree in genealogy software on your computer. Here you'll see how to collect ancestral information and, in one case, enter it into a family tree with sites on the Internet, or "in the cloud" in the current vernacular. There are over 50 genealogy websites, as discussed in Chapter 4. We, of course, can't discuss all of those, but we have picked the two sites that are heavily used and considered among the most useful: Ancestry.com and FamilySearch.org. FamilySearch is a free site, while Ancestry is by subscription. Also, Ancestry is much like genealogy software on your computer, in that you can build a family tree there as well as search for ancestors, while FamilySearch is principally used for searching and research. Look now at how these sites work by actually using them.

Explore Ancestry.com

Ancestry.com is the world's largest and most heavily used genealogy website. Many people believe it is also the easiest to use and provides access to an extensive range of databases in which to search (Ancestry says seven billion genealogy records). Since it has the largest user base, if you are willing to make your family tree public (which is recommended), then you will have the largest audience who can see your work and possibly provide help. Also there are a large number (Ancestry says "millions") of public family trees that are available to you.

Ancestry.com charges for the use of their site, costing between approximately $10 and $30 a month, depending on the service you sign up for, how many months you are willing to pay for in advance, and the specials that are in effect at that time. You can generally get 14 days free to try it out, but you still need to give them a credit or debit card and, be warned, the site is highly addictive. Most people find that the site is well worth the fee that is charged.

Start a Family Tree on Ancestry

To begin using Ancestry.com, enter the information about your family that you want to start with: their names and birth and death dates and places. When you do that Ancestry.com will search on the names that you enter and tell you if there is other information on those names that you can download to help you

extend your family tree. Here is how to get started:

1. Open your browser, such as Internet Explorer or Firefox, and in the address bar type <u>ancestry.com</u> and press **ENTER**. If you have never used Ancestry.com before, you will see a signup page.

2. Type your first and last name, your age, and your email address. Then select your gender, who you want to search for, and click **Get Started**. If you want to create a free trial account in which you do searches and build a family tree, click **Create My Account**. An account will be created for you. Click **Continue**, and you can immediately start on your search.

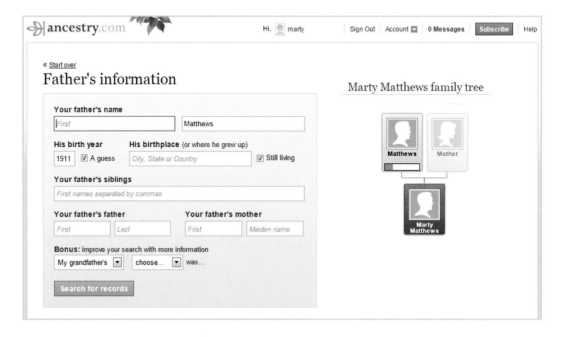

NOTE

You'll see in Figure 5-1 that "Burrel" is spelled "Burrel," "Burrell," and "Burl." This is quite common and you should be prepared for multiple spellings on both first and last names, as well as varying dates and places. This is especially true on the census forms in the 1800s.

3. Type as much of the information as you know about the person you want to search for, and click **Search For Records**. A number of public records may appear that are related to the person you are searching for, as you can see in Figure 5-1.

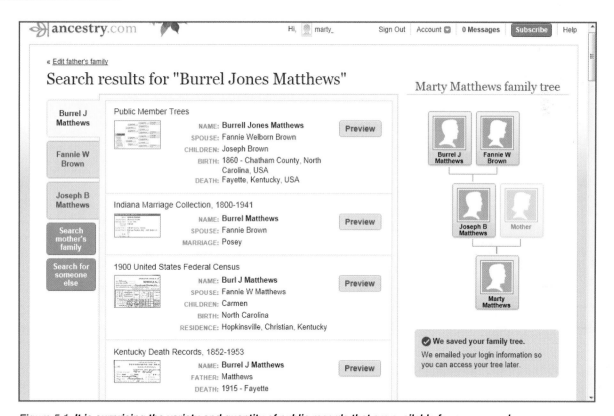

Figure 5-1: It is surprising the variety and quantity of public records that are available for many people.

4. Click **Preview** to preview a record you want to see. If you are using a free trial, you will be told you can see that and other records by signing up for a free 14-day trial. To do that, click **Start Free Trial & View Record**.

5. Select **Focus On The U.S.** or **Expand To The World**, and click **Start Your Free Trial**. Choose the length of prepaid membership you want after your free trial, and click **Start Your Free Trial**. Enter your address and phone number, and click **Continue**. Enter your credit card information and click **Start Free Trial**. You are welcomed to Ancestry and given the facts of your subscription. Click **Continue**. The Ancestry.com Get Started page will open.

6. To return to the public records list you were looking at, in the lower part of the page, under Search, begin to type the ancestor's name you were researching in steps 3 and 4. Ancestry will suggest a name from those you entered. Click that name and then click **Search**.

TIP

To cancel your subscription before the 14 days are up and therefore not be billed on your credit card, go to the My Account section of the Ancestry.com website or call 1-800-958-9022. If you choose to go ahead and keep the account, your credit card will automatically be billed on whatever period (month, quarter, and so on) that you selected until you cancel it.

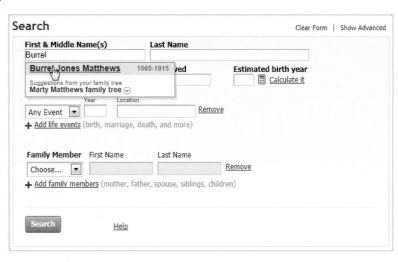

7. The Search page opens, as you can see in Figure 5-2, listing the various records that were found. Click the record you were hoping to look at in step 4. By simply putting the mouse over the link ("hovering"), you'll see a preview of the information.

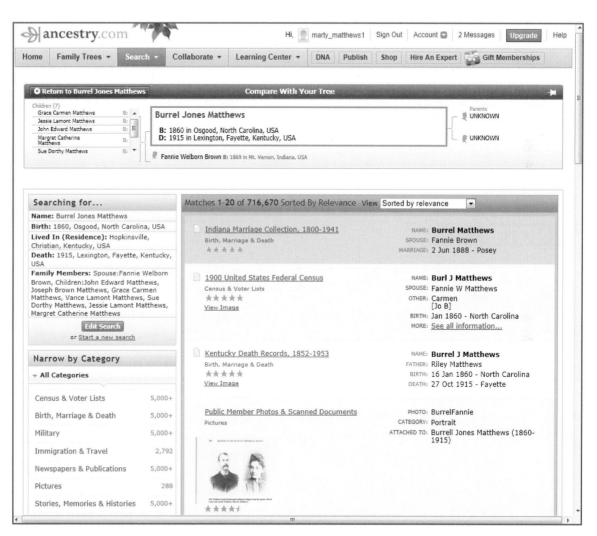

Figure 5-2: When you search for information, Ancestry sorts the results by relevance, which is indicated by the number of stars on the record.

Indiana Marriage Collection, 1800-1941 about Burrel Matthews

Name:	**Burrel Matthews**
Spouse Name:	Fannie Brown
Marriage Date:	2 Jun 1888
Marriage County:	Posey
Source Title 1:	Posey County, Indiana
Source Title 2:	Index to Marriage Record 1850 - 1920 Inclusive Vol
Source Title 3:	W. P. A Original Record Located: County Clerk's Of
Book:	C-10
OS Page:	99

Save This Record
Attach this record to a person in your tree as a source record, or save for later evaluation.

Save ☑

Source Citation: Title: *Posey County, Indiana, Index to Marriage Record 1850 - 1920 Inclusive Vol, W. P. A Original Record Located: County Clerk's Of*; Book: C-10;Page: 99.

8. Click either the record's underlined title (the "link") or **See More** in the preview to open and read the record. If it is something that you want to keep, click **Save** to attach the record to the person you search on, another person, or in your "Shoebox" where you can evaluate it later on.

9. Select where you want to save the record, and click **Continue**. Review the information being added to your family tree, make any needed adjustments, and then click **Save To Your Tree**.

10. You are shown a summary of the information in your tree for the person you selected. To return to the search records, click **Search Records** immediately under the person's photo or the placeholder for it. Repeat steps 8 and 9 for the rest of the search records you want to review and/or save.

11. Some records have an original image attached to them that you can view and save to your tree. Click **View Original Record** to see the image. Figure 5-3 shows a 1900 Census form for my grandparents and their children.

12. If you want to attach the image to your family tree, click **Save** in the upper right, select where you want it saved, and then click **Continue**.

NOTE

The source citation at the bottom of the Indiana marriage record is helpful for your records. Having solid sources throughout your family tree gives you assurance that the tree is accurate.

TWELFTH CENSUS OF THE UNITED ST[ATES]

SCHEDULE No. 1.—POPULATION

State _Kentucky_

County _Christian_

Township or other division of county_____ [Insert name of township, town, precinct, district, or other civil division, as the case may be. See Instructions.] _____ Name of Institution, &

Name of incorporated city, town, or village, within the above-named division, _Hopkinsville City_

Enumerated by me on the _2nd_ day of June, 1900, _Ellis A. Cottrell_

LOCATION		NAME (of each person whose place of abode on June 1, 1900, was in this family.)	RELATION	PERSONAL DESCRIPTION									NATIVITY		
24	25	Perry Louisa W.	Head	W	F	Feb 1843	57	W		2	0	Kentucky	Kentucky	Kentucky
		Newman Arthur P.	Son	W	M	Sept 1876	23	S				Texas	Missouri	Kentucky
25	26	Matthews Burl J	Head	W	M	Jan 1860	40	M	12			N. Carolina	N. Carolina	N. Carolina
		Fannie M.	Wife	W	F	Oct 1869	30	M	12	5	5	Indiana	Maine	Scotland
		Carmen	Daughter	W	F	Jan 1890	10	S				Kentucky	N. Carolina	Indiana
		Susie	Daughter	W	F	Jan 1892	8	S				Kentucky	N. Carolina	Indiana
		Jo B.	Son	W	M	June 1894	5	S				Kentucky	N. Carolina	Indiana
		Margaret	Daughter	W	F	June 1896	3	S				Kentucky	N. Carolina	Indiana
		John	Son	W	M	Apr 1899	1	S				Kentucky	N. Carolina	Indiana
26	27	Carlose James	Head	W	M	Dec 1864	35	M	2			Kentucky	Kentucky	Kentucky
		Mary A.	Wife	W	F	Mar 1862	38	M	2	0	0	Kentucky	Kentucky	Tennessee
27	28	Yost Harris A.	Head	W	M	Jan 1866	34	M	2			Illinois	Kentucky	Kentucky

Figure 5-3: Census records can provide a lot of information, but also some errors, as in the spelling of "Burl" in place of "Burrel."

Use Hints to Expand Your Tree

While you can go through all the people in your family tree and do a search on them as we did in the previous section, Ancestry.com will automatically do a lot of this for you and tell you by way of the Hints icon in the upper-right corner of a person in your family tree.

Fannie Welborn Brown
B: Oct 1869
Mt. Vernon, Indiana, USA
D: 1914
Lexington, Fayette, Kentucky, USA

1 Ancestry hint

View profile · Quick edit · Search records · View her family tree · Add relative

1. Hover over **Family Trees** in top horizontal menu, and click your family tree.

   Family Trees ▾ | Search
   Marty Matthews family tree
   Start a new tree
   Upload a GEDCOM

2. In your family tree look for the leaf icon in the upper-right corner of a person. It will periodically move, or "shake." Hover on that leaf. More information on that person will appear along with several options and a new Hint icon. Click the **Hint** icon.

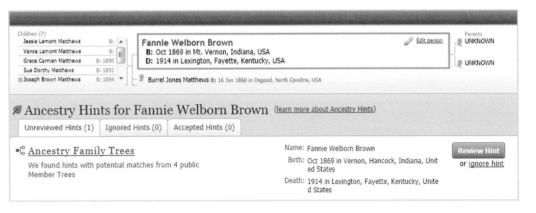

3. The Ancestry Hints page will open and explain the hints that are available. Click **Review Hint** to open a detail page for a particular hint.

4. If there are multiple records on the left, as is the case in Figure 5-4, click the checkbox in the upper-left corner of each record whose content, some or all of it, you want to incorporate into your tree. When you have selected all the records you want, click **Review Selected Tree Hints**.

Figure 5-4: A great benefit of Ancestry.com is the ability to search a large number of other family trees and pick up information from them—but note, it may not always be correct.

5. In the Review Member Tree Hints page, click the facts or people that you would like to add to your family tree, as shown in Figure 5-5, and then click **Save To Your Tree**. If you don't want any of the hints, click **Cancel**.

6. If additional hints appear, follow steps 3 through 5 to review a hint and then possibly save it to your tree. When you see the message that you have no unreviewed hints, you can click **Search Historical Records** to see if there is anything else. If there is, use the steps in "Start a Family Tree on Ancestry" earlier in this chapter to review and possibly save the new information to your family tree.

QUICKSTEPS

IMPORTING A GEDCOM FILE

If you have started to build a family tree in another product, such as Family Tree Maker or Legacy, on your computer, or Legacy.org or RootsWeb.com on the Internet, you can transfer that information to Ancestry.com using a GEDCOM file (GEDCOM, which stands for Genealogical Data Communication, is a standardized file format used to transfer genealogy information). You must first export a GEDCOM file from the other product. See explanations in Chapter 3 about exporting a GEDCOM file from Ancestry.com and later in this chapter for exporting from FamilySearch.org or RootsWeb.com. Given that you have a GEDCOM file on your computer, here is how to import it into Ancestry.com:

1. In Ancestry.com, hover over **Family Trees** in the top horizontal menu, and click **Upload A GEDCOM**.

Continued . . .

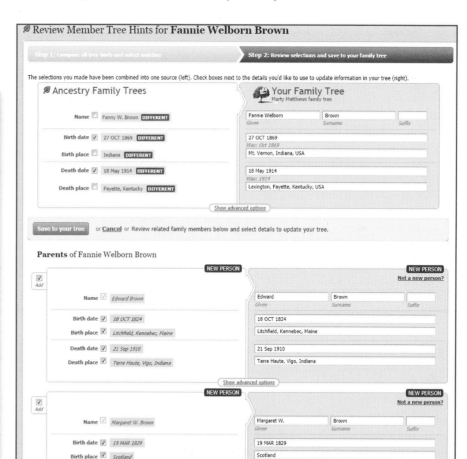

Figure 5-5: A great way to extend your family tree is by finding the parents of one of your ancestors in someone else's public family tree. Once again, they may not always be correct.

IMPORTING A GEDCOM FILE *(Continued)*

2. In the Upload A Family Tree page that appears, click **Browse** opposite Choose File.

Upload a Family Tree

When you upload a family tree file, all of the people in it are placed into a new tree on Ancestry.com sites. The name you choose to give your tree will be visible to your guests and other members of Ancestry.com sites. How do I upload my tree?

Choose file _____ [Browse...]
Find the family tree file on your computer.
Maximum file size is 75MB.

Tree Name _____
Give your new tree a name
☑ Allow others to see my tree as a public member tree
What does this mean?

Description _____

Enter surnames, years, etc., to help people understand what your tree is about. (optional)

☐ I accept the Submission Agreement

[Upload] or Cancel

3. Select the folder in the left pane that contains the file, click the file you want to use in the right pane, and then click **Open**.

4. Back in the Upload A Family Tree page, adjust the tree name, if desired, choose if you want to allow others to see the new tree, add a description if you want, click **I Accept The Submission Agreement**, and click **Upload**.

You'll see a progress dialog box telling you how far along the process is. When it is done, you'll see a message on your home page that Ancestry has finished processing the family tree.

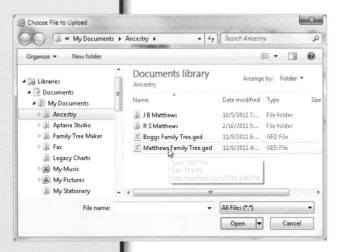

Connect with Others on Ancestry

Ancestry.com provides several ways that you can connect with or utilize the work of others who are building family trees on Ancestry. These include the following:

- Accessing information and media (photos, video, and audio) on other people's family trees if the other person allows their family tree to be public, which is the default. As you saw in the "Use Hints to Expand Your Tree" section and in Figure 5-4 earlier in this chapter, some hints will display information on other people's family trees, which you can choose to include or not in your family tree.

- Seeing on your home page recent activity in other people's public family trees that may relate to your family tree and that you can view and/or copy to your tree if you wish. See Figure 5-6. Move your mouse over each activity to see additional links that you can use to access information or contact the originator of the activity.

- Contacting others on Ancestry if they have chosen to allow that. In either hints or recent activity lists there may be a link to the person who built the tree. Clicking that link opens a dialog box for the person from which you can open their public family trees, view their profile, contact them, or block them from your trees.

- Connecting to others on Ancestry.com using Ancestry's Member Connect Service. As you begin to use Ancestry you will see a page appear introducing Member Connect, as shown in Figure 5-7. Clicking **Next: See New Activity** tells you about seeing the recent activity page shown in Figure 5-6. Clicking **Add To Your Tree** explains how to transfer information from someone else's family tree to yours, as described in the "Use Hints to Expand Your Tree" section earlier in this chapter.

CONTROLLING YOUR INFORMATION ON ANCESTRY

Ancestry.com provides several ways for you to control how you and your information are shared with others, including the privacy of your family trees, setting your site preferences, and inviting others to work on your family trees.

SET FAMILY TREE PRIVACY

You can set your family tree to be

- **Public** where others as well as Ancestry searches can see it and copy information from it.

- **Private** where others cannot see or directly access your information. Ancestry still can search and report information about deceased individuals from it unless you also prevent that.

When you create or import a family tree, you can choose to make it public or private. If you want to change a tree's privacy:

1. Display the tree whose privacy you want to change, mouse over **Tree Pages**, and click **Tree Settings**.

2. In the Tree Settings page that opens, click **Privacy Settings** to display the two options, as you can see in Figure 5-8.

Continued . . .

Tree pages

Family Group Sheet
Tree Overview
Media Gallery
Tree Settings
Share your tree

NOTE

Ancestry.com does not share information about people who it believes are living, which is defined as people under 100 years old without a death date.

Figure 5-6: *Being able to access and use the research of others on Ancestry is one of its greatest assets.*

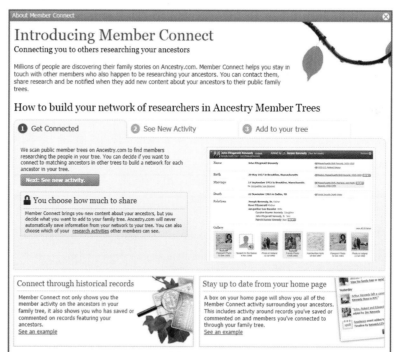

Figure 5-7: *Member Connect allows you to connect with and share research with others interested in people on your family tree.*

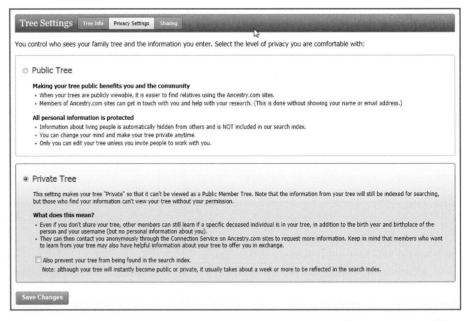

QUICKSTEPS

CONTROLLING YOUR INFORMATION ON ANCESTRY *(Continued)*

3. Read about the two options carefully and then click the option you want to use.

4. If you also want to prevent Ancestry from searching a private tree, click that option.

5. When you are ready, click **Save Changes**.

INVITE OTHERS TO SEE YOUR TREE

You can invite people to see, add to, and possibly change your family tree even if they are not Ancestry.com subscribers.

1. Display the tree you want to invite people to work with you on, mouse over **Tree Pages**, and click **Tree Settings**.

2. In the Tree Settings page that opens, click **Sharing**, and then click **Invite People**. The Invite To dialog box will open allowing you to invite people in three ways:

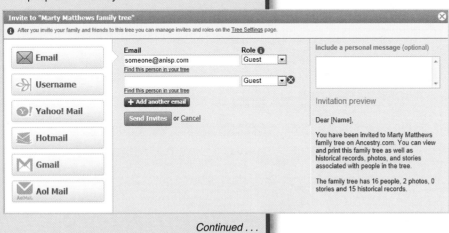

Continued . . .

*Figure 5-8: **In almost all cases you want to leave your family tree public because you will be able to get help on it, whereas you won't otherwise.***

Use FamilySearch.Org

FamilySearch.org provides free Internet access to the huge genealogy library of The Church of Jesus Christ of Latter-Day Saints (LDS). Their claim is that their records span billions of names across hundreds of collections, including birth, marriage, death, probate, land, military, and more. FamilySearch.org is primarily for searching various databases, which is further discussed in Chapter 6. Here we will simply introduce it.

CONTROLLING YOUR INFORMATION ON ANCESTRY *(Continued)*

- **Standard email** where you enter an email address, which can include addresses for Yahoo! Mail, Hotmail, Gmail, and AOL Mail.

- **Username** where you enter an Ancestry.com user name for current subscribers to Ancestry. Alternatively, you can display Ancestry members you have invited to work with you on other trees and select from that list those you want to invite to work on this tree.

- **Contact list** where you open your contact list on Yahoo! Mail, Hotmail, Gmail, or AOL Mail and select from that list those you want to invite to work on this tree.

3. When using the email or user name methods, click **+Add Another** if you want to invite another person. In a contact list, select all the people you want to invite.

4. When you have entered or selected all the people you want to invite, click the down arrow opposite **Guest** in the Role drop-down box and select from among the following:

- **Guest**   This person can view your tree, but not add to or change it.

- **Contributor**   This person can view and add to your tree, but not change it.

- **Editor**   This person can view, add, and change your tree.

Continued . . .

Create a FamilySearch Account

To fully utilize FamilySearch.org, you should create an account.

1. Open your browser, such as Internet Explorer or Firefox, and in the address bar type <u>familysearch.org</u> and press **ENTER**. You will see the initial search page shown in Figure 5-9.

2. Click **Sign In** in the upper-right corner. In the Sign In page that opens, click **Create New Account**.

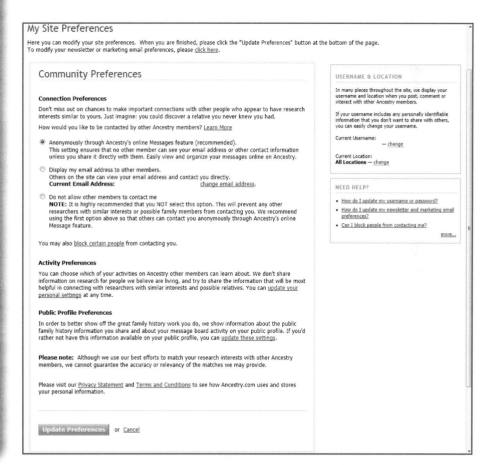

*Figure 5-9: **Being as open as possible with your preferences allows others to work with you and help you solve your genealogy problems.***

CONTROLLING YOUR INFORMATION ON ANCESTRY *(Continued)*

5. When you are ready, click **Send Invites** or **Share Tree**. You'll be told you have invited the number of people you sent invitations to. Click **I'm Finished Sending Invites**. A message will be sent out to those you invited.

You can manage the people you have invited to work with you on the Tree Settings, Sharing page, where you can change their nickname, role, and whether they can see living people, as well as remove and reinvite them.

SET SITE PREFERENCES

Site Preferences is the catch-all for setting the site options not set earlier in this QuickSteps, many of which have to do with how and what other people see about you and your family trees.

1. In any Ancestry.com window, mouse over **Account** at the top of the window and click **Site Preferences**. The Site Preferences page opens as you can see in Figure 5-10.

2. Read through the various preferences. Click **Learn More** to understand how you are contacted by others.

3. Select from among the three ways you can be contacted or prevented from being contacted by other Ancestry users.

Continued . . .

3. Indicate if you are an LDS member and want to use your LDS account. Otherwise, click **FamilySearch Account**.

4. Enter the registration information requested, enter the letters in the picture, and click **Register**. An email message will be sent to you that you must respond to within 48 hours.

Search for an Individual

Explore FamilySearch by doing a search on an individual.

1. Open your browser, such as Internet Explorer or Firefox, and in the address bar type familysearch.org and press **ENTER**. You will see the initial search page shown in Figure 5-9.

2. Try an initial search by entering one of your ancestors, like your father or great-grandmother. Click in the **Given Name** text box and type your ancestor's first and possibly middle name or initial.

CONTROLLING YOUR INFORMATION ON ANCESTRY (Continued)

4. Click **Change Email Address** to do that, and click **Block Certain People** to enter the Ancestry user name of each of the people you want to block.

5. Click **Update Your Personal Settings** to choose which of your activities on Ancestry others can learn about. Read the options, make any needed changes, and click **Update Your Settings**. Click **Return To Site Preferences**.

6. Click **Update These Settings** to customize what others see in your public profile about the work you've done on your family tree and posts you've made on the message board. When you are finished, click **Update Preferences** and then click **Return To Site Preferences**.

7. When you have made all the changes you want to make on the Site Preferences page, click **Update Preferences** and then click **Return To My Profile**.

TIP

Using "Exact" can severely limit what you see, while not using it can give you many more records than you want. Try various combinations to see what works best for you.

Figure 5-10: FamilySearch starts out assuming you want to simply search their records.

3. If you only want to search for the exact name you typed, click in the checkbox on the right of the Given Name text box.

4. Press **TAB**, type the person's surname or last name, and click the **Exact** checkbox if you want that.

5. To improve the search, click one of the life events—probably most important is birth— if you know it. If so, enter the location and then the range of years. Add as many life events as you want and know, and click **Exact** if you want.

6. When you are ready, click **Search**. You will get a list of historical records that match the information you entered, as shown in Figure 5-11.

7. If you want to change what you search on, click the **Refine Your Search** down arrow, make the changes you want, and once again click **Search**.

8. If you want to filter your search results to limit what is shown, click the category on the left and then click the parameter in the box that opens. Your list of records will be limited to those matching the parameter(s) you chose.

9. To remove a filter, click the **X** on the left of the parameter.

10. To look at the detail for a record, click the person's name. The detailed record will appear, as you see in Figure 5-12.

11. Detailed census records, like the one in Figure 5-12, may have additional family members' names listed in blue. Click a name to see the related detailed record.

12. When you have explored the search results as much as you want, click **FamilySearch** on the top-left corner to return to the FamilySearch Home page.

NOTE

You can use either "FamilySearch.com" or "FamilySearch .org," and capital or lowercase letters are interchangeable (you don't need to make the "F" and the "S" capitals). The capitals are shown only to make it easier to read.

TIP

By clicking the down arrow on the far right of a historical record entry in FamilySearch.org, you can get a preview of the information in a record. You can then drag across the information to highlight it, press **CTRL+C** to copy it, open a program and document where you want to store the information on your computer, and press **CTRL+V** to paste the information there. Figure 5-14 shows a preview open in FamilySearch and the same information copied into a Microsoft Word document.

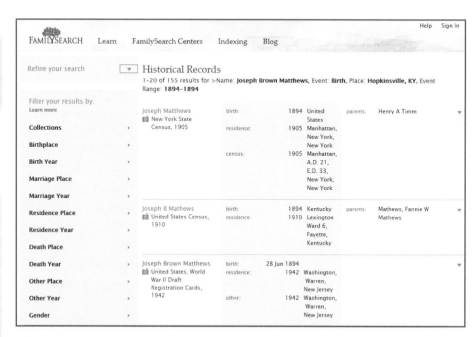

Figure 5-11: *FamilySearch.com sorts search results by relevance, with the more likely results first.*

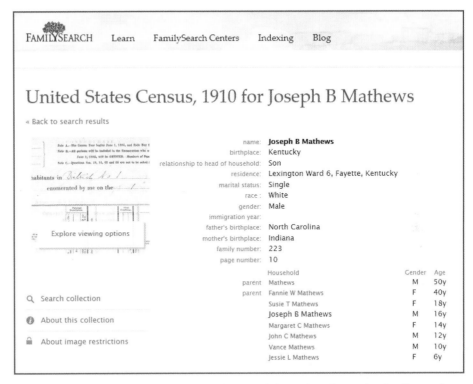

*Figure 5-12: **A detailed census record can give you information about other family members.***

Search for a Family Tree

FamilySearch.org allows you to search on a complete family unit.

1. From the FamilySearch Home page, click **Trees** under Discover Your Family History. The Trees page will open, as shown in Figure 5-13.

FINDING SOURCES

As you build your family tree and search for your ancestry, it is important to have as many solid sources as possible. Government census, birth, marriage, and death records, as well as military and immigration records, are all strong sources (although not 100 percent foolproof). For example, while you are building your family tree on Ancestry and you enter some event, such as a birth, marriage, or death that you heard about, you should try to find one or more good sources for it. If you don't find exactly what you want on Ancestry, then you need to look on other sites.

A case in point is the marriage of Marty's paternal great-grandparents, W. Riley Matthews and Lydia Catherine Riddle (see the genealogy story in Chapter 2). In Ancestry, after entering the names, a hint on Lydia showed that another family tree had Lydia marrying Riley on 13 Dec 1855, in Moore County, North Carolina, but the hint did not have any source documents, which Marty felt he needed.

SEARCH IN ANCESTRY.COM

To try and find a source record in Ancestry (this procedure is using Lydia as an example):

1. From the family tree, hover over Lydia and click **Search Records**. The list displays 387,914 records.

2. To narrow the results, click **Birth, Marriage & Death** under Narrow By Category. This provided 27,252 records.

3. To narrow further, click **Marriage & Divorce**. This brought the results down to 13,342 with a lot of people with a last name of Matthews.

Continued . . .

Discover Your Family History

Records   Trees   Catalog   Books

First Names

Last Name

Birth Year   Birth Place

Death Year   Death Place

Father, First Names   Father, Last Name

Mother, First Names   Mother, Last Name

Spouse, First Names   Spouse, Last Name

Marriage Year   Marriage Place

Search   Advanced search

Ancestral File Number (AFN)

Find

FAMILYSEARCH   Help   Sign In

Learn   FamilySearch Centers   Indexing   Blog

rootstech LEARN MORE ▶

Get early bird pricing for RootsTech 2012 in Salt lake City, Feb. 2–4.

Go to previous site

Free U.S. Civil War Records

U.S. CIVIL WAR PROJECT
Free Access to Civil War Era Records

Find your Civil War ancestors and help preserve more records.

Want to give back?

Start indexing records to make them searchable online

Figure 5-13: *A complete family search can sometimes better focus on finding your ancestors.*

QUICKSTEPS

FINDING SOURCES *(Continued)*

4. Click **Edit Search** to edit Lydia's record that was being searched. Shorten the name to just Lydia Riddle, add the marriage date and spouse name, select the **Female** gender, and click **Search**. The result was 645 records.

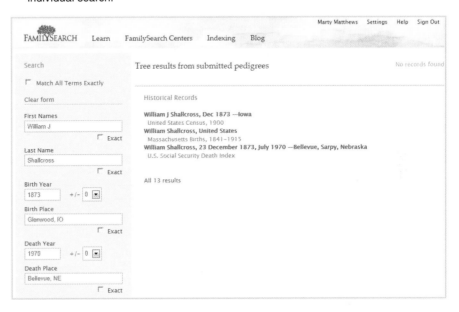

5. Select **North Carolina Marriage Collection**. This produced 15 records, as you see in Figure 5-15. Unfortunately, none were Marty's great-grandparents.

Continued . . .

2. Enter as much of the information as you can, and click **Search**. If a complete pedigree has been previously submitted for the family you entered, you will see that pedigree. In addition, you will see similar search results to those you saw for an individual search.

3. Change any of the parameters on the left, and click **Search** again to see those results. Also, you can click **All xxx Results** to see the possible, but less likely, results.

QUICKSTEPS

FINDING SOURCES (Continued)

SEARCH IN FAMILYSEARCH.ORG

In FamilySearch:

On the Records page, enter <u>Lydia Riddle</u>; click **Marriage**; enter <u>Moore County, North Carolina, 1855</u>; click **Spouse**; enter <u>W. R. Matthews</u>; and click **Search**.

The immediate results, shown in Figure 5-16, are Marty's great-grandparents with the source "North Carolina Marriages 1759–1979."

As discussed in Chapter 6, searching on a number of sites is often needed to find the source documents.

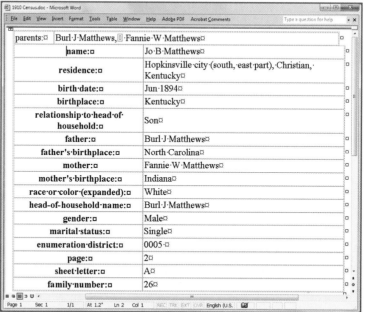

Figure 5-14: You can copy and paste information from FamilySearch to other documents.

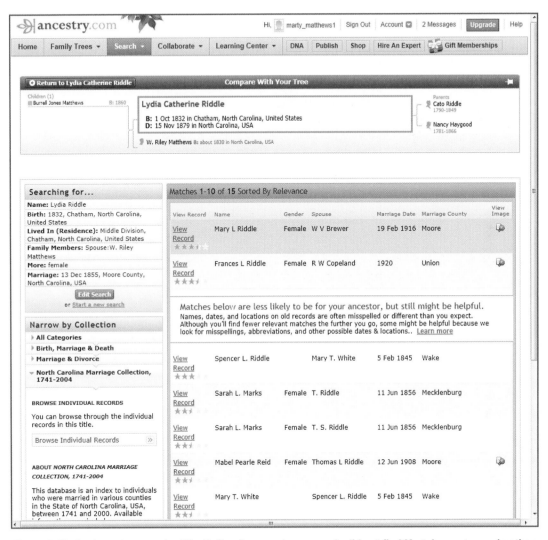

*Figure 5-15: **An Ancestry search of North Carolina marriage records did not find Marty's great-grandmother.***

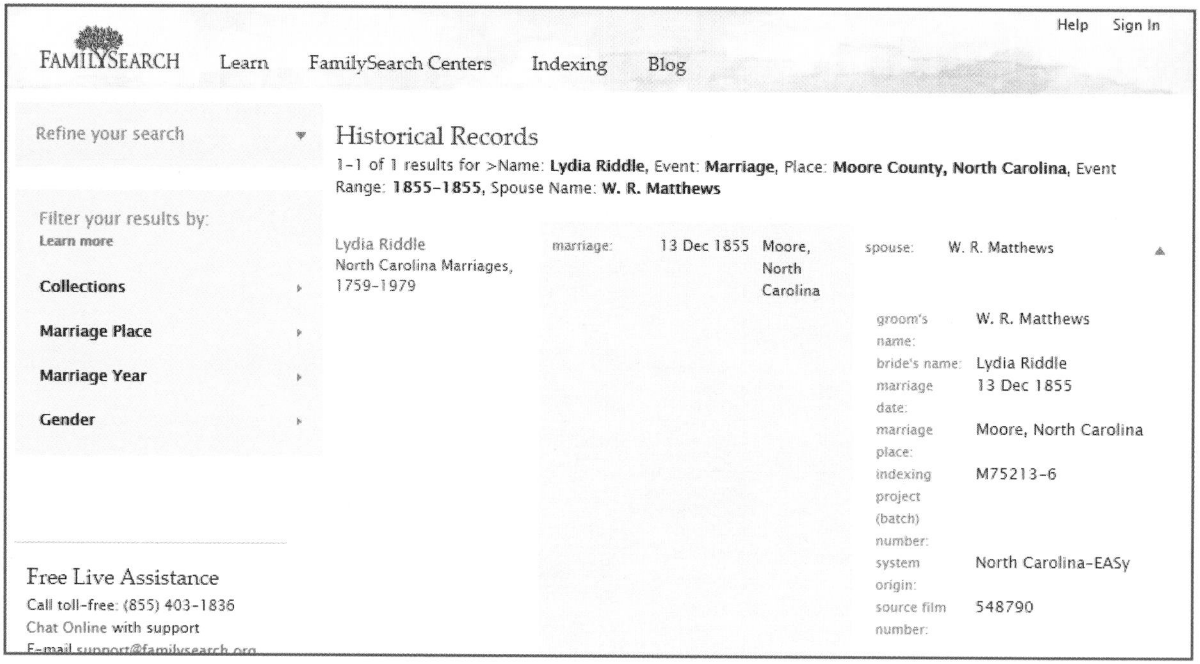

*Figure 5-16: **The same search on FamilySearch did find his ancestors.***

TOM'S STORY

Thomas Harold Beard, 62, Whidbey Island, WA

OVERVIEW

My mother's paternal line has been well documented back 11 generations to 1636, where my ancestors lived in Guilford, Connecticut, having emigrated from England. Her maternal line is known back four generations to 1816 in Dublin, Ireland. I have traced with strong evidence my father's paternal line back five generations to 1802 in Adair, Kentucky, and, as a result of a DNA link, I have identified a possible lineage back several more generations to 1735 in Scotland. My father's maternal line is known back five generations to 1781 in William County, Tennessee. In my genealogy work I have used Ancestry.com, RootsWeb.com, FamilySearch.com, HeritageQuest.com, and FindAGrave.com websites, as well as Family Tree Maker 2010.

STORY

The first flickering of interest in my ancestry was around 1970 when I saw some pedigree forms, which I bought and gave to my grandmother to fill out (she did, and they have been helpful). But over the years I all but forgot the forms until in 2005 my daughter had a school project in which she was to write a story about her ancestors. I got out a book I'd gotten from my mother entitled *The Munger Book* (see Figure 5-17) that had been written in 1915 about my mother's paternal ancestry. In this book my daughter found a story about her relatives as children in the 1600s getting put in stocks for talking together outdoors after dark unchaperoned. This spiked my interest. I knew through this book and other sources a lot about my mother's family, but almost nothing about my father's family before my grandfather. I decided to change that.

GETTING STARTED

As I started out I knew my grandfather's name, George Cleveland Beard; that he died in 1948; that he had lived in Texas; that his father, my great-grandfather, was called Simpson Beard; and that Simpson had died around 1890. From a friend I heard that a good and free online genealogy database called Heritage Quest was available at the local public library,

so I started there with a search on my grandfather's name. I found him on the 1910 Census (see Figure 5-18) and was able to learn that he was living with his brother, that he was 24 years old (meaning he was born in 1885 or 1886), and that he was born in Arkansas (see Figure 5-19 for more detail). In addition, I found he was a schoolteacher and had three brothers: John H., Roy, and Noah. Later on I got a picture of him at this time, as you can see in Figure 5-20.

Doing some more hunting through older censuses, I found in the 1880 Census a 21-year-old Simpson Beard in Sugar Loaf, Boone County, Arkansas, but born in Texas, with a wife Susan M. and a one-year-old son John H., which would correspond with 31-year-old John H. Beard on the 1910 Census (see Figure 5-21). Continuing on, I went to the 1860 Census for Denton County, Texas, and found a one-year-old Joel S. Beard, son of William H. and Mary A. Beard, both born in Tennessee (see Figure 5-22). Here I learn for the first time that the person I've

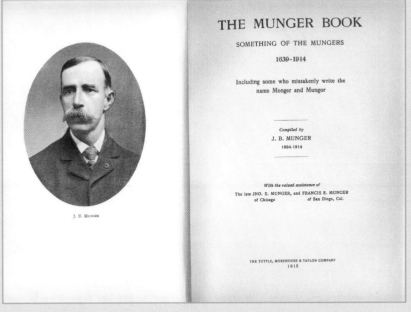

*Figure 5-17: **One of my mother's ancestors had produced and printed a very detailed record of her paternal line.***

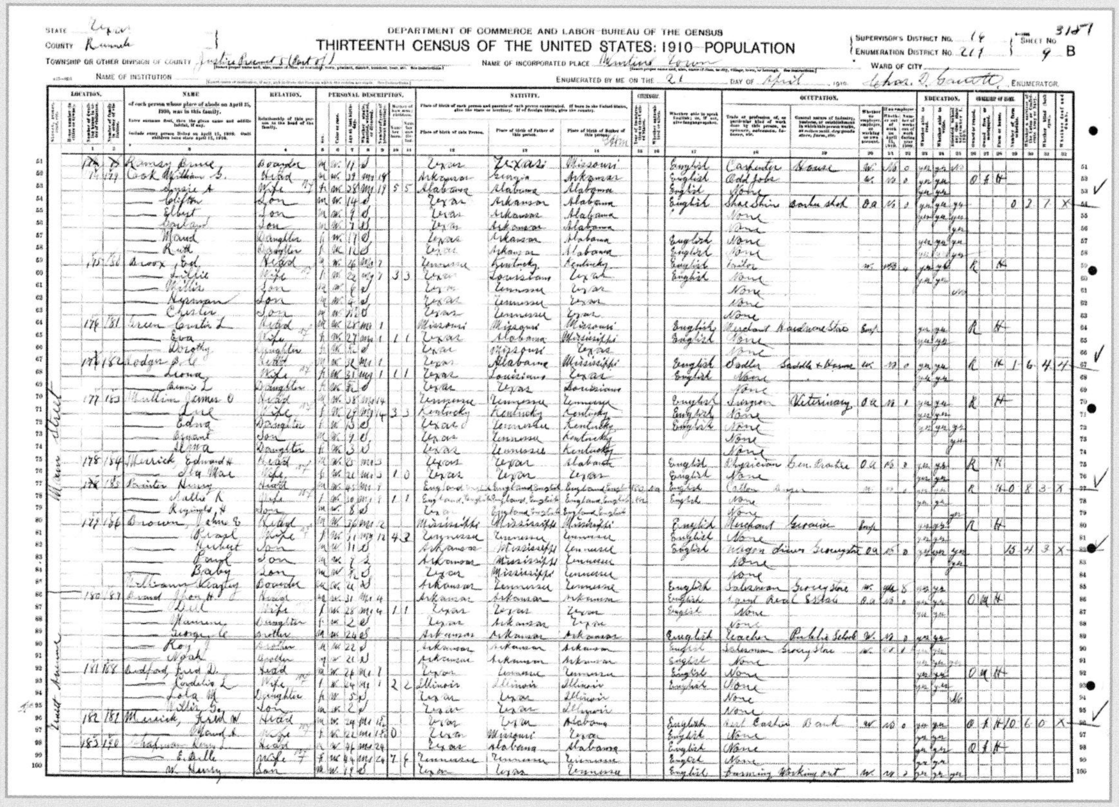

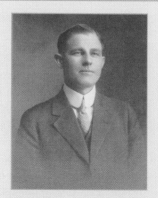

Figure 5-18: *I have found that census records were very helpful in supplying facts about my ancestry that helped me go back in my family tree.*

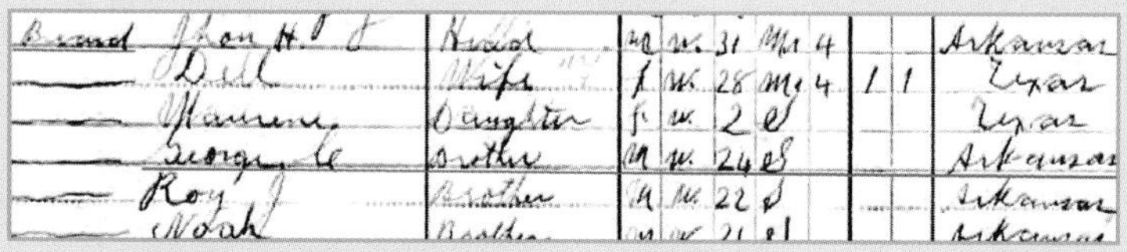

Figure 5-19: *1910 Census detail*

Figure 5-20: *George Cleveland Beard, my grandfather, about 1910*

been calling Simpson Beard is actually Joel Simpson Beard whose parents are William H. and Mary A.

During this time I began using other genealogy websites on my own computer, including RootsWeb, FamilySearch, and Ancestry, and building a public family tree on the latter (see Figure 5-23). Through the public tree I connected with several others who are researching the Beard family. These contacts and my research helped me fill in a number of facts about the family, including that William H. Beard was William Henry, and that his father was Sevier Beard, who I also found on the 1850 Census (see Figure 5-24). I also began to see a number of interesting tidbits of family history. For example, William Henry Beard's sister married William Henry's wife's (Mary Tyson's) brother (a brother and sister married a sister and brother).

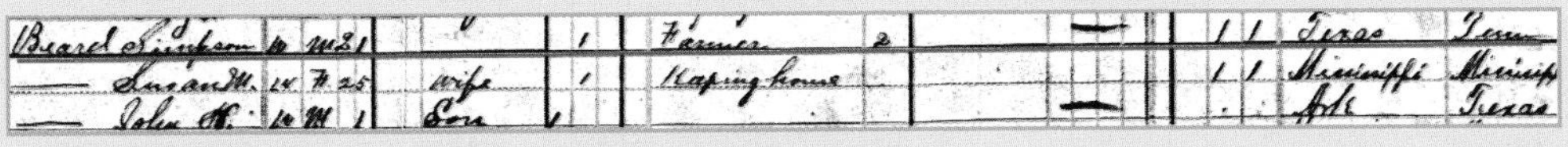

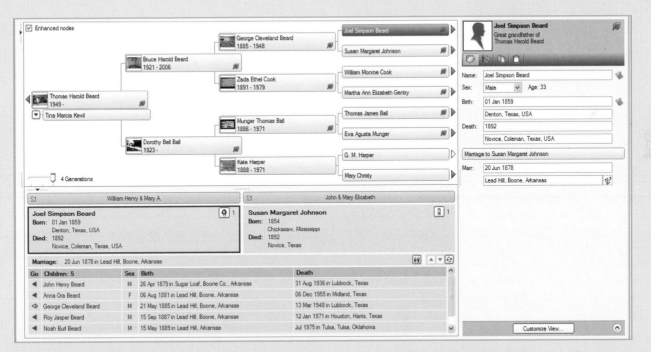

Figure 5-21: *1880 Census detail*

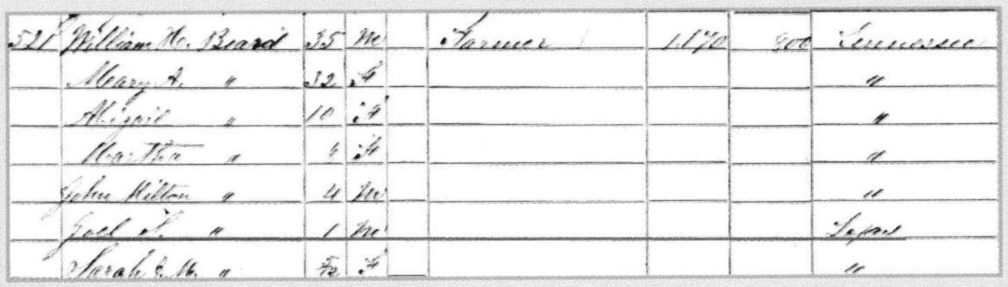

Figure 5-22: *1860 Census detail*

CHALLENGES

At the point of reaching Sevier Beard five generations back (my great-great-great-grandfather), I was at a dead end. I could not find who his parents were, although I knew he was born in Adair County, Kentucky. It might help to go back there and search physical records, but I haven't had that opportunity. After reading about DNA family projects, I decided to submit a sample to the Bard, Baird, Beard Project. It cost approximately $100 to test for 12 markers. They send you a kit with several cotton swabs. You rub the swabs on the inside of your cheek, package them up, and return them. They match your DNA to other people who sent in their DNA samples (it does not try to match to samples of historical DNA). Initially, there were no matches to mine, but within a relatively

Figure 5-23: My initial family tree through Joel Simpson Beard (my great-grandfather) was straightforward.

Figure 5-24: *Using census records and birth, death, and marriage records, along with the helpful work of others, I was able to go back to Sevier Beard, who was born in 1802.*

short time I got an email message that another person has submitted DNA that was a close match to mine. I contacted that person and found they had done quite a bit of ancestral research, which they would let me use (see the first paragraph of a long email they sent back to me in Figure 5-25). It showed a lineage dating back to Scotland in the 1700s (see the first bit of this lineage in Figure 5-26). The problem is that it is not clear what the exact connection is with my ancestors. It looks like a John Beard had a son Sevier Beard, the end of my known line. The problem is that there were two John Beards, a father and a son, or possibly two brothers, both John. Therefore, is Sevier Beard the son of John I, making him the brother of John II, or the son of John II and grandson of John I, or some other combination if the two Johns are brothers?

Letter Resulting from DNA test for Beard Relatives

Thomas:

Here is a summary of what Jim Beard and I think about your Sevier and his ancestors. Please know that we are simply looking at all the facts we have and making inferences and that everything is subject to change. As new information comes in, we can discard theories or firm them up. This is a simple version, without document notes, census recitations, etc. That will make the basic story easier to follow. As you digest this, you can add your own factual documentation and open a dialog with us as to what and why---Jim has researched this family for a number of years and I believe he has an excellent grasp of the movements and relationships, which I find to be the most difficult. He has a keen mind for interpreting the few facts we can find on these old families. I know that you will already have some of the information but I include what we know, just in case. I also plan to use this "story" for my particular family line of <u>Beards</u>, who are now saying to me, "okay, we did the DNA, now give us the story"!

First, a quick view of the ones we feel **may** be the first of our Beard ancestors to come to America. Martin and John Beard came to Philadelphia in 1739, from Scotland or from that part of Ireland that was settled by Scots. There are immigration records for them. They stayed in PA a short while and then moved down the wagon road to the area that would be Botetourt Co, VA.

Figure 5-25: *The first couple of paragraphs of a long email received as a result of DNA testing*

```
                Outline Descendant Report for Martin Beard

.....  1  Martin Beard b: Abt. 1720, d: 1818
.....    + Mary Shafor
.......       2  Hugh Beard b: 1750 in Virginia, d: Scott Co., Kentucky
.......       2  Samuel Beard b: 1754 in Botecourt County, Virginia, d: 1834 in Henderson, Tennessee
.......       2  George Beard b: 1757
.......       2  John Beard b: 1758 in Virginia, d: 1814
..........         + Mary Margret _____
.............          3  Sevier Beard b: 1802 in Adair Co., Kentucky, d: 1884 in Marion, Arkansas, USA
................            + Catherine Hills b: 1802 in Rutherford Co., North Carolina, m: 09 Mar 1825 in Adair Co.,
                            Kentucky, d: Abt. 1886 in Arkansas
...................              4  William Henry Beard b: 25 Dec 1825 in Adair Co., Kentucky, d: 09 Apr 1886 in Lead
                                 Hill, Boone, Arkansas
```

Figure 5-26: *A possible lineage from William Henry Beard back to Martin Beard*

OBJECTIVES

My objective is to document enough of our family history that my brother and I can pass on to our children. This may be in the form of a book or a website. I know I want to include as many photos and documents as I can get a hold of, such as the photo and marriage license of Joel Simpson and Susan Beard shown in Figure 5-27. I also want to include as many stories about the family as I can find. For example, one that I got from an online search of the Battle of Hightower that I heard about from the correspondent whose DNA I share:

> Captain John Beard and John Sevier, Beard's superior officer, were dispatched by the Tennessee territorial governor to calm a group of Cherokee Indians shortly after the Revolutionary War. The Indians would not be calmed, so Captain Beard attacked and killed a number of them at the Battle of Hightower. This upset President George Washington who ordered Beard arrested and court-marshaled. John Sevier, Beard's superior, supported Beard's actions and he was exonerated. It is possible that Sevier Beard, John's son (possibly) was named after John Sevier.

Figure 5-27: *Photos and historical documents make a book or website on one's ancestry come alive.*

How to...

Chapter 6

Searching the Internet for Information

Searching is one of the most common uses of the Internet. But how do searches really work? What do you need to understand about search terminology? This chapter will explain in depth how searches work, explain the differences and similarities between search types, provide some tips to make your searches more successful, and explore a number of genealogy search sites.

Use Techniques for Advanced Searching

Understanding how to phrase your request, using the specialized tools that online search sites (also called "search engines") make available, and understanding how both people and search engines process your requests are keys to successful

TIP

When creating a request for genealogy information, proofread every entry. It is too easy to type an incorrect date or leave out a letter when typing a name.

QUICK**FACTS**

CITING YOUR SOURCES

When students write academic papers, they are required to "cite their sources" to ensure that the information they include in those papers can be verified by outside means. It is no less important in genealogy to be able to cite the source from which you obtain your information. Consider how many hands touch the data before you include it in your family tree. For example, a birth may be recorded in the church register, the county vital records office, and the family Bible, and mentioned in a letter written to another family member. Any of the people recording the information might have misspelled the name of a parent, put down the incorrect date, transposed two letters, or just written the information incorrectly. If you have ever seen a handwritten census record, you can see what abbreviations and poor penmanship can do for recordkeeping. If possible, photocopy the original document or microfilm copy and include that copy in your files. Reference the copy's location in your family tree so that anyone who chooses can access the data.

There are several things to consider when including any information in your family's history:

- What document or record was used to find the information?
- What entity created the document?
- Who provided the information to that entity?
- How did *you* find the information?

Continued . . .

genealogy searches. While each type of search has its own rules, there are some general suggestions when working with genealogy requests.

State a Query

There are several methods by which you can ask for information. You could write a letter, telephone a family member, send an email to a specific location, or send a blanket email to a large group, such as the members of a mailing list. Today, many requests start with an entry into the search box of a search engine. But whatever method you choose to ask for information, consider the following conventions:

- Make your request specific to one name or event.
- Include one name and date (or time period) and, if possible, a location.
- Write out the full name without abbreviations. For example, use William rather than Wm.
- When using a location, include the complete name. Include as much information as possible, especially when posting to a message board.
- Use complete dates. Most genealogy dates are shown as day, month, and year in this format: DD MM YYYY, for example, 15 03 1847, or use a three-letter abbreviation or the month, 15 Mar 1847. If you don't know the exact date, use an approximation, such as "died about 1787" or "born circa 1671." Using "abt 1787" for "about 1787" is also common.
- Include *your* name and the address or method by which you want to be contacted if you are requesting a reply. It's also a good idea to state how you are related to the person about whom you are sending the query.

Use Indexes and Compilations

Indexes are ordered lists of items that include information about the location of a specific item. They are used by government agencies, libraries, courthouses, and others to list what documents or records are available and where those documents or records can be found. With the advent of the Internet, there are giant database indexes used by search engines and other websites to help the user access information. While indexes are very useful for family historians, they are only as good as the person or entity that created the index. If the index was created by hand, the underlying documents may be misclassified or left out

QUICKFACTS

CITING YOUR SOURCES *(Continued)*

- What alternative sources are available to verify the information?
- Is the information from an original document or a copy?
- When was the document created?
- If you traveled to the location of the document, could you see the original or only a copy?

After you have used a document in your family's history, cite its information and location in the history itself. There is a fine article on the Genealogy.com site entitled "How to Cite Sources" that explains the process well.

completely. Since most indexes are created later than the original document, see if you can obtain a copy of the original document to verify information. Also consider that some records have two references, such as marriage records that refer to the groom's name in one location and the bride's in another.

Compilations are defined as collections of information or data in a more useful format. An encyclopedia could be considered a compilation, for example. Among the numerous websites that are compilations of data are Wikipedia for general information and Cyndi's List, RootsWeb, and the U.S. and WorldGenWeb Projects for genealogy information.

Search Primary Genealogy Sites

Every site has its own tips and tricks for most effective searching. We've included some ideas and suggestions for each of the main sites as well as some of the other sites available.

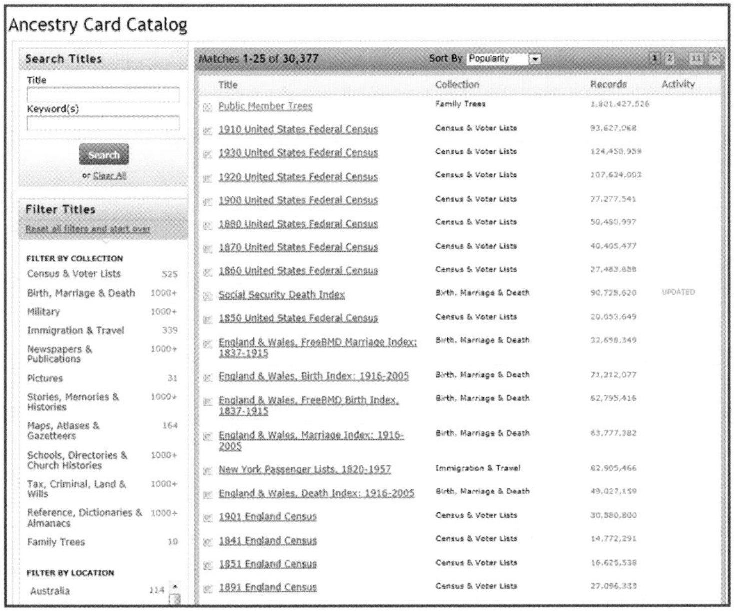

Search Ancestry.com

In addition to the search tools seen in the following illustration that are found on the Search menu from the main Ancestry.com page, your subscription to Ancestry.com offers access to dozens of databases from which to search for information. You can choose specific historical records such as census records, tax rolls, military records, or vital records such as birth or death records.

To find the billions of records that have been digitized by Ancestry .com, consider using the card catalog listing. To use the card catalog:

1. At the Ancestry.com home page, click **Search**.

2. From the Search menu, click **Card Catalog**. At the date of this writing, there are more than 30,000 collections that include millions of records as seen in Figure 6-1.

*Figure 6-1: **The card catalog in Ancestry.com includes links to more than 30,000 records.***

3. At the left of your window, click a filter to make your search more specific, as seen in the next example. In this same window, you can further limit your search by location and/or dates.

4. From the list at the right of your window, choose the database you want to search.

5. Enter the first and last name and any other information you may have. Click **Search**.

6. Close the results to return to your home page.

To return to the main search page from any other location in Ancestry, click the **Search** button at the top of the page. The right side of the main Ancestry search page includes a listing of all the available search categories as well as a link to the card catalog, as seen here. From each database, you can find additional, more specific databases to perform additional searches. As each group of results appears, you may scan through them to find likely matches to your search.

Explore Genealogy.com

Another member of the Ancestry.com family is the Genealogy .com site. It, too, requires a subscription. At the time of this writing, there are three levels of membership, all of which include the Family Tree Maker software package and access to the Genealogy Library. Like Ancestry.com, the site includes message boards and the ability to create a personal webpage for your family.

Genealogy.com was purchased by Ancestry.com in 2002, and some of the tips and references on the Genealogy.com pages refer back to that time. However, a very useful forum is available in the site's Expert Tips section. To access this forum:

1. In any browser, type Genealogy.com in the address bar.

2. From the Genealogy.com home page, hover over **Learning Center**.

3. From the drop-down menu, choose **Expert Tips**.

USING ANCESTRY.COM *(Continued)*

Another way to search for a specific person is to use the wildcards that are built in to Ancestry.com. For example:

- To search for a name that differs by only one letter, use a "?". In this example, typing "Swans?n" would return both "Swanson" and "Swansen."

- If you are looking for a name that has several alternate spellings, such as "Anderson," you can use an "*" for up to five unknown characters. An example would be "Ander*" which might return "Anderson," "Andersen," "Anderssen," and so on.

- You may also use the "*" at the beginning of a name, such as "*son."

There are several rules for using wildcards in Ancestry.com:

- Either the first or last character in a search must be a letter, not a wildcard character. For example, "*nderson" is okay, but not "*nders*."

- Your searches must contain at least three non-wildcard characters. For example, "Swa*" is fine, but not "Sw*."

- Wildcard characters do *not* work with Soundex searches.

TIP

If you are searching for a female's name in the United States, voting records will not help you before 1920. It was not until 1920 that women were allowed to register and vote in the United States.

4. Click **Genealogy Tip**s in the More Great Tips column as shown here.

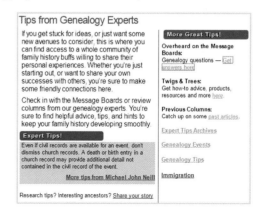

5. The Helpful Tips For Genealogists forum appears. This forum, as seen in Figure 6-2, has current information.

6. Click the browser's **Back** arrow to return to Genealogy.com.

While both Ancestry.com and Genealogy.com offer similar databases, you may find some database records appear on only one of the sites. For example, Ancestry .com may offer the marriage records for one state, while the records for another state are found in Genealogy.com's databases.

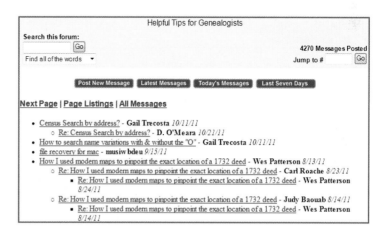

*Figure 6-2: **Genealogy.com has current tips for genealogists.***

QUICKSTEPS

ADDING SECOND MARRIAGES IN ANCESTRY.COM

In earlier days, after the death of a spouse, there were often second (or more) marriages. You can add this type of information in Ancestry.com family trees.

To add a second spouse:

1. In Pedigree view, select the person for whom you want to add the spouse, and click **View Profile**.

2. Click the **Edit This Person** button that appears below the name, birth, and death fields at the top of the page.

3. Click the **Relationships** tab.

4. Scroll to the **Spouses** area, and click **Add A Spouse**.

5. Enter the appropriate information and click **Save**. Enter the marriage information and click **Submit**. You are returned to the Edit page. Make any additional changes or return to your family tree.

TIP

Remember that the backup tool in Ancestry.com backs up only the current tree. Should you have multiple family trees, you must back up each separately.

Some of the best resources on the Genealogy.com pages are the series of genealogy lessons found in the Learning Center. To access these free lessons:

1. Hover over **Learning Center** at the top of the page.

2. Click **Free Genealogy Classes** from the drop-down menu to open the list shown next.

3. Scroll through the classes that are offered. It's usually a good idea to start at the beginning of a series, as each lesson refers to earlier lessons.

Use FamilySearch.org

FamilySearch.org is a free site, operated by The Church of Jesus Christ of Latter-day Saints. According to its main page, it offers "billions of names across hundreds of collections" throughout the world. Chapter 5 describes how to register and begin using the site. If you need some help, you can use the built-in help and learning resources.

To access the learning resources,

1. Click **Learn** on the horizontal menu bar at the top of the window, as seen in Figure 6-3.

2. In the Getting Started window that appears, click **Get Started Now** to start the basis steps to your research. You are introduced to a series of short video instructions for each step.

3. Scroll down on the page to the additional resources and lessons in the What's In Learning Resources section to see the Resource Wiki, Research Courses, and Discussion Forums. As seen in Figure 6-3, each section has links to get more information. There are also technical tips for smart phone and other electronic gadget users.

   a. The Research Wiki is a site on which researchers can share their information and provide tips to other researchers. A "wiki" is a website that allows anyone visiting the site to add information to it.

Genealogy Classes
Click any link below to start learning!

Beginning Genealogy
by Genealogy Research Associates

- Part 1: Your Great Ancestral Hunt (Six lessons)
- Part 2: Record Groups as Building Material (Eight lessons)

Internet Genealogy
by Online Pioneers

- Part 1: Getting Started on the Net (Sixteen lessons)
- Part 2: Powerful Tools for Internet Research (Fifteen lessons)

Tracing Immigrant Origins
by Genealogy Research Associates

- Part 1: Introduction (Twelve lessons)
- Part 2: Post Civil War Immigrant Sources (Six lessons)
- Part 3: Between 1820 and 1865 (Six lessons)
- Part 4: Pre-1820 Immigration (Seven lessons)
- Part 5: European Sources (Nine lessons)

Researching with Genealogy.com

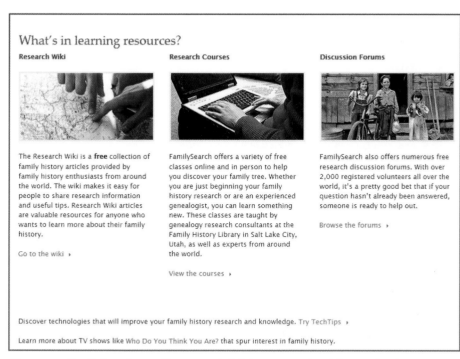

What's in learning resources?

Research Wiki

The Research Wiki is a **free** collection of family history articles provided by family history enthusiasts from around the world. The wiki makes it easy for people to share research information and useful tips. Research Wiki articles are valuable resources for anyone who wants to learn more about their family history.

Go to the wiki ›

Research Courses

FamilySearch offers a variety of free classes online and in person to help you discover your family tree. Whether you are just beginning your family history research or are an experienced genealogist, you can learn something new. These classes are taught by genealogy research consultants at the Family History Library in Salt Lake City, Utah, as well as experts from around the world.

View the courses ›

Discussion Forums

FamilySearch also offers numerous free research discussion forums. With over 2,000 registered volunteers all over the world, it's a pretty good bet that if your question hasn't already been answered, someone is ready to help out.

Browse the forums ›

Discover technologies that will improve your family history research and knowledge. Try TechTips ›

Learn more about TV shows like Who Do You Think You Are? that spur interest in family history.

*Figure 6-3: **FamilySearch.org offers many helpful resources for visitors to its site.***

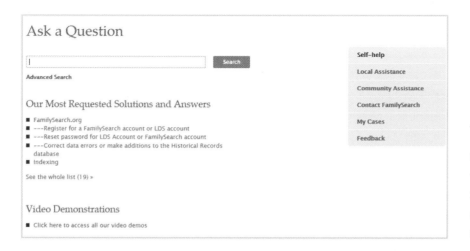

Ask a Question

| | Search |

Advanced Search

Our Most Requested Solutions and Answers

- FamilySearch.org
- ---Register for a FamilySearch account or LDS account
- ---Reset password for LDS Account or FamilySearch account
- ---Correct data errors or make additions to the Historical Records database
- Indexing

See the whole list (19) »

Video Demonstrations

- Click here to access all our video demos

Self-help

Local Assistance

Community Assistance

Contact FamilySearch

My Cases

Feedback

b. Research Courses can be filtered by place, skill level, subject, format, and language, as seen next. Short videos, interactive slides, long presentations, and audio courses are available.

What are you looking for?

Place
Argentina (1)
Australia (4)
Canada (2)
Europe (3)
France (4)
Germany (10)
India (1)
Ireland (7)
Italy (5)
Latin America (7)
Netherlands (3)
New Zealand (1)
Poland (7)
Portugal (3)
Russia (5)
Scandinavia (4)
South Africa (1)
Spain (4)
United Kingdom (70)
United States (100)

Skill Level
Advanced (48)
Beginner (56)
Intermediate (220)

Subject
Birth, marriage and death (50)
Business records and occupations (8)
Census, taxation, and voter lists (25)
Court, land, and wills (14)
Directories (1)
Ethnic, political, or religious groups (14)
Family trees (55)
Geographic aids (5)

c. Discussion Forums can help answer your questions, give you ideas when you've hit a roadblock, and offer both technical and research support.

Click **Help** to the left of the Sign In link at the top of the home page to ask more specific questions or to find answers to frequently asked questions. You can even access video demonstrations from this window, as seen at left.

QUICKFACTS

UNDERSTANDING GENEALOGY INDEXING

Many records of life events, such as marriages, births, and deaths, are kept by government and church officials in their records. Indexing helps make those records available when you search on the Internet.

For example, the Social Security Death Index lists all persons registered with the Social Security Administration whose death has been reported. If you have U.S. ancestors who were alive in 1935 but have since died, chances are good that that person had a Social Security number and their death will be reported in that index list. Using this information, you can ascertain where your ancestor was living when he or she died as well as where the original Social Security card was issued. Some, but not all, records include the decedent's date of birth as well.

Several websites offer the opportunity for volunteers to help create indexes that can be searched online. FamilySearch.org is in the process of indexing its microfilm records and the information submitted by its members, and is actively seeking volunteers to help in that process.

Indexes are not always accurate or complete, but they do offer another means to locate information about your ancestors. As always, original documents are the best sources, but indexes may help point the way to locate those documents.

IMPROVE FAMILYSEARCH.ORG SEARCHES

Each field in the search form has specific tips to help your search:

- Given Name:
  - Use both the first and middle names of the person. If you do not get any results, omit the middle name.
  - Try using nicknames—for example, for someone named William, try Bill.
  - Many early records abbreviated first names, using "Wm." instead of writing out the first name. This is especially true on census records.
  - FamilySearch allows the use of wildcards. The * is used to replace one or more characters, and the ? is used to replace one character.
  - If you don't know the first name, leave the field blank and use the spouse or parents fields to enter the information you do know.
- Surname:
  - Use spelling variations.
  - For women, try using a maiden name. If that doesn't work, try her married name.
  - If you do not know a woman's maiden name, leave the surname field blank and enter her spouse's name in the Spouse field.
- Checkboxes:
  - The checkboxes by each name can be checked if you want an exact match.
  - If nothing is found by using exact matches, clear the checkbox and try again.
- Life events:
  - After you have chosen a life event, such as marriage, try including a location. For example, if you are not sure of a city, try using just the state name.
  - Use the Any option to find immigration dates or military service information.
  - If you have entered a date range, increase or decrease the range.
- Refine your search:
  - After you have performed a search, a column appears at the left of the records that were returned. Click **Refine Your Search** to add or delete information.

Search RootsWeb.com

Accessing RootsWeb.com may seem daunting at first glance. However, it has links and indexes to millions of family trees, surname lists, and mailing lists.

**Search Family Trees
at WorldConnect**

<u>Advanced Search</u>

More than **640 million** names on file

Surname

Given Name

[GO]

or -- jump to a specific database

Database

[GO]

or -- find a database by keyword(s)

[GO]

or -- find a database by surname(s)

[GO]

About WorldConnect

• <u>WorldConnect History</u>
• <u>RootsWeb's Acceptable Use Policy</u>
• View <u>current count</u>, and rate of growth.

Surname	Cornelius	Exact ▾	Father	
Given Name		☐ omit living	Mother	
Birth Place		☐ omit blanks	Spouse	
Birth Year	Exact ▾		Skip Database	
Death Place	Washington	☐ omit blanks	Updated Within	Forever ▾
Death Year	Exact ▾		☐ Has Descendants	
Marriage Place		☐ omit blanks	☐ Has Notes	
Marriage Year	Exact ▾		☐ Has Sources	
Fuzzy Search ☐ (uses soundex)	Search			
	Reset			

*Figure 6-4: **The Advanced Search dialog box in the RootsWeb site may return more information than a simple search.***

While much of the information found at the site is user-generated, there are links to the Social Security Death Index as well as death records from several states.

Since the stated purpose of RootsWeb.com is to connect genealogy researchers with others, many of the links are to existing databases. One of the most ambitious is the WorldConnect group of family trees that currently includes more than 663 million surnames.

To use the WorldConnect Project to find information on your ancestor:

1. Type <u>RootsWeb.com</u> in the address bar of any browser.

2. The home page of RootsWeb.com appears. In either the Search Engines And Databases or the Family Trees section, click **WorldConnect Project**.

3. The search page for the WorldConnect Project appears as seen here. Enter a surname and, if you choose, enter the given name as well. Click **Go** to start your search.

If you have additional information other than the name, you may want to use the Advanced Search dialog box as shown in Figure 6-4. Follow steps 1 through 3 as shown earlier, but click the **Advanced Search** button to open the form. Enter the data you have and click **Search**.

Any results appear as shown in Figure 6-5. Note that the location you entered may not be what appears on the results. In our example, only two of these results are from the state of Washington although Washington is part of the location.

The Other Matches column on the right provides links to census records, newspapers, and other sources. These links will take you directly to the record in the Ancestry.com pages.

USE ROOTSWEB MAILING LISTS

The more than 32,000 mailing lists currently available in the RootsWeb.org pages can help you find when your ancestor arrived in Massachusetts, for example, or connect you with cousins who may also be working on the family history.

Cornelius, Dorice Mildred	16 NOV 1893	BEACONSFIELD, TAS	1966	BUNBURY, WA	:3368426		Census Newspapers Histories
🔍 🔲	Father: John Gilbert Cornelius Mother: Sarah Moore Spouse: Charles Daniel Prior						
Cornelius, Eber Lewis	29 APR 1852		01 APR 1942	Whitman County, Washington, USA	funstonfamilies	🛒	Census Newspapers Histories
🔍 📖	Spouse: Sarah Cecelia Funston						
Cornelius, Edward Harry	30 MAY 1919	Virgin, Washington, Utah, United States	26 APR 1944	Virgin, Washington, Utah, United States	breamefford	🛒	Census Newspapers Histories
🔍 🔲 📖	Father: Henry Cornelius Mother: Emma Bradshaw						
Cornelius, Elizabeth A.	17 JUL 1852	Cornelius, Washington Co., Oregon	23 OCT 1933	Cornelius, Washington Co., Oregon	jf-63	🛒	Census Newspapers Histories
🔍 🔲	Father: Thomas Ramsey Cornelius Mother: Florentine Wilkes Spouse: George H. Shaw						
Cornelius, Elmer Delmar	01 NOV 1908	New Mexico, United States	30 OCT 1974	Virgin, Washington, Utah, United States	breamefford	🛒	Census Newspapers Histories
🔍 🔲 📖	Father: Henry Cornelius Mother: Emma Bradshaw Spouse: Myrtle Lela Wilcox						

Figure 6-5: *Location results may not be what you expect when receiving information from databases.*

A mailing list sends a duplicate email to each of its subscribers when new information is posted or someone sends in a question.

To subscribe to a mailing list in RootsWeb.org:

1. From the RootsWeb.org home page, click **ROOTS-L Mailing List** in the Mailing Lists section.

2. Click the link to **ROOTS-L-Request@Rootsweb.com** near the top and enter the word "subscribe" in the message section of your email.

USE MESSAGE BOARDS IN ROOTSWEB.ORG

Message boards are similar to the bulletin board you may see at your local grocery store. People post a message, and you can answer it or respond as you please. Most message boards are web-based and require you register with the site that hosts the board. There may or may not be a charge for this service. The message boards on RootsWeb.org are free to the public to search and read messages. However, you must have registered with either RootsWeb.org or Ancestry.com to reply or add to a message. Ancestry.com and RootsWeb.org share the same message boards. There are several types of message boards, including surname, locality, and topic. Chapter 8 discusses message boards in more depth.

Search MyHeritage.com

MyHeritage.com is an online family network site where people can build and share their family trees, find new relatives, and use these links to explore their past. In November 2011, MyHeritage.com acquired FamilyLink.com and WorldVitalRecords.com so it will now provide historical records in addition to helping family historians build their family's tree. This acquisition means that searchers will have access to many more records from the United States as well as Canada, Australia, the United Kingdom, and Ireland.

One of the best features of MyHeritage.com is the free genealogy software program, Family Tree Builder. To download this program:

1. In the address bar of any browser, type MyHeritage.com.

2. The home page of MyHeritage.com will open. At the top of the page, click the **Downloads** tab.

3. As seen in Figure 6-6, the download button for the latest version of Family Tree Builder will appear. Click **Free Download**.

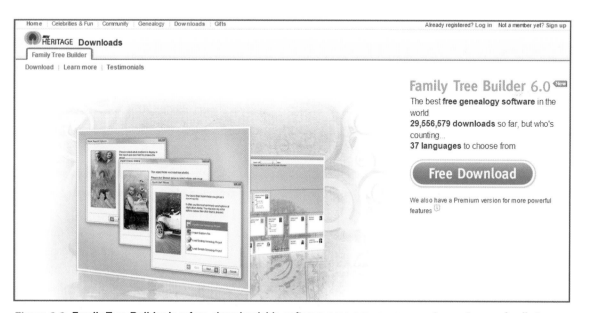

Figure 6-6: Family Tree Builder is a free, downloadable software program you can use to create your family tree.

4. Depending on your browser, somewhere on the page a message will appear asking if you want to run or save the file, as seen here. The easiest choice is to run the file to install the program right away.

Do you want to run or save **family_tree_builder_5365i.exe** (27.0 MB) from **a.netdna.mhcache.com**?   [Run] [Save] ▼ [Cancel] ✕

5. A message appears asking what language to use. Make your choice and click **OK**.

6. Follow the on-screen prompts to install the program.

7. When the installation is complete, you may choose to open the program to use it right away, or close it and return to the MyHeritage.com site.

In addition to the family trees you can build online as well as with free software, you can also use the MyHeritage.com site for searching as seen in Figure 6-7.

To access the search function from the MyHeritage.com home page:

1. Click the **Genealogy** tab at the top of the page.

2. Click the **Research** tab to open the search form. In our example we have opted to use the Advanced search section, which is shown.

3. Enter the information and click **Search**. Depending on the number of databases being searched and the speed of your Internet connection, this may take a few minutes.

4. The results are displayed for you to view. Click each link to view the sources of the information.

Build a Website at MyFamily.com

Another one of the Ancestry.com group, the fee-based MyFamily.com site offers a place to create a family website that can be accessed by others or kept private at your discretion. At the present time, one can create a family group for a subscription fee of $29.95 per year that allows anyone you approve to share photos, videos, and stories. In addition to the website, subscribers can create a family blog, keep an online calendar, and access the site from an iPhone with a free app. The online family tree function is

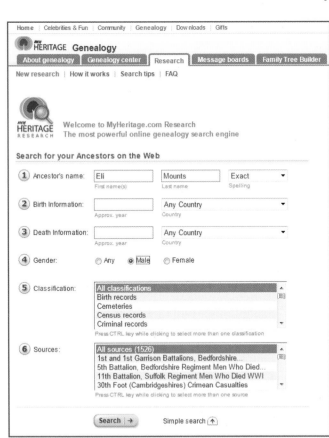

Figure 6-7: **You can set the search criteria for both the classification and the sources in MyHeritage.com.**

provided by Ancestry.com, and the information you include in those trees is available to members of Ancestry.com as well as those using MyFamily.com.

Get Documents from Fold3.com

Fold3.com (formerly Footnote.com) is a fee-based website offering millions of documents that have been scanned and indexed for online availability. Since changing its name, the site is emphasizing military records, which makes sense, as they work with the National Archives and Records Administration offices. Some documents are available for viewing at no charge. You must register to become a member. Free membership does not allow access to all of the documents available through the site. Check your local library, as some make the site available for their patrons at no additional charge.

The site's home page offers several short videos and a number of text tutorials to help users understand what documents and records are available. You can search based on keywords or name.

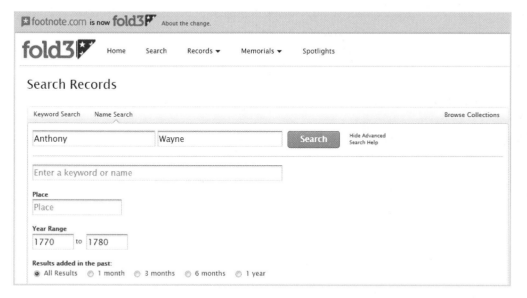

To search the site:

1. Type <u>Fold3.com</u> in the address bar of any browser.

2. From the home page, click **Search** at the top of the page. Click either the **Keyword Search** tab or the **Name Search** tab. Click **Advanced Search** for additional options as shown here.

3. Enter the information for which you are searching, and click **Search**.

4. The results will appear in a new window. You can quickly make changes to your search criteria by entering additional information in the You Searched For section at the left of the window as seen in Figure 6-8.

Figure 6-8: *Most searches can be refined to narrow the results.*

5. Click the **Search Tips** link at the upper right of the search results to get additional help in phrasing your search terms as seen at left.

6. Click **Home** to return to the main Fold3.com page.

Search Other Genealogy Sites

There are currently more than 7 million genealogy sites on the Internet. In addition, there are libraries, cemeteries, courthouses, and many other resources from which you can glean family history. We have included several sites that have unusual databases or other features that may prove useful.

SEARCH ACCESSGENEALOGY.COM

One of the key features of this site is the Native American genealogy database. It also contains numerous biographies, cemetery records, and an online history and genealogy library. The Native American genealogy records include Native American Rolls and Records and information about many of the Native American tribes. Much of the tribal information is historical rather than genealogical, but useful to the historian for the additional links specific to each tribe.

SEARCH ANCESTORHUNT.COM

This delightful site offers an obituary search portal as well as state indexes and death records. It has links to the vital records provided by each state, some old newspapers that include online data, and family Bible records that have been indexed by surname for research. Some of these family Bible records include pictures. There are links to each state's genealogy website as well as several other free directories and search links. Unique among genealogy websites are prison records that date back to the Civil War and, on the other side, links to U.S. sheriffs and police officers. This website is free and growing each week.

USE CYNDISLIST.COM

One of the most well-known genealogy sites on the Internet, Cyndi's List has been online since 1996, when the owner of the list created a website that contained bookmarks that could be used by her local genealogy society. Currently there are more than 290,000 links, as seen in Figure 6-9, all of which have been cataloged and arranged to be as useful as possible for each visitor. It is considered one of the top online research websites and is totally free, supported solely by Cyndi and those who make donations to keep the list alive. She includes the name of each person making a donation, and the names can be found in the Why Donate Money To Cyndi's List section on the page.

Figure 6-9: Cyndi's List offers thousands of cross-referenced links.

Genealogy Categories

A	B	C	D	E	F	G	H	I	J	K	L	M
N	O	P	Q	R	S	T	U	V	W	X	Y	Z

▸ Acadian, Cajun & Creole (127)
Updated November 20, 2011

▸ Adoption (191)
Updated November 21, 2011

▸ Africa (86)
Updated June 2, 2011

▸ African-American (681)
Updated November 10, 2011

▸ Ancestry.com: The Basics (174)
Updated October 31, 2011

▸ Antarctica (41)
Updated December 5, 2010

▸ Asia & The Pacific (295)
Updated November 8, 2011

▸ Australia (1094)
Updated November 11, 2011

▸ Austria / Österreich (219)
Updated October 31, 2011

▸ Baltic States: Estonia, Latvia & Lithuania (213)
Updated October 31, 2011

▸ Baptist (118)
Updated September 24, 2011

▸ Beginners (163)
Updated October 7, 2011

▸ Belgium / Belgique / België (156)
Updated October 31, 2011

▸ Biographies (240)
Updated September 24, 2011

▸ Births & Baptisms (556)

▸ Norway / Norge (333)
Updated September 11, 2011

▸ Novelties & Gifts (72)
Updated November 14, 2011

▸ Numbering Systems (37)
Updated August 29, 2011

▸ Obituaries (509)
Updated November 27, 2011

▸ Occupations (386)
Updated November 19, 2011

▸ Odds & Ends (55)
Updated July 5, 2011

▸ Oral History & Interviews (121)
Updated November 26, 2011

▸ Organizing Your Research (224)
Updated October 31, 2011

▸ Orphans (160)
Updated September 3, 2011

▸ Outer Space (10)
Updated September 5, 2011

▸ Passports (56)
Updated October 7, 2011

▸ Personal Home Pages (10632)
Updated November 27, 2011

▸ Philippines (62)
Updated July 25, 2011

▸ Photographs & Memories (632)
Updated November 18, 2011

▸ Podcasts for Genealogy (28)
Updated November 18, 2011

Figure 6-10: **Each category in Cyndi's List shows the number of links and the latest update.**

Each link is categorized, as seen in Figure 6-10, and each category includes the number of links as well as the date of the last category update. Most category lists include a How To section in the index as well as related categories that may be useful.

SEARCH ELLISISLAND.ORG

The EllisIsland.org website is operated by the Statue of Liberty-Ellis Island Foundation. Its first goal was to restore the Statue of Liberty, and since 1986, the foundation has focused on restoring Ellis Island and maintaining the Ellis Island Immigration Museum. In 2001, the American Family Immigration History Center was opened, which contains archives of more than 22 million passengers that entered Ellis Island between 1892 and 1924. Many of these records are now online for your research. Remember, however, that not all immigrants came through Ellis Island but landed at other locations in both the United States and Canada.

To research the name of a passenger:

1. Type ellisisland.org in the address bar of any browser.

2. From the main page, click **Passenger Search** and then click **New Search** from the drop-down menu. Enter the passenger's name as seen here, and click **Start Search** to start the search.

3. If there is no exact match, you are prompted to widen the search by using only the first initial, just the last name, or an alternative spelling. Make your choice and click **Search** in the Checked Name Change area.

4. Your results appear as shown in Figure 6-11. If you want more information about a name, click that name. If you have not yet registered with the site, you are prompted to register.

5. Complete the registration information, and the passenger record will appear. You may see a copy of this passenger's record, a copy of the ship's manifest, and a picture of the ship, and purchase any of the records for your files.

6. When you have completed your review, click **Sign Out**.

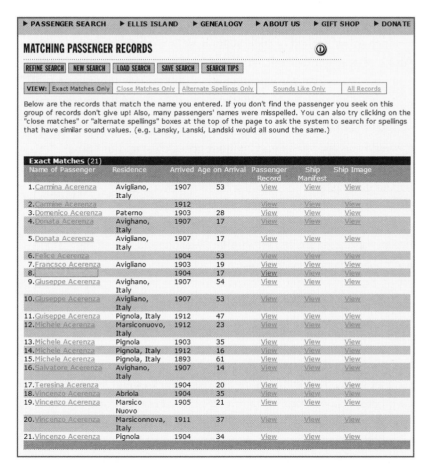

Figure 6-11: **From the passenger lists found on the Ellis Island site, you can link to additional information.**

SEARCH FINDAGRAVE.COM

This site can be searched at no cost. However, if you want to add a name or something else to the database, you must register so that the database can be updated with who submitted what information and when that information was submitted. To become a member costs nothing but your time. The site states that its primary purpose is to create a graves registration website in addition to providing a remembrance and genealogy resource site.

USE GENEALOGYTODAY.COM

This website offers tips, links, instructions, and articles on researching and organizing your family history. Its links are, for the most part, free and very useful. It is not a catalog or family tree creation site, but rather a site for those new and not-so-new to researching their family's history to learn more about the process. It partners with genealogy suppliers and offers links to purchase forms and other genealogy supplies and gifts.

SEARCH GENEASEARCH.COM AND GENEALOGYPAGES.COM

These free sites offer similar links to help you find surnames and offer other online resources for your research. Of the two, GeneaSearch has the most options and offers suggestions to aid your search.

USE GENGATEWAY.COM

This catalog site offers a number of links and resources, many of which are free. It includes links to sites in the United States, Ireland, Scotland, and the United Kingdom. While many of the sections do not yet contain information, it may be worth your time to explore the site for any information that may be relevant to your search.

USE GENI.COM

This site, which was launched in 2007, states it aims to create a "world family tree" by using private family trees, which can be linked on the "world family tree" by common ancestors. You can join for free, but the site offers additional services, advanced research tools, and other incentives for paid subscriptions.

SEARCH GENSOURCE.COM

This site, owned and operated by an amateur genealogist and full-time computer programmer, provides databases to help you in your research. There are three main databases:

- I Found It! is described as a "directory" rather than a complete index. When using this database, follow the instructions found in Search Instructions. This database includes such lists as ship passenger lists, software, family mailing lists, and others.
- Common Threads offers a database search to find other people who may be researching the same surname. You can add an entry so they can find you.
- The I Found It! Archive contains records that have been transcribed by researchers and indexed by the owner of the page.

SEARCH ONEGREATFAMILY.COM

This subscription-based site merges all individually entered family trees into one tree so that you can see connections between your tree and theirs. This automatic process creates a unified family tree that can save information and time. The page states that it will automatically find your ancestors, safeguard your data, and connect you to research that has already been completed. With an Internet connection, you can access your data from any location.

SEARCH WORLDVITALRECORDS.COM

This valuable website offers databases that show census, birth, marriage, death, military, court, and other records from throughout the United States and Canada. There are newspaper and parish register records, family trees, and hundreds of other databases to search. While it is a fee-based site, some libraries in the United States offer access with your library card.

| United States | UK & Ireland **Updated!** | Canada | Australia | World | | Become a fan | Follow us on | Share via Email |

Pick a state or country. See all of the records we have for that location. This feature works well if you know the place where the information may be. The collections here are divided in time by decades.

Alabama	Hawaii	Michigan	North Carolina	Utah
Alaska	Idaho	Minnesota	North Dakota	Vermont
Arizona	Illinois	Mississippi	Ohio	Virginia
Arkansas	Indiana	Missouri	Oklahoma	Washington
California	Iowa	Montana	Oregon	West Virginia
Colorado	Kansas	Nebraska	Pennsylvania	Wisconsin
Connecticut	Kentucky	Nevada	Rhode Island	Wyoming
Delaware	Louisiana	New Hampshire	South Carolina	
District of Columbia	Maine	New Jersey	South Dakota	
Florida	Maryland	New Mexico	Tennessee	
Georgia	Massachusetts	New York	Texas	

Featured Collections

PIONEER COLLECTION - Over 13.8 Million Names in 534 Databases

Military - Nearly 300 Million Records

Census and Voter Lists - Almost a Billion Records

Birth, Marriage and Death - More Than 290 Million Records

Collections of the Month

PIONEER COLLECTION - Over 13.8 Million Names in 534 Databases

Massachusetts Vital Indexes Prior To 1850 - search over 3.2 million names.

*Figure 6-12: **The WorldVitalRecords.com website has links to records from each state and several other countries.***

As seen in Figure 6-12, there are pioneer collections from the United States as well as databases from the United Kingdom, Ireland, Canada, Australia, and other countries. Each month the site offers new collections from which its members can search.

Search Census Data

Many family historians rely upon census data to locate their ancestors. Nearly every government has taken a census, some of which date back centuries. Census records have provided a basis for taxation, military service, and government planning. In the United States, the sole purpose for the census that is taken every ten years, according to the U.S. Constitution, is "for apportioning direct taxes and representatives among the several States."

UNDERSTAND CENSUS DATA

Each of the censuses taken in the United States since 1790 has been handled a bit differently. Early census takers often had to provide their own supplies, and many did not heed the established boundaries, thereby double-counting some residents and missing others altogether. The information collected has varied by census as well. For example, the 1820 Census asked such questions as

- The name of the head of the household
- The number of free white males by age
- The number of free white females by age
- The number of other free persons except Indians
- The number of slaves
- The number of persons not naturalized
- How many persons engaged in agriculture, commerce, or manufacturing

By 1870, the requested information was more complete:

- Name, age, sex, and color of every person in the household.
- The occupation of each male.
- The occupation of each female.
- The value of owned real estate.
- The value of personal property owned.
- The birthplace of every person in the household.
- Whether or not the person was married within the year.
- Whether or not the parents of the persons were of foreign birth.
- Did the person attend school within the year?
- Can the person read and write?
- Is the person a male citizen over 21?

As you can see, each census asked different questions and provided different data. Add to that the problem of penmanship, abbreviations, and mistakes, and the census data may prove only a starting point for your research.

LOCATE CENSUS DATA

Many states now have early census records available online. Try censusfinder .com to see if your ancestor's state is among them. Ancestry.com and WorldVitalRecords.com both have extensive U.S. census records as well as some records from the United Kingdom, Ireland, and Scotland. Many libraries offer microfilm copies of state census results. Consider using voting records, city directories, tax records, and even local newspapers to verify information from that time period. Family History Centers throughout the United States may also have microfilm copies of census data. Go to FamilySearch.com to find the center nearest you. You can also find microfilm records of the 1930 Census in Washington, D.C. and at one of the 13 regional offices throughout the United States. For more information about this census, see the National Archives and Records Administration website at 1930census.archives.gov.

NOTE

As mentioned in earlier chapters, the U.S. census from 1890 was destroyed in a fire in 1921.

VERIFY CENSUS DATA

As with any genealogy record, census information must be verified before it is accepted. Before you assume that the John Jacobs found in the 1870 Census was the John Jacobs that married Sally Jones in 1880, verify birth dates through other sources. As with all historical records, two (or preferably three) records that show the same information are better than one.

Search Other Sites

Besides the general search sites and specialized genealogy sites, there are a number of other resources for your online family history research. A number of immigration sites as well as military and ecclesiastical sites can provide information for your records.

Search Immigration Sites

While the Ellis Island site may be the one that first comes to mind when thinking about immigration to the United States, only a small percentage of immigrants arrived through that portal. Following are a few possibilities that may help you get started in your immigration search.

SEARCH THE U.S. CITIZENSHIP AND IMMIGRATION SERVICES

The U.S. Citizenship and Immigration Services site provides access (for a fee) to immigration and naturalization records for deceased immigrants. Two types of services are offered: an index search based on your (the researcher's) data, and a record copy request that provides copies of both immigration and naturalization records. To access the forms and learn more information, type uscis.gov in the address bar of your browser and click **Genealogy** under Services on the left.

SEARCH THE NATIONAL ARCHIVES

To access this website, type nara.gov in your browser's address bar, type Immigration Records in the search box, and press ENTER. For example, microfilm copies of passenger lists for all arrivals from foreign ports are in the archives for the years between 1820 and 1982. Access the website for more information.

This website, described earlier in this chapter, contains links to the ships' passenger lists project being researched by other family historians.

SEARCH SHIP PASSENGER LISTS AND IMMIGRATION RECORDS

This information, found at researchguides.net/immigration/index.htm, provides links to passenger lists for ships arriving in the United States between 1820 and 1840. It also provides tips for determining the port at which your ancestor arrived.

Search Military Sites

A useful site for military records in the United States is the same research site described in the "Search Ship Passenger Lists and Immigration Records" section at researchguides.net/military/index.htm. This site offers links to military records from the War of 1812 through World War II, as well as tips on locating information.

Another useful site is barbsnow.net/Military.htm (the "M" must be capitalized). This site offers links to various military records as well as general information about searching for this data.

National archives in both the United States and Canada can help you get started finding information about the military service of your ancestors. Go to archives.ca for Canadian information and archives.gov for information about U.S. service members.

Search Ecclesiastical Sites

Church records are perhaps the most thorough type of records over the centuries other than census records. The issue becomes identifying the type of records, how, and where they are kept. Different denominations keep different types of records. Your first problem may well be identifying which church records to search. In many families there are as many religious affiliations as there are people.

Once you have established the denomination to which your ancestor belonged, do a general search for that denomination. Many groups have online archives, such as the Evangelical Lutheran Church in America whose website at elca.org offers a number of links when you enter genealogy in the search box.

Another site for those with Baptist ancestors is found at the RootsWeb.com site. Type homepages.rootsweb.ancestry.com/~baptist in the address bar of your browser. An example is seen in Figure 6-13.

Whatever denomination you find, look online for that denomination and see if there are websites for churches in the area in which your ancestor lived. Often an email to a local church can get you started on your search.

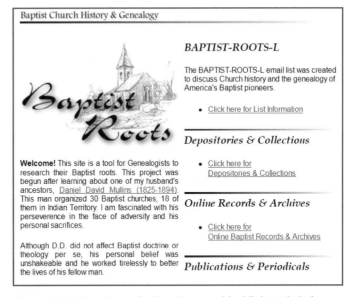

Figure 6-13: **Many denominations have archival links to help in your genealogy research.**

Pam Brager, 43, Whidbey Island, WA

OVERVIEW

For me, it's all about the stories. I grew up listening to my grandfather telling stories about the island on which I'd grown up. Some of the family had even done ancestral charts that fit in with the stories. The family reunions I attended always had a new chart prepared by my mom's cousin, who had traveled to places like the National Archives, cemeteries, and other places the rest of the family couldn't go. Our family started taping stories when I was quite young, and I got hooked on the idea of creating my own *Little House on the Prairie* series customized for my children.

Grandpa Gabelein got prostate cancer when he was about 72, so I knew there was a deadline. He loved banana splits served with hot fudge sauce, so we started meeting for a "banana split break" every Sunday. I'd turn on my tape recorder and ask, "Grandpa, what about the time…" and he'd be off. For me, the smell of my dad's hot fudge sauce will always bring back Grandpa's voice and those stories. And yes, it is my *dad's* hot fudge sauce!

STORY

I was born Pamela Sue Sires. Both of my parents were from the Pacific Northwest, and yet my mother's mother and father's father came from the Midwest. My maternal grandmother was a Dust Bowl kid from Scotts Bluff, Nebraska. When she was 12, her father and mother packed up the family and moved to Seattle because a friend had written there was work to be found out here. My great-grandfather knew he couldn't impose his family of seven on his bachelor friend permanently, so he moved the family to Whidbey Island where he found work logging.

The youngest child, standing on the running board in Figure 6-14, is my maternal grandmother, Dora Norene Mellroth. When it was time to move from Nebraska, they packed up a car like the one shown here and hooked a trailer to it. Her oldest siblings rode in that car, while her father drove a second car with the rest of the family. Nebraska roads were flat and planned on a grid. But going over the Rockies to Washington was like a scary carnival ride with all those twists and turns, especially with her brother driving!

Figure 6-14: *My grandmother's father moved the family from Nebraska to the Pacific Northwest to find work.*

Grandpa Gabelein's family came from Germany to Wisconsin and then to Whidbey Island in about 1908. The picture in Figure 6-15 was taken about the same time as they arrived on Whidbey. I've never been able to ascertain if the families knew each other before they arrived in the Pacific Northwest.

Figure 6-15: *The Gabelein family came to Whidbey Island from the Midwest at the turn of the 20th century.*

Figure 6-16: **According to Grandpa Gabelein, the Kramers visited Whidbey Island only once, the week of his father's funeral.**

The tall boy in the back is my mother's grandfather, Arthur Frederic Gabelein, who lived from 1888 to 1925. Arthur was killed when a well he was building collapsed around him, leaving his pregnant wife with six children. Minna Juliana (Kramer) Gabelein not only kept the family together, but lived to see all of her grandchildren.

Minna's parents also hailed from Nebraska. They came out for Arthur's funeral and immediately returned to Nebraska. My grandfather always remembered the white beard sported by his grandfather, as seen in Figure 6-16.

GETTING STARTED

It seems like I've always been collecting information about our family. Somehow, the family pictures and stories are so interwoven with my life, it's hard to remember a time when I wasn't collecting. Because of the close connection I felt with my mother's father, I created a book of his stories, as seen in Figure 6-17. I published the book for my children and all of my cousins after he died.

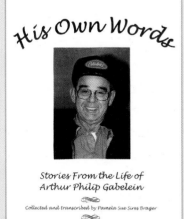

Figure 6-17: **I wrote this book for my family from the tapes of Grandpa Gabelein's stories.**

One of my favorite mementos is a letter written to my Grandmother Gabelein from her brother during World War II. In it, Uncle George described a "scrape" he had gotten into overseas and asked his sister (my grandmother) to help him out with some money, but "please don't tell mamma." A picture of the envelope is shown in Figure 6-18. The "scrape" must not have been too bad, because as you can see, the letter was passed through by the censor.

As I continue my searching, one of my goals is to find information about my father's side of the family. My father's mother, who was born in Everson, Washington, was married prior to marrying my grandfather, which was a big scandal in those days. I have not yet been able to unearth the details of that marriage, but think I have the wedding ring from it.

I've traced my father's family through several generations to a great-great-great-great-grandfather in Kansas named John Shell. In 1888 the family, with several of their Kansas neighbors, chartered a train and arrived in Whatcom County in Washington Territory on May 10, 1888. Two generations later, my paternal grandmother, Marguerite Shell, met and married Miron William Sires. I've traced the Sires family to a great-great-great-grandfather born in England in 1820. He was an immigrant to Indiana, and after the Civil War the family migrated north and west. Some lived in the Pacific Northwest and some in the Dakotas, where my paternal grandfather was born in 1909. It is rumored that his family moved to the Bellingham, Washington, area because of the fertile land and tall timber,

Figure 6-18: **My Uncle George asked Grandma Gabelein for money during World War II to help him out of a "scrape."**

although I don't yet have any documentation supporting this. Miron was one of several siblings, and he loved to tell the story about how he learned to milk a cow at a very young age. His father would say, "Melvin, go milk the cow." Melvin said, "Glenn, go milk the cow." Glenn said, "Miron, go milk the cow," and he (Miron) got stuck with the milking. Miron said he had to put his arms up and look up at the udder to milk. Milking at the age of five, he didn't sit next to the cow; he sat under it!

I've created a wall hanging of the pictures I've been able to find of the Sires and Shell families, as you can see in Figures 6-19 and 6-20.

CHALLENGES

As I continue my searching, I've run into additional issues on older generations because I cannot read Swedish or German, the languages of my earlier ancestors. And, as I mentioned before, I really have not found out much about my paternal grandmother's first marriage. I continue to use online resources and even local telephone books trying to find relatives that might help.

Figure 6-20: **The Shell family pictures date back five generations.**

Figure 6-19: The Sires family photos that I've been able to locate to date

OBJECTIVES

In addition to updating the book I published for our family in 1999, I've created a large poster-sized family tree for my children on both my husband's and my family's side (see Figure 6-21). I plan on continuing that research, especially on my husband's side, and hope to encourage my children's interest in their heritage by continuing to tell stories.

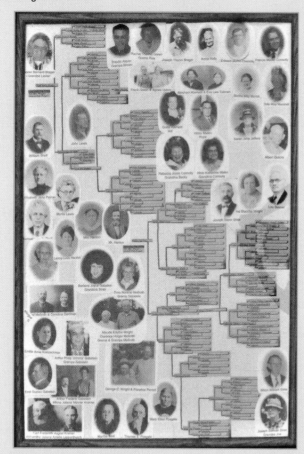

Figure 6-21: **The giant poster of our family is already a treasure for my children.**

Chapter 7
Researching Outside the Internet

For many years before the Internet, family historians have laboriously drawn family trees with pen and ink, tried to identify ancestors from blurry photographs or hand-drawn sketches, and pored over microfilm to find connections. Others spent hours in dimly lit courthouse libraries, used tracing paper to record information from old tombstones, and traveled many miles to verify the connection between their maternal great-great-great-grandmother and a name they found in an old family Bible. In this chapter we discuss how you can find information from a variety of locations, as well as provide some hints to help you in your research.

Visit "Brick and Mortar" Resources

A term often used by on-site businesses when describing how they differ from an online store is "brick and mortar," referring to the fact that there is a real store rather than a page on the Web. In this section, we share methods by which you can discover information that may not be available on the Internet.

Use Local Libraries

Consider using your local library card as the entry point for your genealogy research. Nearly every public library has a genealogy department as well as access to a variety of databases. Check your local library for a list of databases to which they subscribe. With your library card number, you may be able to access some database information from home. While these databases can help you start your search, you will often have to go into the library to access items you have discovered in the online catalogs and databases.

INSPECT PAPER, MICROFILM, OR MICROFICHE RESOURCES

Local libraries often hold many resources that have not been digitized. To use these resources may require a trip to your local library. Many libraries require you use them only while in the library. Some examples of resources that you might find in a local public library are

- City directories.
- Family histories.
- Local histories of counties, cemetery records, probate records, and towns or villages.
- Maps and gazetteers, both historic and current.
- Local and regional newspapers. While many older newspapers may be available in microfilm or microfiche, some libraries hold the printed copies as well.
- Telephone directories. Many early telephone directories included street addresses, and some date to the early 1900s.
- Community newspapers, many of which contain information, such as local events, not found in larger papers.
- School yearbooks.

NOTE

A gazetteer is much like a dictionary for geography information. It may contain information on physical features, such as mountains, rivers, and roads. Other gazetteers include locations of places within an area, population, and even literacy rates. The gazetteer is usually used in conjunction with a map or atlas, and can prove very valuable for genealogy research.

You may be allowed to photocopy items from library collections. At the least, you can take notes as to the location, publication date, source, and author of the information.

DISCOVER CATALOGS, INDEXES, AND DATABASES

In addition to the books, periodicals, and other resources held by a library, most contain extensive catalogs, indexes, and access to specialized online databases.

- **Catalogs** Often, the best way to start a new search of any type is through the library catalog. Catalogs are listings of the resources found within the library itself, or available through a library consortium. These resources may be books, anthologies, indexes, maps, CDs, or DVDs. There are also online catalogs that list items available in other libraries throughout the world. Online catalogs, often referred to as OPAC (Online Public Access Catalogs), are the online catalogs of individual libraries or groups of libraries and allow you to search for information by such criteria as author, title, keyword, or subject. An example is the Library of Congress Online Catalog seen in Figure 7-1 (catalog.loc.gov). See the QuickFacts "Understanding Library Catalog Systems" elsewhere in this chapter for more information about library catalog systems.

- **Indexes** Indexes are lists of printed articles, book or journal chapters, topics, abstracts, stories, or other items that appear in published works. Indexes provide "pointers," such as date, volume or page numbers, or other identifiers, that show you how to get to that area of the publication. One example of an index of interest to family historians is the BGMI (Biography and Genealogy Master Index), which is an index to printed publications that contain information about more than 15 million names. This index is available through Ancestry.com, as shown in Figure 7-2, by clicking **Search | All Categories | Stories, Memories, & Histories | Family Histories, Journals, & Biographies | Biography & Genealogy Master Index (BGMI)**.

- **Databases** Today's databases are often online indexes that may provide access to the entire text of an article or chapter.

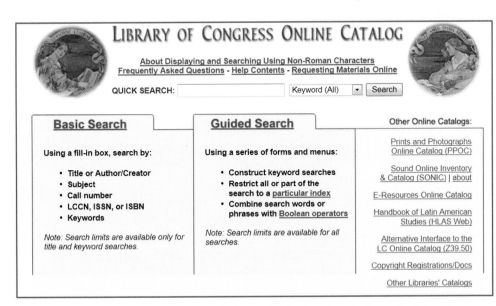

Figure 7-1: *Online catalogs can help you find material that is not available on the Internet.*

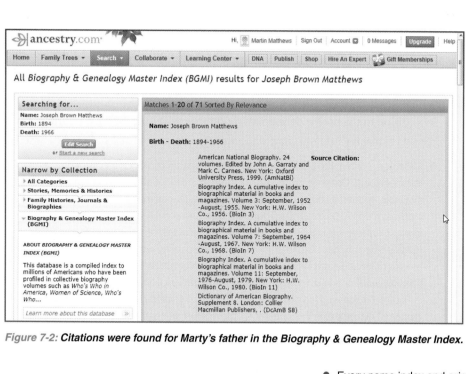

Figure 7-2: *Citations were found for Marty's father in the Biography & Genealogy Master Index.*

USE THE ANCESTRY LIBRARY EDITION

You are normally able to access this valuable genealogy resource, owned by ProQuest, only onsite at your local library. You may be required to enter a user name and password (which is normally supplied by the librarian), as seen next. It includes the following:

- Every name index and original images of every U.S. federal census from 1790 to 1930 (except 1890)

- Canadian collections, including census records and the Drouin Collection, which contains baptism, marriage, and burial records from Quebec for the period 1621 through 1967

- Name indexes and original images for the UK and Ireland censuses of 1871, 1891, and 1901, as well as birth, baptism, marriage, and death records for periods ranging from 1521 through 1938

- Original images of passenger and immigration lists from New York from 1851 through 1891, San Francisco from 1893 through 1953, and New Orleans passenger lists from 1820 through 1850

- Original images of World War I draft cards, Civil War Service Records, and military prisoner information from World War II and the Korean War

- The 200-volume American Genealogical-Biographical Index

- The Federal Writers Project Slave Narratives

- The Daughters of American Revolution Lineage Books

TIP

If you live near a community college or university, you may be able to access research information through their library.

UNDERSTANDING LIBRARY CATALOG SYSTEMS

Most libraries today have modern versions of the *card catalog* system, which you may remember. A card catalog was a citation on small (often 3 × 5) index cards that listed the title, author, and subject of each item in the library. These card catalogs were often kept in big wooden cabinets at the back of the main library room. With the advent of computer technology, many of these catalogs have now been digitized and are available online. Understanding how this catalog information is kept can save you valuable time.

THE DEWEY DECIMAL CLASSIFICATION SYSTEM

Public libraries in the United States, Canada, and the United Kingdom usually list their inventory using the Dewey Decimal system. You may remember the Dewey Decimal system divides books into categories and each of the broad categories is assigned a three-digit number, such as 100 for philosophy and psychology and 900 for geography. There have been many changes to the Dewey Decimal system since the advent of computers. There are now websites that discuss how the classifications are assigned and how to use the various classifications. The Online Computer Library Center (oclc.org/dewey), which has owned the system since 1988, has an explanation and other resources you may use to better understand the system.

Continued . . .

While much (but not all) of the information is also available on the Ancestry.com website, if you are a member you might want to search the ProQuest site first. The resource may be available at your local library without a subscription to Ancestry.com.

DISCOVER OTHER PROQUEST RESOURCES

In addition to the Ancestry Library Edition, ProQuest distributes many useful research tools through public and academic libraries. While not all libraries have access to all of ProQuest's products, ask your local library if they have access to any of the following:

- HeritageQuest Online has primary source material as well as local and family histories.
- ProQuest African American Heritage has many references for family history research.
- ProQuest Historical Newspapers and ProQuest Black Historical Newspapers contain thousands of archives for digital newspaper research.
- Historic Map Works Library and ProQuest Sanborn Maps Geo Edition offer digital editions of both historic and U.S. municipal maps.

Explore Other Libraries

In addition to your local public library there are university libraries, some of which may be used by nonstudents; medical libraries; and specialized reference libraries. There are even online libraries, such as the OCLC (Online Computer Library Center) at oclc.org and the IPL (Internet Public Library) at ipl.org, as seen in Figure 7-3. From the IPL site you can find directories of libraries around the world, research millions of resources, and even connect with a librarian who will answer general research or reference questions by email. There are a number of genealogy-specific libraries as described next.

THE FAMILY HISTORY LIBRARY AND FAMILY SEARCH CENTERS

The largest genealogy facility in the world is the Family History Library in Salt Lake City, Utah. It is available to the public at no charge and is normally open six days a week. Because of its vast size (more than 142,000 square feet), it's

QUICK**FACTS**

UNDERSTANDING LIBRARY CATALOG SYSTEMS *(Continued)*

THE LIBRARY OF CONGRESS CLASSIFICATION SYSTEM

While public libraries use the Dewey Decimal system, academic libraries in the United States usually use the Library of Congress Classification system. This system divides works into 21 basic classes and uses letters rather than numbers to identify each subject area. The classes range from General Works (A) to Bibliography, Library Science, and General Information Resources (Z). Within each class are various subclasses, also indicated by two (and occasionally three) letters. For example, Technology (T) has several subclasses: Bridges (TG) and Photography (TR). The Library of Congress website has a complete discussion of this system at loc.gov/catdir/cpso/lcc.html.

Figure 7-3: *The Internet Public Library connects users with libraries throughout the world.*

best to plan your visit carefully. Some suggestions before using this facility's resources include the following:

- Verify the hours the facility is open on the day you plan to visit. The library is often closed on holidays, so check their website at familysearch.org/locations/saltlakecity-library before your trip. Also, check for parking and transportation around the library.

- Before traveling to Salt Lake City, consider using one of the Family Search Centers nearer to your home to see the types of materials and tools available in Salt Lake City. You can find a location near you at familysearch.org/locations.

- The Family History Library has an online catalog (familysearch.org/#form=catalog) from which you can select records and verify their availability before your trip. This site even allows you to preorder microfiche and microfilm items that may be in storage so the records are available when you arrive. Some items can be loaned to Family History Centers throughout the country as well.

THE LIBRARY OF CONGRESS

As mentioned in Chapter 4, the Library of Congress in Washington, D.C. has more than 119 million documents and, reportedly, the largest map collection in the world. While the main function of the library is to meet the needs of members of Congress, it is open to others, including genealogy researchers. If you plan to visit the library, use its website at loc.gov (click **Library Catalogs**) before you go to ascertain what records are available. The library suggests the following for researchers using its facility:

- Use local public and academic libraries for preliminary research to determine just what you need to view before coming to the Library of Congress.

- Researchers must show a passport or current driver's license and obtain a Reader Identification Card to enter reading rooms or request materials from closed collections. Researchers over high-school age have no other restrictions. High-school-age students must meet further conditions as shown on the Library of Congress website.

- Use the Library of Congress catalog to answer questions and find information that is available at the site. The direct address for the catalog is catalog.loc.gov.

THE DAUGHTERS OF THE AMERICAN REVOLUTION LIBRARY

This facility in Washington, D.C. is open to the public and contains biographies, histories, directories, manuscripts, abstracts, and directories pertaining to U.S. history that may not be available through any other facility. It is open to all researchers, but be sure to check for hours of operation and any fees that may be involved to use its voluminous collection. Go to dar.org to access the site. Click **Genealogy** to see the options shown in Figure 7-4. Members of the society have donated cemetery record transcriptions, family Bible records, unique histories, and many other items that are exclusive to this library. Photocopies from resources as varied as an index of Revolutionary War pensions to specific family records are available for a fee. The Daughters of the American Revolution (DAR) has very extensive electronic databases covering over 1.5 billion names and their related census, military, land, court, and vital (birth, marriage, and death) records, but these are only accessible from the DAR Library's computers and are not accessible online.

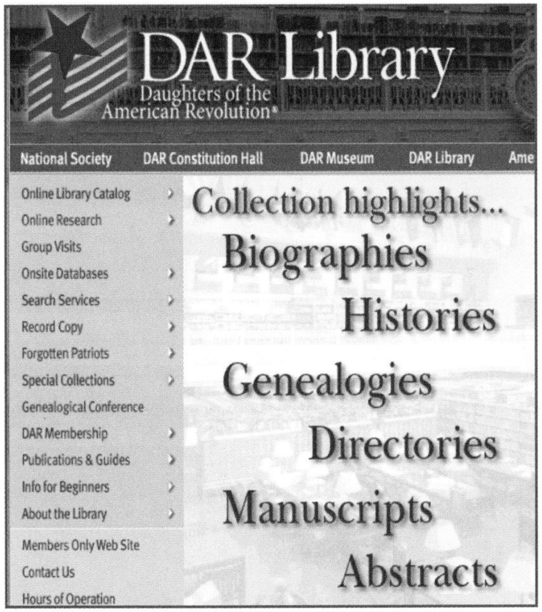

Figure 7-4: *Many unique records are stored in the DAR Library.*

THE NEWBERRY LIBRARY

This Chicago, Illinois, facility is a genealogy-research library. Its collection has a large number of items relating to colonial America; a large collection of Native American information; and manuscripts, maps, and articles relating to the

Midwestern United States. Before you visit, the library suggests the following:

- Review the Online Catalog and Research Guides at newberry.org/catalogs-and-guides to ensure the library has the material you want to see.
- Review the Newberry Reading Room Policies and Procedures.
- Obtain a Reader's Card. This card, available to those 16 years of age and older, requires a photo ID and proof of a current home address, and a specific interest in researching one of the library's collections.

THE NEWBERRY
Chicago's Independent Research Library Sin

| Visit | About | Research | Programs a |

Core Collections
Core Collections
Catalogs and Guides
Catalogs and Guides
Publications and Dig
Resources
Publications and Digital Resources
Services for Readers
Researchers
Services for Readers and Researchers
Research Centers

REGIONAL AND STATE LIBRARIES

There are many other genealogy libraries throughout the United States. Do an Internet search to see what is available. Also, check with local genealogy groups, as they may sponsor libraries in conjunction with state or regional societies. The three listed here are some of the largest and contain many useful resources:

- The New England Historic Genealogical Society Lending Library in Boston, Massachusetts, is one of the leading research centers for family historians. Go to americanancestors.org/visit/ for directions, hours of operations, and fees.
- The New York Public Library has volumes of regional and international information. From your browser's address bar, you can access their page by typing nypl.org for information about the facilities. Especially useful are their biographical resources.
- The Allen County Public Library in Indiana has a wonderful genealogy section. Go to www.acpl.lib.in.us (you need the "www") and click the **Genealogy** tab at the upper right of the page.

Investigate Courthouse Records

Often, the major events in a person's life have been recorded in some government archive. In the United States, this information is often found in courthouse records. While perhaps the most time-consuming of research tasks, going through vital records in a courthouse may yield much more information than other resources. While birth, death, and marriage records are the more common records found, there are others you may find as well. A few of the record types that may be found in courthouses throughout the United States (and many other countries) are

- **Adoption**   While some jurisdictions seal adoption records, you may find limited information about the adoptive parents, and in some cases, the birth parents as well. Some jurisdictions may require that you obtain a court order to see copies of the records.

- **Civil actions**   Civil legal actions may help ascertain that your ancestor was living at a certain date and in a certain place. Look as well for actions that may have taken place after the ancestor moved from one place to another. Statute-of-limitation laws make it possible to sue someone even after they have moved from an area.

- **Criminal actions**   Besides finding that a great-great-uncle was accused of cattle rustling in 1871, criminal actions can reference relatives about whom you may not have known. For example, Bobbi found a previously unknown maternal relative whose death prompted the first murder trial in Washington Territory.

- **Divorce and separate maintenance**   These records vary by date and locality, and are sometimes incomplete. However, most records will supply at least the date of marriage, the names and/or ages of any minor children, and in some cases, previous residences of the couple in question.

- **Guardianship**   Before women were granted legal rights, adult males were often named guardians of minor children when their father died. These records are often included with probate records and include the names and birth dates of the children, and in some cases, the names of other relatives.

- **Naturalization**   While many of these records now are found in the National Archives, early naturalization records were kept in the courts where the naturalization occurred.

- **Property line and other real property disputes**   Real estate boundary and fence line issues were often settled in court when property owners could not agree. These records can provide verification of land ownership and proof of residency in a certain location at a specific time.

- **Wills and probate records**   Probate records are meant to establish a will's legality. These records often contain the names of the deceased's relatives and the relationship to the deceased. Property named in the will may prove residence and ownership of a specific plot of land, building, or other assets.

Frequently Asked Questions	
Does the recording department supply blank documents or notary services?	Documents must be presented for recording as they are intended for public record. We can not provide forms or notarize signatures, as this constitutes "legal advice".
Does the recording department have birth and death certificates?	Original birth and death records after 1907 are maintained by the Regional Health District, Vital Statistics Office at 678-7351. There are only a few original records beginning with 1891 through 1907 available in the recording department.
Where do I obtain information regarding divorce records or annulments?	Please contact the Clerks Office at 679-7359 (option 6) for information regarding these items.
Are wills recorded for public records?	Wills can be recorded for public record, but it is not advised. To probate a will, contact the Clerks Office at 679-7359 (option 6).
What kinds of documents are recorded in the recording department?	The recording office records Real Estate documents, liens, military discharges, maps and surveys. Copies of these documents are available for a fee. We also issue marriage licenses and County business licenses. For information regarding City business licenses, please contact the city your business will be in. For State business licenses, call 360-664-1400.

Figure 7-5: Record availability varies by location. Some records may be obtained online, while others require a fee.

NOTE

Consider volunteering to help with indexing projects. For example, the Family Search Center has a current indexing project. Go to familysearch.org/volunteer/indexing to learn more.

You may find the records are kept in several formats. Certainly, paper records are the most common. Some jurisdictions may require that an employee handle the records while you look at them. There may be fees for this service. Other records may have been preserved on microfilm or microfiche. While you might be allowed to obtain photocopies, there is usually a small fee for each copy.

Today, some court records have been published and even digitized. Before you go to a specific location, contact the court and learn their hours of operation, what access you have to which type of records, and any fees that you might incur. An example of what may be available is seen in Figure 7-5.

TIPS FOR SEARCHING IN COURTHOUSE RECORDS

Depending on the locality, you may find both paper and microfilm records. Most courts do not have cross-indexed records, and even the Family History Library's information, while quite extensive, may not be completely indexed. Consider these ideas when searching court records:

● Look for both defendant and plaintiff court indexes. Sometimes the names are kept in separate books.

● Review the final disposition of the case, often found in judge's records, court journals, and other court books.

● Try to obtain the entire case file for review. You may find additional information about relatives, children, or property.

● Consult court record books for any additional information. Early records were often transcribed into a court record book and the original documentation destroyed.

● Examine the court dockets for the time period involved.

Tour a Cemetery

Cemeteries are history books carved in stone. From gravestones one can find birthplace locations, dates of birth and death, maiden names, spouse and parent names, religious affiliations, and military service information. If the grave is in a family plot, you may find names of other relatives and their data. In many pioneer cemeteries, neighbors had adjoining plots, as they had adjoining properties in life, so take the time to search around in other areas of the cemetery.

HOW TO BEGIN YOUR CEMETERY SEARCH

After you have ascertained where your ancestor died, the death record, obituary, or even the funeral card may show the name of the cemetery in which he or she was buried. If you cannot find a record showing the name of the cemetery, contact a funeral home in the area to ask for the names of local cemeteries. Some cemeteries have offices with records that list the names and locations of each grave.

Consider using tax or census records to find out where your ancestor lived, as often people were buried near where they lived. If you can find a locality map that shows cemeteries in the area, you may see a cemetery close by.

The following records may help you find the cemetery name:

- Death certificates can show the name and location of internment.

- Burial permits are sometimes issued by the county or other governmental agency and will list the name of the deceased as well as the date and location of the internment.

- Internment ledgers or sexton records are kept by some cemeteries listing the name, date of death, sometimes the cause of death, and where within the cemetery the person is buried. A sexton is the person responsible for the care of the cemetery. Their records can contain plat maps, plot records, and burial registers.

- Cemetery deeds are sometimes recorded as land purchases and may be recorded in the county courthouse. These records show the location of the plot and the names of the purchaser and seller.

Once you have located the cemetery, consider the time of year when you plan your visit. Older cemeteries are often overgrown with foliage, and visiting in

CONSIDERING TOMBSTONE RUBBINGS

Because tombstones erode over time, many people over the centuries have taken "rubbings" using crayons, charcoal, and other substances to transfer the carvings from tombstones onto paper. Today the practice has become very controversial because many old gravestones are fragile and while the stone may look very sturdy, sometimes the slightest touch can damage or destroy the stone.

Many areas do not allow the practice at all, while others require permits and deposits to ensure the stones are not damaged nor any residue left on the stone. Some areas have established laws against the practice, and those caught rubbing may face arrest and steep fines. Even cleaning can damage some gravestones or, at the very least, make the stone more susceptible to destruction.

To ensure you are following all the rules, contact the cemetery before your visit to ascertain what is and is not allowed. Many cemeteries have posted the regulations online. If the site does not have a web presence, call the sexton or overseer to see if they will mail you that facility's regulations.

NOTE

Some genealogy researchers are using DNA in their quest. See Chapter 9 for more information on genealogy DNA searches.

the early spring before the leaves appear might mean you can locate overturned stones more easily. Wear sturdy, long-sleeved clothing and gloves for protection from bugs, snakes, and other critters. If your visit takes place in summer, bring sunscreen and wear a hat. Consider taking a hoe and clippers to clear out areas around gravestones, and go with at least one other person. If the cemetery is on private land, get permission from the land owner before you venture in. Bring the following:

- A camera with extra film, for a film camera, and extra memory card and/or batteries, for a digital camera.

- Writing material such as paper, pencils, and a way to ensure they stay dry.

- Water, both for drinking and to clean gravestones and markers. Old rags and soft-bristle nylon brushes are good for cleaning stones as well. Do not use bleach, stiff-bristled brushes, or other potentially damaging materials on gravestones. See the QuickFacts "Considering Tombstone Rubbings" for more information.

Contact Houses of Worship

Ecclesiastical records are those records that are maintained by a house of worship. Marriages, baptisms, confirmations, and funerals are conducted and usually recorded by the institution in which the ceremony was held. However, before you can obtain information about these records, you must first ascertain their location.

Once you have found the location of the records, consider looking for your ancestor's name in these religious records as well:

- Membership lists
- Donation records
- Church bulletins
- Committee reports
- Office and administrative notes

All of these sources can both verify information and provide new clues to further your search. The records of each religious group are private, so respect those rights. Try to contact the church, temple, synagogue, or mosque in person and be respectful of their wishes.

CREATING A FAMILY MEDICAL HISTORY

Using your current genealogy records, you can quickly create a family medical history to share with your healthcare provider. For this history, you can use a blank family tree, as seen in Figure 7-6, or make a copy of one you have already created. Often going back only three or four generations will yield a lot of information.

1. For each person, enter the birth date and date of death.

2. Enter the cause of death. If you do not know, refer to death certificates, obituaries, or even family letters.

3. Enter any known health problems, such as asthma, chronic bronchitis, osteoporosis, or diabetes.

4. Enter any known illnesses, such as cancer, polio, addiction, or pneumonia.

5. For women relatives, show the number of children. Include any miscarriages she may have suffered.

6. Enter any additional information relating to health you can find.

You may see records that show the cause of death as palsy, dropsy, or other terms used in earlier times. Take a moment to perform an Internet search for old medical terminology to find the modern name for such conditions.

Use Medical Facility Records

Today's privacy laws prohibit hospitals from revealing information about their patients to anyone but the patient, or after death, the next of kin. And again, today, many hospitals keep their records for no more than ten years. However, some facilities have saved records from the 1800s, and there are some archival medical records available through the Family History Library in Salt Lake City.

If you have a copy of an obituary or death certificate that gives the name of a facility, you can contact the records department of that facility to start your inquiry.

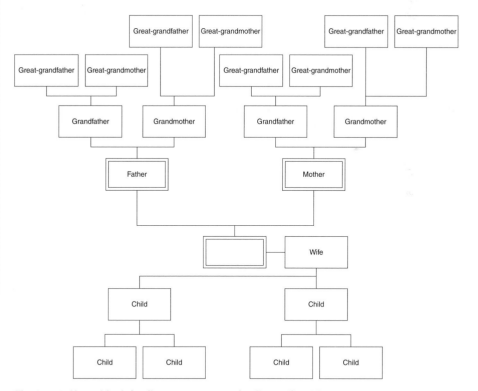

Figure 7-6: **Use a blank family tree to create a family medical history.**

FAMILY MEDICAL HISTORIES

With the strides in genetic research, many families are creating a family medical history. Similar to genealogy research, medical records are being used proactively to help family members allay or prevent recurrences of problems as genetic traits are passed down through families. Along with such features as hazel eyes, small noses, and big feet, a genetic legacy may also mean allergies, asthma, or a propensity for heart disease. Being aware of your family's medical past can help prevent future generations from developing the same maladies.

Search Foreign and Ethnic Records

As family historians research their ancestors, many find the need to investigate records from other countries. Many of these records are now available on the Internet, including governmental records such as census or immigration sources, birth and marriage information from parish records, and even real estate transactions.

Find International Records

Thanks to the Internet, you can find ship passenger lists, obituaries, cemetery transcriptions, and other information published by other countries from the comfort of your own computer workspace. A first step might be to use the Tracing Immigrant Origins guide available from the LDS church. To access this guide, go to familysearch.org/eng/search/RG/guide/tracing_immigrant_origins.asp. This tool, seen next, offers suggestions for obtaining records as well as modern spellings of old names and many other useful tips.

Consider joining ethnic or nationality-specific genealogy groups to establish contacts and gain information about your ancestor's point of origin. There are genealogy societies throughout the world, and many now maintain websites.

Several other good starting points are shown next.

RESEARCH GUIDANCE

Tracing Immigrant Origins
Research Outline

Table of Contents

USE GENEALOGYLINKS.NET

This website states it has more than 50,000 free links for many European countries as well as Australia, Canada, England, Ireland, New Zealand, Scotland, and Wales. There are additional links for China, India, South Africa, Israel, and Jewish genealogy. This site includes parish registers, censuses, passenger lists, city directories, and much more from around the world, as seen here.

Genealogy**links**.net
Your Online Resource for Family History Research

Welcome
Genealogylinks.net consists of 4,500 pages of more than 50,000 Free Genealogy Links; for US, UK, England, Scotland, Wales, Ireland, Europe, Canada, Australia & New Zealand.

I have endeavoured to add sites that either have online genealogy records through which you can search for your ancestors or sites that provide helpful information to aid in your research..

The types of records you can find using Genealogylinks.net include parish registers, censuses, cemeteries, marriages, passenger lists, city directories, military records, obituaries and more.

Good luck with your research!

TRY SEARCHFORANCESTORS.COM

This site uses interactive directories to link you to many free genealogy search engines, as seen next. Enter searchforancestors.com, and click **Get Started Here** to see unique ideas for starting your genealogy searches. This link is geared to the beginner, but scroll down to find additional, lesser-known resources.

> **NOTE**
>
> Do not enter ancestorsearch.com to get to this site, as that address belongs to FamilySearch.org. Use the SearchForAncestors.com link.

ANCESTOR SEARCH ...Find your family history

FREE Genealogy Records by Country

Search for your ancestors using this interactive directory of the best free genealogy search engines. Search top world-wide & specialized genealogy databases from one genealogy search site! The Ancestor Search site also has unique custom genealogy search engines found no where else.

| Home | Ancestry | Getting Started | Google Searcher | Surname Finder | Surname Origins | Freebies | Tools | Help |

EXPLORE IMMIGRATION INFORMATION

A substantial amount of immigration and other information is available on a worldwide volunteer genealogy site: worldgenweb.org. This site has links to the country websites of many GenWeb projects, as well as query pages, message boards, and mailing lists. As seen in Figure 7-7, you can also find historical data from many countries, including census records, cemetery records, biographies, bibliographies, and family/surname registration websites.

The WorldGenWeb Project

MAIN MENU

Home ▸ How To Get Started

* Home
* Advisory Board
* Country Index
* FAQ
* **How To Get Started**
* Policies and Procedures
* Special Projects
* Web Links
* Whats New
* WorldGenWeb Archives

REGIONAL WEBSITES

* AfricaGenWeb
* AsiaGenWeb
* BritishIslesGenWeb
* CaribbeanGenWeb
* CenEuroGenWeb
* EastEuropeGenWeb
* MediterraneanGenWeb

How To Start Your Research

If you are new to internet research and don't know how to begin your search this page should help you get started. If you need further assistance, please visit the **Country Project** and email the coordinator for specific help!

Getting Started

Before you begin your world research you should have solid information leading back to the oldest known ancestor in your home country (where you live now). Example: before I begin researching my Irish ancestor, I need to trace his line back to when he actually came from Ireland to America (Pennsylvania to be exact). Many researchers skip this step completely and assume that they can begin searching in the country of origin with just a surname (last name). This process is like searching for a needle in a haystack - difficult at best, almost impossible in most cases.

Information you must have to begin your search in a foreign country:

* Full name of your ancestor (given, middle and surname)
* Place of birth (country and county - parish, town, prefect, etc. preferred)
* Religion of your ancestor (important in many instances to access local records)
* Date of birth (date range is ok, example 1790's)
* Names of spouse and children (helpful)

*Figure 7-7: **The WorldGenWeb Project uses volunteers throughout the world to maintain its site.***

In addition to this site, immigration information can be found at the Ellis Island, Ancestry, and RootsWeb sites, as discussed earlier in this book. Go to the following sites for passenger lists of immigrant ships:

* TheShipsList.com is a site from which you can search passenger lists, newspaper, and shipwreck reports, and find the names of ships on which immigrants arrived.

* Cyndislist.com/ships is a master link that leads to links about passenger lists, ship names, ports of departure, and points of entry. It even contains links to migration routes once an immigrant arrived.

* Immigrantships.net, a website operated by Immigrant Ships Transcribers Guild volunteers, has ethnic research sites; emigration sites; and links to libraries, archives, and maritime information.

Travel to Ancestral Locations

For most Americans, their family history is available in local archives for only a few previous generations. At some point, many of our ancestors came here from somewhere else. Whether that "somewhere" is in another state or another country, at some point you may want to travel there for additional research. The more you prepare before you leave, the more successful you will be when you return home.

Plan Your Trip Carefully

Most successful genealogy trips are for specific purposes: to find information that can only be found in person, to locate relatives who might have documents or information relating to your ancestor, or to find evidence of a marriage that cannot be found anywhere but the parish church where the marriage took place.

Whatever reasons you have for traveling, plan well. Determine your time, decide what you want to accomplish, and when you can accomplish that task. Leave plenty of time for unexpected events, travel glitches, and other unforeseen happenings. Give yourself time to explore and research while you are at your destination as well.

RESEARCH BEFORE YOU TRAVEL

After you have determined the reasons for your trip, research what resources are available at your planned destination:

- Create a "trip folder" for papers, names, research information, and any other paperwork you might need for reference while you are at your destination. Use photocopies of documents you are using for reference so that you do not lose any originals.

- Use the Internet to locate any libraries, archives, or other record repositories at your destination that may contain information about your subject.

- Take time to use the Internet to find genealogy groups and societies in the area you plan to visit. Whether your trip takes you overseas or to the next state, many societies will offer advice and assistance.

- Determine what records are available and, if necessary, order microfilm or other resources so they are available when you are there. If possible, download the information about call numbers or other identifying numbers from any online catalogs. Print this information and put it in your "trip folder."

- Determine the hours of operation and driving directions to your resource's location. Find out about parking, public transportation, and any fees that may be involved.

- If you are traveling out of the country, ensure there will be someone available to translate if you do not speak the language. Take a phrase book or dictionary with you as well.

- Obtain any necessary paperwork required for access to private or protected venues. Keep photocopies of any correspondence in your "trip folder" as backup.

- Create empty folders or binders in which you can save the information you obtain on the trip.

- If you are meeting relatives, consider taking copies of your researched family tree to share.

- Send letters or emails, or telephone people or places with whom you want to meet to schedule appointments.

- Make sure you have made hotel reservations and reserved a rental car if necessary.
- Create an itinerary for the entire trip, again leaving significant chunks of time for visiting with newly discovered relatives or for more research.

OVERSEAS RESEARCH

A good place to start when planning a trip to another country is a search for the national archives of the country in question. Many countries include an English translation of their website. For example, we recently did a search for the "national archives of Finland," and the first result was the Finnish National Archives page in English, as seen in Figure 7-8.

Many countries also maintain national websites that you can sometimes access directly. In the address bar of your browser, enter the name of the country and the country's domain extension. For example, type denmark.dk in your browser's address to open the official Danish website. If you access some of

*Figure 7-8: **Many nations have websites with links to their national archives.***

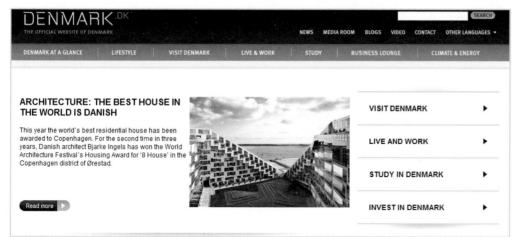

the official pages from an English-speaking location, the site may appear in English, as seen next. You can find a complete list of country domain extensions by typing iana.org/domains/root/db in the address bar of any browser.

ORGANIZE YOUR MATERIAL

As you are getting ready for your trip, organize your files, your "trip folder," and all of your resource material so that you can access necessary information quickly. The method you use does not matter. Some family historians file their data in separate folders or binders by surname, using maiden names for women. Others file by year; still others by geographic location. Whatever method works for you is the method you should use.

Make sure you have your still or video camera, perhaps a digital voice recorder, plenty of batteries, digital storages, and/or film. Do you use Post-It Notes to mark information? Pack plenty. Extra-large manila envelopes and/or large Ziploc bags are easy to pack and are especially handy to ensure you don't lose or soil precious slips of paper. Consider taking a portable scanner. Today, many smart phones can take moderate-to-good-resolution pictures, so they can be used as a scanner for some purposes.

CAUTION

The material you take on a trip should only be copies, never your originals, to eliminate the chances of losing anything.

Contact Individuals and Institutions

Before your trip, email or write a letter to everyone with whom you plan to connect. If you are contacting distant relatives, ask them to talk to other family members about your upcoming visit. Consider offering them some of the research you have completed to help their compilations. There is nothing as valuable as the personal contacts you make before you arrive at your destination.

GET ANSWERS NOT AVAILABLE ON THE INTERNET

While there is valuable information on the Internet, there is much you cannot learn without talking to someone, reading old notes, and, indeed, actually standing on the same ground where your ancestor lived. Ask others for stories, memories, and ideas where you can look for additional information.

GATHER STORIES BY LISTENING

Much of the information you gather when at an ancestral location can be learned by listening. Family stories, local legends, and even tall tales can give you clues for further research. Ask leading questions and then let the other talk. This is a perfect time for that digital voice or video recorder, if your family members agree.

Becky Foote, 59, Whidbey Island, WA

OVERVIEW

It seems my family has always been searching for its roots. On my mother's side, we can verify one branch of our family back to 1418, as my mother's research has shown in Figure 7-9. On my father's side we have traced back to the Pilgrims in Salem, Massachusetts. My mother started our genealogy journeys based on stories her mother had written on snippets of paper. The search has become as exciting as the facts it uncovers, and the more mysteries we solve, the more exciting the quest becomes.

STORY

I was born Rebecca Foote in Seattle, Washington. While my parents were originally from Ohio and Minnesota, I grew up in the Pacific Northwest. They were both in the military, as seen in Figure 7-10, and after World War II, I was a Boeing brat. I cannot remember a time when family history was not a part of my life because my mother was so interested. After I graduated from high school, she invited me to join her on these amazing genealogy adventures.

I got interested in the Wilder branch of the family because at some point, I remember my mother mentioning that her mother (my grandmother) had seen a family plaque that stated Benjamin Wilder (my maternal great-great-grandfather) was a colonel in the Confederate Army and was married to a daughter of Jefferson Davis. The journey I undertook to prove or disprove this mystery started an entirely new quest. Figure 7-11 shows the snippet of paper on which my grandmother recorded the information about Benjamin Wilder's wife, Elizabeth Davis.

GETTING STARTED

My latest search was a journey to obtain more information about the Wilder branch of my mother's family. To get started, my husband and I took a van trip in 2007 and stopped for a week in Washington, D.C. so I could start researching at the DAR museum. I had done work online using various sources and been able to verify some of the information on the Wilder family pedigree that dated

---

Descendants of John Wylder

Generation No. 1

1. JOHN[1] WYLDER was born 1418 in Bohemia, Czech Republlic, and died 1489 in Normandy, France. He married MRS WYLDER. She was born Bet. 1460 – 1521.

Notes for JOHN WYLDER:
My Have Lived in Germany Then Moved to Normandy,France

Child of JOHN WYLDER and MRS WYLDER is:
2. i. NICHOLAS[2] WYLDER, b. 1465, Normandy, France; d. 1542, England.

Generation No. 2

➤ **2.** NICHOLAS[2] WYLDER (*JOHN[1]*) was born 1465 in Normandy, France, and died 1542 in England. He married ANN OR ELIZABETH 1490 in England. She was born 1475 in Nunhide, Eng, and died 1505.

Notes for NICHOLAS WYLDER:
Nicholas Wilder,

Children of NICHOLAS WYLDER and ANN ELIZABETH are:
   i.   JOHN[3] WILDER.
   ii.   THOMAS WILDER, b. Abt. 1460.
   iii. RICHARD WILDER, b. 1494; d. 1560, Greenmoor Hill South Stoke, Oxfordshire, England.
3. iv.   JOHN WILDER, b. Bet. 1495 – 1505, Nunhide, Eng.; d. 1583, Combe Hants, Eng.
4. v.   NICHOLAS WILDER, b. Bet. 1496 – 1519, Sulham Berkshire, England; d. Bef. 1600.
   vi.   WYLLYAM WILDER, b. Bef. 1522.
   vii. HENRY WILDER, b. Abt. 1542.

Generation No. 3

➤ **3.** JOHN[3] WILDER (*NICHOLAS[2] WYLDER, JOHN[1]*) was born Bet. 1495 - 1505 in Nunhide, Eng., and died 1583 in Combe Hants, Eng. He married AGNES ALICE 1550 in Nunhide, Eng.. She was born 1509 in Birkshire, Eng., and died 1585 in Birkshire, Eng..

Children of JOHN WILDER and AGNES ALICE are:
5. i.   AGNES[4] WILDER, b. 1548, Nunhide, Eng; d. 1580, Nunhide, Eng..
6. ii.   HENRY WILDER, b. 1550, Burghfield, Eng.; d. 1592, Combe Hants, Eng..
7. iii. JOHN RICHARD WILDER, b. 1552, Nunhide, Eng.; d. Aft. 1588, Combe Hants, Eng.
8. iv.   RICHARD JOHN WILDER, b. 1560; d. 1588.
    v.   THOMAS WILDER, b. 1572, Nuhide Sulham, Berkshire, Eng; d. 1630; m. MARTHA KEENE; b. Abt. 1580, Berkshire, Eng; d. 20 Apr 1652, Hing.
9. vi.   AGNES WILDER, b. Abt. 1585; d. Abt. 1650.

4. NICHOLAS[3] WILDER (*NICHOLAS[2] WYLDER, JOHN[1]*) was born Bet. 1496 - 1519 in Sulham Berkshire, England, and died Bef. 1600. He married UNKNOWN ALICE Abt. 1539 in England. She was born Abt. 1520 in England.

Child of NICHOLAS WILDER and UNKNOWN ALICE is:
   i.   JOHN[4] WILDER, b. Bef. 1539, Berkshire, Eng; d. Bef. 1610.

Generation No. 4

5. AGNES[4] WILDER (*JOHN[3], NICHOLAS[2] WYLDER, JOHN[1]*) was born 1548 in Nunhide, Eng, and died 1580 in

1

*Figure 7-9: **Our roots on the Wilder side have been traced to 1418.***

Figure 7-10: ***My parents, John Foote and Margaret (Leitch) Foote, during World War II.***

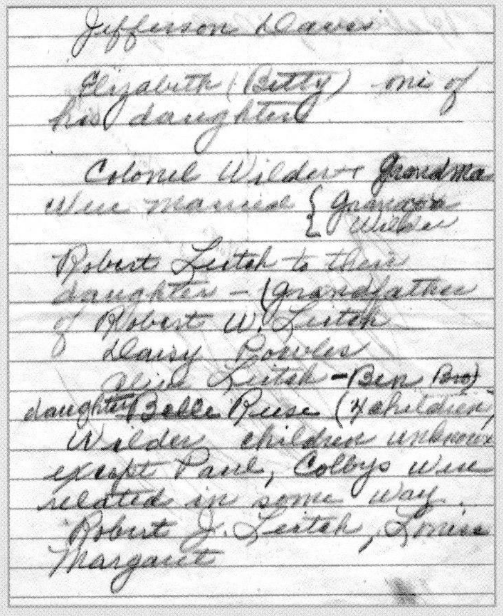

Jefferson Davis

Elizabeth (Betty) one of
his daughters

Colonel Wilder + Grandma
were married { grandpa
                 Wilder

Robert Leitch to their
daughter - Grandfather
of Robert W. Leitch
Mary Bowles
Alice Leitch - (Ben Bro)
daughter Belle Reese (4 children)
Wilder children unknown
except Paul, Colbys were
related in some way.
Robert J. Leitch, Louise
Margaret

Figure 7-11: ***My Grandmother Leitch kept her genealogy records on small scraps of paper.***

back to 1418 (see Figure 7-9). From that research I had learned that Martha (Dandridge) Washington was a distant cousin of mine. Also, Col. Benjamin Wilder's father, Jacob Wilder, fought in the Revolutionary War in Capt. Andrew Haskell's company.

In the museum, I found the Wilder DAR file (see Figure 7-12), which discussed both Jacob and his son, Col. Benjamin Wilder. This file contained information about that family branch including Benjamin's birth in 1795. I had simply asked at the information desk for information on Jacob Wilder. For a small fee, the printing costs, and less than two hours of my time, I found all of the information for which I had been searching. Before our trip, I had spent time on the DAR website preparing for my visit there.

One of the discoveries I'd made was that Benjamin Wilder actually fought in the War of 1812, not the Civil War. Therefore, the information on the paper my grandmother had kept all those years was not correct. Benjamin Wilder had never fought for the Confederacy. However, my next trip will be to South Carolina to seek information on his wife, Elizabeth Davis. Perhaps she was actually related to Jefferson Davis. That trip is yet to come.

My research showed that Jacob Wilder had been granted a pension for his service in the Revolutionary War in 1818, as seen in Figure 7-13. From that data, I learned he had been living in Woodstock, Vermont, when his pension was granted. From Washington, D.C. we traveled to Woodstock, where Jacob had settled. Lo and behold, at the first cemetery we stopped, there were Jacob and Mary Wakefield Wilder's graves, with the sun shining just as if the stones had been waiting for us. Figure 7-14 shows what we saw.

In Woodstock, I went to the local library, a stop I make on every genealogy adventure, and got the history of Woodstock, which had been published in 1889. There was an entire page on Jacob Wilder, as seen in Figure 7-15. From this I found that Jacob had been one of the earliest patriots and was a founding father of Woodstock, Vermont (not to be confused with Woodstock, New York, where I had gone earlier trying to find him). I learned that during the Battle of Bunker Hill he had drawn picket duty and therefore did not actually participate, which may have led to his long life. I learned he did fight in the Battle of Monmouth. After the war he moved first to Plymouth, Vermont, and became captain of the first military

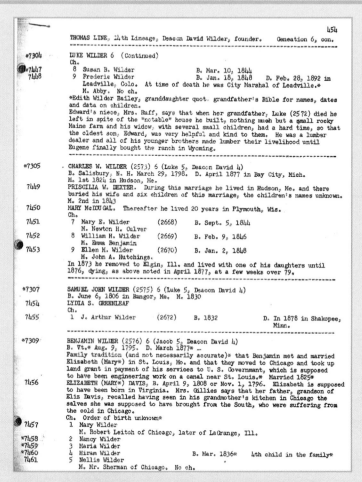

THOMAS LINE, 14th Lineage, Deacon David Wilder, founder.   Generation 6, con.

----

*7304   LUKE WILDER 6 (Continued)
           Ch.
*7447   8 Susan B. Wilder   B. Mar. 10, 1844
 7448   9 Frederic Wilder   B. Jan. 18, 1848   D. Feb. 28, 1892 in
            Leadville, Colo. At time of death he was City Marshal of Leadville.*
            M. Abby. No ch.
         *Edith Wilder Bailey, granddaughter quot. grandfather's Bible for names, dates
         and data on children.
         Edward's niece, Mrs. Ruff, says that when her grandfather, Luke (2572) died he
         left in spite of the "notable" house he built, nothing much but a small rocky
         Maine farm and his widow, with several small children, had a hard time, so that
         the oldest son, Edward, was very helpful and kind to them. He was a lumber
         dealer and all of his younger brothers made lumber their livelihood until
         Eugene finally bought the ranch in Wyoming.

*7305   CHARLES W. WILDER (2573) 6 (Luke 5, Deacon David 4)
           B. Salisbury, N. H. March 29, 1798. D. April 1877 in Bay City, Mich.
           M. 1st 1824 in Hudson, Me.
 7449   PRISCILLA W. DEXTER. During this marriage he lived in Hudson, Me. and there
           buried his wife and six children of this marriage, the children's names unknown.
           M. 2nd in 1843
 7450   MARY McDOUGAL. Thereafter he lived 20 years in Plymouth, Wis.
           Ch.
 7451   7 Mary E. Wilder   (2668)   B. Sept. 5, 1844
            M. Newton H. Culver
 7452   8 William H. Wilder   (2669)   B. Feb. 9, 1846
            M. Emma Benjamin
 7453   9 Ellen M. Wilder   (2670)   B. Jan. 2, 1848
            M. John A. Hutchins.
         In 1873 he removed to Elgin, Ill. and lived with one of his daughters until
         1876, dying as above noted in April 1877, at a few weeks over 79.

----

*7307   SAMUEL JOHN WILDER (2575) 6 (Luke 5, Deacon David 4)
           B. June 6, 1806 in Bangor, Me. M. 1830
 7454   LYDIA S. GREENLEAF
           Ch.
 7455   1 J. Arthur Wilder   (2672)   B. 1832   D. In 1878 in Shakopee,
                                                            Minn.

----

*7309   BENJAMIN WILDER (2576) 6 (Jacob 5, Deacon David 4)
           B. Vt.* Aug. 9, 1795. D. March 1877* _
           Family tradition (and not necessarily accurate)* that Benjamin met and married
           Elizabeth (Mary*) in St. Louis, Mo. and that they moved to Chicago and took up
           land grant in payment of his services to U. S. Government, which is supposed
           to have been engineering work on a canal near St. Louis.* Married 1825*
 7456   ELIZABETH (MARY*) DAVIS, B. April 9, 1808 or Nov. 1, 1796. Elizabeth is supposed
           to have been born in Virginia. Mrs. Gillies says that her father, grandson of
           Eliz Davis, recalled having seen in his grandmother's kitchen in Chicago the
           salves she was supposed to have brought from the South, who were suffering from
           the cold in Chicago.
           Ch. Order of birth unknown*
 7457   1 Mary Wilder
            M. Robert Leitch of Chicago, later of LaGrange, Ill.
*7458   2 Nancy Wilder
*7459   3 Maria Wilder
7460   4 Hiram Wilder   B. Mar. 1836   4th child in the family*
 7461   5 Nellie Wilder
            M. Mr. Sherman of Chicago. No ch.

Figure 7-12: The DAR file on the Wilder family provided a lot of information on that branch.

company in Plymouth and was always afterward known as Captain Wilder, as seen carved on his gravestone in Figure 7-14. He moved in 1790 to what is now Woodstock, Vermont.

While doing my research at the DAR Library, I found that some of the Wilders had migrated to the Chicago area. This fit well with some research I wanted to do on the Leitch family (my mother's father's family), who homesteaded what is now LaGrange, Illinois. I spent time at The Newberry Library in Chicago, one of the best genealogy libraries around. In its collection are thousands of stories of Chicago-area families, family histories, and newspaper articles from all the

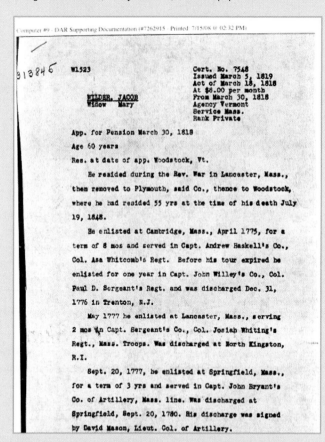

Computer #9 - DAR Supporting Documentation (#7262915 - Printed: 7/15/08 @ 02:32 PM)

313846   W1523   Cert. No. 7548
                                           Issued March 5, 1819
                                           Act of March 18, 1818
                                           At $8.00 per month
            WILDER, JACOB   From March 30, 1818
            Widow   Mary   Agency Vermont
                                           Service Mass.
                                           Rank Private

App. for Pension March 30, 1818

Age 60 years

Res. at date of app. Woodstock, Vt.

He resided during the Rev. War in Lancaster, Mass.,
then removed to Plymouth, said Co., thence to Woodstock,
where he had resided 55 yrs at the time of his death July
19, 1848.

He enlisted at Cambridge, Mass., April 1775, for a
term of 8 mos and served in Capt. Andrew Haskell's Co.,
Col. Asa Whitcomb's Regt. Before his tour expired he
enlisted for one year in Capt. John Willey's Co., Col.
Paul D. Sergeant's Regt. and was discharged Dec. 31,
1776 in Trenton, N.J.

May 1777 he enlisted at Lancaster, Mass., serving
2 mos in Capt. Sergeant's Co., Col. Josiah Whiting's
Regt., Mass. Troops. Was discharged at North Kingston,
R.I.

Sept. 20, 1777, he enlisted at Springfield, Mass.,
for a term of 3 yrs and served in Capt. John Bryant's
Co. of Artillery, Mass. line. Was discharged at
Springfield, Sept. 20, 1780. His discharge was signed
by David Mason, Lieut. Col. of Artillery.

Figure 7-13: Jacob Wilder lived in Woodstock, Vermont, when his pension was granted in 1818.

Figure 7-14: Jacob and Mary Wilder are buried in Woodstock, Vermont.

JACOB[5] WILDER   451

JACOB[5] WILDER

Thomas,[1] John,[2] Ebenezer,[3] David[4] Wilder, b. 1705; m. 1st. in Lancaster, Mass., June 10, 1739, Mrs. Anna (Willard) Prentice, widow of Samuel Prentice; m. 2nd. 1745, Eunice Jennison, b. 1720; d. 1750; m. 3rd. Martha White, b. Nov. 24, 1717; d. Nov. 6, 1811, dau. of Josiah White, Jr. and Abigail (Whitcomb) White.

JACOB[5] WILDER, son of David[4] Wilder and Martha (White) Wilder, b. July 2, 1757, Lancaster, Mass.; d. 1848, Woodstock, Vt.; bur. in River St. Cemetery; m. 1794, Mary Wakefield, b. 1756, Hartford, Vt.; d. Feb. 27, 1852, dau. of William Wakefield. Jacob enlisted in the American Army at the commencement of the Revolutionary War. At the time of the Battle of Bunker Hill he was on picket duty in the vicinity and therefore not in the fight. He was in the Battle of Monmouth and served faithfully where duty called him. After the war he immigrated to Plymouth, Vt. where he resided several years. He was Captain of the first military company in Plymouth and thereafter known as "Captain Wilder". He removed to Woodstock, Vt. about 1790; was a builder and constructed a fine house "the old Hutchinson House" on the Woodstock Green and a covered bridge over the Quechee river. At one time he had a linseed oil mill.

Issue of Jacob[5] Wilder and Mary (Wakefield) Wilder:

1. Benjamin[6] Wilder, b. Aug. 9, 1795; d. Mar. 1877; m. 1825, Elizabeth (Mary) Davis, b. Apr. 9, 1808. Issue: Mary, Nancy, Maria, Hiram, Nellie, Caroline and George Wilder.

2. Mary[6] Wilder, b. Nov. 1, 1796; m. David Watson.

3. Frederic[6] Trask Wilder, b. Sept. 13, 1798; m. Rachel Runnels.

4. Nancy[6] Wilder, b. Aug. 25, 1800; m. David Marsh.

5. Lucy[6] Wilder, b. Nov. 23, 1802; d. Apr. 28, 1811.

6. Louisa[6] Wilder, b. Aug. 1805; d. Aug. 10, 1821.

7. George[6] Wilder, b. Oct. 8, 1807.

8. Jacob[6] Wilder, b. Oct. 24, 1810; d. Apr. 9, 1811.

9. Lucy[6] Wilder, b. Oct. 31, 1811; m. Joshua Woodbury.

10. Clariss[6] Wilder, b. Sept. 28, 1814; m. Thomas B. Marcy.

11. Martha[6] M. Wilder, b. Aug. 3, 1817; m. Lucius Green.

Figure 7-15: Jacob Wilder was featured on an entire page of the Woodstock, Vermont, history published in 1889.

early Chicago papers. Chicago newspapers before 1871 were destroyed in the Chicago Fire, but the Newberry has extensive files of papers after that time. I did learn that some of the suburban areas have earlier information, but since my research was centered on Chicago and LaGrange, those references were not an option on this trip. While reading papers from the 1880s, we discovered that Benjamin Wilder had been involved in some legal matters after his wife's death that was covered extensively in the local papers. I also found the obituary for my great-aunt Olive Leitch, who never married and lived her entire life in the Chicago area. A photocopy of that obituary and a picture of Aunt Olive are seen in Figure 7-16.

One of the most well-known pioneer cemeteries in Chicago, the Rosehill Cemetery, was another resource. During our visit there we found that Benjamin Wilder had purchased an entire section in the cemetery, three entire lots. At the same time, we discovered that the gates of the cemetery were designed by a relative of Benjamin Wilder, William W. Boyington. While reading, we found the same Mr. Boyington designed the famous Chicago Water Tower and was quite well known.

Most of the Wilder plots at the Rosehill Cemetery are not used, so they are still available for my family's use. However, the time and money involved in putting those lots on the market is prohibitive and, who knows, some great-great-grandchild of mine may someday want to use them.

Olive L

OBITUARIES

Miss Olive A. Leitch

Miss Olive A. Leitch, 60, member of an old Chicago family, suffered a fatal heart attack yesterday in front of 19 Quincy st. She was pronounced dead at St. Luke's hospital. Miss Leitch lived at the Majestic hotel. Her family were early settlers in the stock yards district, owned considerable land in the area, and at one time held much of the land in what is now La Grange. Miss Leitch was a graduate of Chicago Law school, but did not practice law. Her nearest relative is an aunt, Miss Dollie F. Leitch, Los Angeles, Cal.

Figure 7-16: Obituaries, such as this one for Olive Leitch, offer a lot of genealogy information.

CHALLENGES

My challenges at this time are the same as everyone has: proving the information, following through to solve the dead-ends, and so on. I'm further frustrated when I'm in other locations at the time constraints of having to leave to return home just as I've discovered another trail to follow.

OBJECTIVES

I want to explore the other family branches, as seen in Figure 7-17. Eventually, I want to put the information into a family biography to pass on to my children and their children some day. I'd like to get all the documents scanned and digitized to protect against fire. My sister-in-law and I have talked about establishing a family website at some future date.

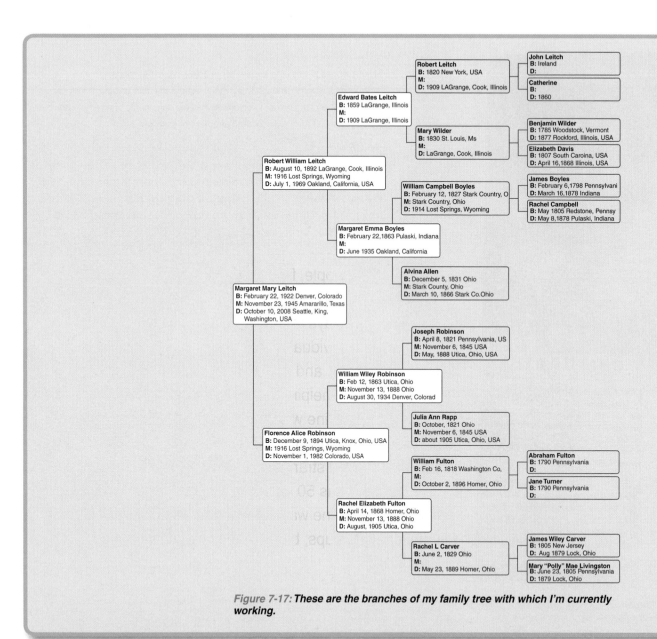

Figure 7-17: **These are the branches of my family tree with which I'm currently working.**

Chapter 8
Working with Others

People helping people, facilitated by the Internet, is one of the most powerful forces in current-day genealogy. There are a number of ways that this happens, from online forums, online support individuals and groups, blogs, individual and group online chats, and social networking to simple email. Of course, people helping people with genealogy is not new and all the offline ways of libraries and librarians; local, regional, and national genealogy clubs and societies; and family, friends, and strangers helping each other is just as valid today as it was 50 years ago. In this chapter we'll look at many of the online ways of working with others, including forums, chats, groups, blogs, and social networking.

8

Connect Through the Major Genealogy Sites

Many of the major genealogy sites provide ways of connecting people together to solve genealogy issues. Here we'll look at three of those sites: Genealogy.com, RootsWeb.com, and Ancestry.com.

Work with Genealogy.com

Genealogy.com has several ways in which you can work on genealogy with other people within the Community section. Two of these are the message boards, which provide a number of forums for people to place messages that others can respond to, and family home pages, which allow you to search for a person's name on other people's home pages.

USE THE GENEALOGY.COM FORUMS

The Genealogy.com forum is one of the most active and therefore one of the best genealogy forums. Marty has personally made good use of it. You'll remember from Marty's story in Chapter 2 that he started out knowing almost nothing about his great-grandfather except that he was called "Riley Matthews," his wife was Catherine Riddle, they were from North Carolina, and their son, Marty's grandfather, was Burrel Jones Matthews who was born in 1860. With that information, Marty went on the Genealogy.com forum and followed these steps:

1. Open Genealogy.com, hover over **Community**, and then click **Message Boards** to open the GenForum shown in Figure 8-1.

2. This provides several choices of how to access the forum:

   • Marty could type <u>Matthews</u> in the Forum Finder and click **Find**. This provides a link to the Matthews Family Genealogy Forum. There a search could be made, such as for W.R. Matthews, or a question could be asked, as shown in Figure 8-2.

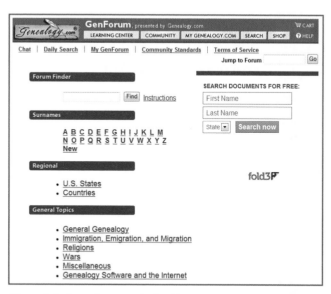

*Figure 8-1: **Genealogy.com's GenForum provides a number of alternative message boards to either search or ask questions.***

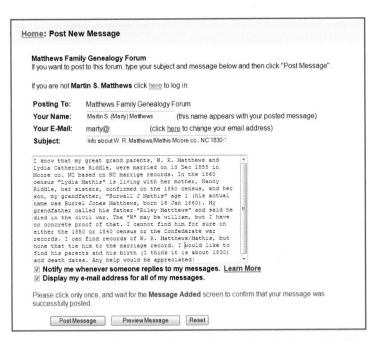

Figure 8-2: When asking a question in a forum, it is wise to provide all immediately relevant information so you don't get back information you already know.

- ● <u>North Carolina</u> could also be typed in the Forum Finder and **Find** clicked. This provides a link to the North Carolina Genealogy Forum, which can be searched or a question asked.

- ● **M** can be clicked and the list scrolled to "Matthews," which when clicked opens the Matthews Family Genealogy Forum, discussed earlier.

- ● **United States** can be clicked and then **North Carolina** clicked to open the North Carolina Genealogy Forum, also discussed earlier.

In Marty's query using the Matthews forum shown in Figure 8-2, he had not gotten a response at the time this was written. In Marty's initial foray into the GenForum, he chose to use the North Carolina forum (see Figure 8-3), which provided many more potential respondents who responded very quickly and in amazing depth, as shown in Figure 8-4.

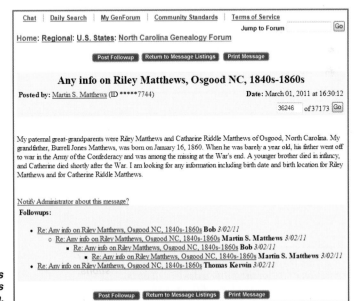

Figure 8-3: Marty's initial GenForum query was seeking information about his great-grandparents from the North Carolina Genealogy Forum.

Re: Any info on Riley Matthews, Osgood NC, 1840s-1860s

Posted by: Bob (ID *****0272) Date: March 02, 2011 at 09:11:40

In Reply to: Any info on Riley Matthews, Osgood NC, 1840s-1860s by Martin S. Matthews 36248 of 37173 Go

Hi Martin,

Catherine's full name was Lydia Catherine Riddle.
Riley was your great-grandfathers middle name. His first name may have been William? (just guessing)

Kentucky Death Records, 1852-1953
Name: Burrel J Matthews
Death Date: 27 Oct 1915
Death Location: Fayette
Age: 55
Gender: Male
Ethnicity: White
Birth Date: 16 Jan 1860
Birth Location: North Carolina
Father's Name: Riley Matthews
Father's Birth Location: North Carolina
Mother's Name: Lydia C Riddle
Mother's Birth Location: North Carolina

1860 United States Federal Census
Name: Burwell J Mathis (Matthews)
Age in 1860: 1
Birth Year: abt 1859
Birthplace: North Carolina
Home in 1860: Middle Division, Chatham, North Carolina
Gender: Male
Post Office: Pittsboro
Household Members:
Nancy Riddle 70, NC
Polly Riddle 35, NC
Piety J Riddle 30, NC
Antionett Riddle 20, NC
Lydia Mathis 27, NC
Archibald T Burnes 3, NC
Burwell J Mathis 1, NC

Groom's Name: W. R. Matthews
Groom's Birth Date:
Groom's Birthplace:
Groom's Age:
Bride's Name: Lydia Riddle
Bride's Birth Date:
Bride's Birthplace:
Bride's Age:
Marriage Date: 13 Dec 1855
Marriage Place: Moore, North Carolina
Collection: North Carolina Marriages, 1759-1979

1850 United States Federal Census
Name: Lydia Riddle
Age: 17
Estimated Birth Year: abt 1833
Birth Place: North Carolina
Gender: Female
Home in 1850: Lower Regiment, Chatham, North Carolina
Household Members:
Nancy Riddle 60, NC
Mary Riddle 33, NC
Martha Riddle 25, NC
Piety J Riddle 19, NC
Lydia Riddle 17, NC
Eliza Riddle 15, NC
Antionet Riddle 10, NC

Here's a tree containing Lydia's family (I don't know how accurate it is).

http://trees.ancestry.com/tree/10866786/person/-564431892/?o_cvc=Image-SavedPublic;PersonPage

Footnote; Osgood is in present day Lee County.
Lee County was formed in 1907, from parts of Moore & Chatham Counties.

Hope this helps.
Bob

*Figure 8-4: **This response to Marty's query shows documentation of his grandfather's death and birth, his great-grandparents' wedding, and his great-grandmother's 1850 census record.***

SEARCH HOME PAGES

An effective way to find out about your ancestry is to find others who have done research on your ancestors by searching for them on other people's home pages.

1. Go to Genealogy.com and click **Community** to display the Family Home Pages search.

2. Type, at a minimum, the last name you want to search for. If you can add a first and middle name, it will get you closer to the person you are trying to find. Click **Go**. The search may take some time. The first part of the results after typing "Thomas Lamont" (an early ancestor of Marty's) is shown in Figure 8-5.

Family Home Pages

Search
Search for home pages that contain a particular name.

First Name:
Middle:
Last:

Go!

Page Author Browse
To locate a page created by someone with an *uncommon* name, click a letter. Warning: Browsing for common names (Smith, Thompson) can be slow.
A B C D E F G H I J K L M N O P Q R S T U V W X Y Z

*Figure 8-5: **Searching for an ancestor on other people's family trees can be a powerful method of advancing your research.***

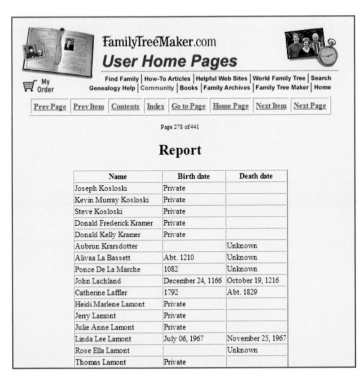

3. To refine the search, enter as much as you can of the birth and death dates and places, and then click **Search Again**. A detailed search with all the dates and places can take some time.

4. The results of a detailed search may be extensive and, given the time it takes, you may want to save them by clicking **Save This Search**, and then clicking **OK** to acknowledge the completion of the save.

5. Look at the number of stars on the left of the findings, and begin your review with the items that have the most stars. Then open the individual links. What you get depends on the type of item you started with (family home pages, historical records, GenForum) and what the user put up. Two common results are shown in Figure 8-6.

Connect Using RootsWeb.com

RootsWeb is primarily a large collection of links to information, search engines, family trees, mailing lists, message boards, and websites, as you can see on RootsWeb's home page shown in Figure 8-7.

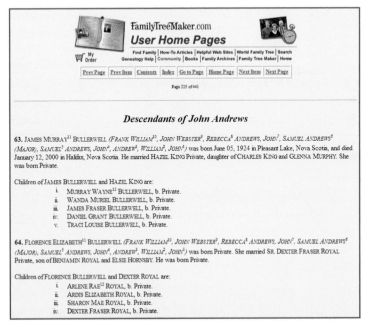

Figure 8-6: *The results of searching family home pages can be difficult to use but may hide some gems.*

Getting Started	**Websites**
Getting Started at RootsWeb	Websites at RootsWeb
Ancestry Tour	Websites on RootsWeb's Freepages
RootsWeb's Guide To Tracing Family Trees	Requests for Web Space
RootsWeb Review Archives | Subscribe	
What's New | RootsWeb Newsroom	**Other Tools and Resources**
	ROOTS-L Library | State Resources
Search Engines and Databases	RootsLink URL Registry | Add A Link
RootsWeb Surname List/RSL (Surname	Blank Charts and Forms
Listings)	RootsWeb Graphics
MetaSearch (Multiple Databases and Files)	Soundex Converter
Social Security Death Index (Deaths)	
U. S. Town/County Database (Locations)	**Volunteering at RootsWeb**
WorldConnect Project (Family Trees)	How to Volunteer
Index of All Search Engines and Databases	
	Hosted Volunteer Projects
Family Trees (WorldConnect)	World Archives Project
WorldConnect Project Main Page	Books We Own
Search Family Trees	CanadaGenWeb
Submit Your Family Tree	FreeBMD (England and Wales)
Edit Your Family Tree	FreeReg (UK)
	Obituary Daily Times
Mailing Lists	WorldGenWeb Project
Find a List Search	WorldGenWeb Archives
Index (Browse All Lists)	
ROOTS-L Mailing List	**Help**
Surname List Finder	FAQs & Help-Related Resources
Archives Search	Address Changes
Archives Browse	Password Central
Requests for Mailing Lists	Contacting the HelpDesk
(New or Adoptable)	
	Buy
Message Boards	Visit the Ancestry.com Store
Message Boards Home Page	
Surnames | Localities | Topics	**Contributing to RootsWeb**

*Figure 8-7: **The links that are available in RootsWeb make it a major starting point for expanding your genealogy research.***

All of these links represent ways to connect with others on the subject of genealogy. Here we'll look at their lists of mailing lists and websites.

USE ROOTSWEB MAILING LISTS

RootsWeb has a large and unique set of genealogy mailing lists that you can join to converse with others interested in the same areas of research as you.

1. Open Rootsweb.com and, in the left column of links, click **Find A List Search**. A Keyword search dialog box opens. Type a keyword, most likely a surname (for example, Marty might type Matthews), and click **Search**.

2. The result, if any, is a list of mailing lists relating to your keyword. Click one of the lists to open it, and you'll see a page similar to that in Figure 8-8.

3. Use the links to subscribe, unsubscribe, search, or browse the archives, or contact the administrator.

4. If you search the archives, you can search for words in the body or subject of the email, or who the email is from, or the date it was sent. The results are emails that contain the words that you searched for, as shown in Figure 8-9.

5. Click an individual email to open it. You will be able to see who it is from and read the email.

MATTHEWS
Surname and Family Lists

Please select a list of interest, or scroll down the page:
[MATTHEWS] [MATTHEWS-HUGH]

MATTHEWS-L

lists2

Topic: the MATTHEWS surname and variations (e.g., Mathissen, Mathes, Matherson, Mathias, Marthaws)

For questions about this list, contact the list administrator at MATTHEWS-admin@rootsweb.com.

- **Subscribing.** Clicking on one of the shortcut links below should work, but if your browser doesn't understand them, try these manual instructions: to join **MATTHEWS-L**, send mail to MATTHEWS-L-request@rootsweb.com with the single word *subscribe* in the message subject and body. To join **MATTHEWS-D**, do the same thing with MATTHEWS-D-request@rootsweb.com.
    - Subscribe to MATTHEWS-L
    - Subscribe to MATTHEWS-D (digest)
- **Unsubscribing.** To leave **MATTHEWS-L**, send mail to MATTHEWS-L-request@rootsweb.com with the single word *unsubscribe* in the message subject and body. To leave **MATTHEWS-D**, do the same thing with MATTHEWS-D-request@rootsweb.com.
    - Unsubscribe from MATTHEWS-L
    - Unsubscribe from MATTHEWS-D (digest)
- **Archives.** You can search the archives for a specific message or browse them, going from one message to another. Some list archives are not available; if there is a link here to an archive but the link doesn't work, it probably just means that no messages have been posted to that list yet.
    - Search the MATTHEWS archives
    - Browse the MATTHEWS archives

*Figure 8-8: **RootsWeb can get you on a mailing list discussing a topic important to your research.***

Archives Search Engine

Keyword	Advanced

Body: Moore Co, North Carolina

Subject:

From:
(email address of poster)

List: MATTHEWS
(limit search to one mailing list)

Date:
(e.g. 10 Jun 2005, Jun 2005, or 2005)

[Search] Search tips

Searching for: +path:matthews +(+moore +co +north +carolina)

Viewing 1-2 of 2 matches from **38,244,050** documents

---

1. **[MATTHEWS] Capt.Sam Matthews** [1]

This is from the files of LL Watson...Hope it helps. Regards, Mark W.Matthews Canyon Lake,Tx. Below you will find some of the info I have on my Matthews kin. Let me know if ti helps. I have this in gedcom form if you need it and can determine your ancestry from it. Good Luck, LL Watson FIRST GENERATION 1. Governor Samuel MATTHEWS was born in 1592 in England. He died on 13 Mar 1660 in VA. Came to VA in 1622 onboard Ship SouthHampton with servants and relatives. settled on south side of James River in

- http://archiver.rootsweb.ancestry.com/th/read/matthews/2001-10/1003080707
  Date: Sun, 14 Oct 2001 12:31:47 -0500

  From: "Mark & Leslie Matthews" < sammy@gvtc.com >

2. **Re: [MATTHEWS] Immigrant Samuel Mathews I & France Grevill** [0.997604]

Thank you Greg. Yes, we did correspond last year and I enjoyed your insight into this family. I definitely agree with you that there is no evidence that James Matthews is descended from Governor Samuel Matthews (or the Governor's parents). It has always been this intriguing connection with the Collier family that has left me wondering (i.e., that Isaac Collier married a descendant of Frances Grenvill). I am not a Collier researcher by any means, but if you refer to Posting #4043 on the Collier Fo

- http://archiver.rootsweb.ancestry.com/th/read/matthews/2008-01/1199506288
  Date: Fri, 4 Jan 2008 20:11:28 -0800 (PST)

  From: DAVID BROWN < dbrown544@prodigy.net >

Viewing 1-2 of 2 matches from **38,244,050** documents

*Figure 8-9: **Searching the RootsWeb email archive can produce clues as well as useful pointers for your research.***

CONSIDERING THE ROOTS-L MAILING LIST

The Roots-L mailing list is for anybody interested in genealogy worldwide. Open it by clicking **Roots-L Mailing List** on the lower-left corner of the RootsWeb home page. Roots-L is a community discussion where people can talk about genealogy issues, both their own questions and research, as well as general discussions on genealogy topics. By Internet standards, it is old, starting in 1987, and over the years it has grown into the largest genealogy mailing list in the world and has spawned thousands of new mailing lists for special-interest areas. There are two types of subscriptions:

- Send an email message to roots-l-request@rootsweb.com with the single word "subscribe" (without the quotation marks) in the message to be placed on the mailing list and start receiving email messages, which you can respond to, or send out your own message. Be sure you and your inbox are ready for a deluge of email; it can be quite large.

Continued . . .

ROOTS-L

Message Archive (over 10 years!)
Recent Messages
ROOTS-L Library

United States Links
- Alabama
- Alaska
- Arizona
- Arkansas
- California
- Colorado
- Connecticut
- Delaware
- District of Columbia
- Florida
- Georgia
- Hawaii
- Idaho
- Illinois
- Indiana
- Iowa

What is ROOTS-L?

ROOTS-L is a mailing list for people who are interested in any or all aspects of genealogy, anywhere in the world. We're the original Internet genealogical mailing list (our first messages were posted in 1987), and the largest. But that doesn't mean we're not interested in new faces, new queries, new knowledge. Please join us!

To subscribe, just send an e-mail to ROOTS-L-request@rootsweb.com with the message

        subscribe

To later unsubscribe (yes, not everyone chooses to stay with us), just send to that same address the message

        unsubscribe

If you'd prefer digest mode instead of mail mode (single messages), send your subscribe message instead to ROOTS-D-request@rootsweb.com. For more information, you might want to consult our Welcome File for more details, or our various help files.

TIP

In the RootsWeb links to websites there are a number of sites dedicated to African American and Native American ancestries.

EXPLORE WEBSITE LINKS FROM ROOTSWEB

Another unique feature of RootsWeb.com is its very large registry of genealogy-related websites. Many of the sites are family genealogy pages, often based on the common surname, but there are also many websites for state and local genealogy societies and other organizations.

1. In Rootsweb.com, click the **Web Sites** tab to open the registry shown in Figure 8-10.

2. Start with regional sites by clicking **United States** and then clicking the state you are interested in. For example, in Marty's case, he is interested in North Carolina.

3. Within the state you can then look at counties you may be interested in or local genealogy or historical societies. Marty picked the Moore County Genealogical Society because his great-grandparents were married there. Clicking that link opened the society's website shown in Figure 8-11.

4. Back on the website registry click in the alphabetical surname list to begin a search down that path. In the list of names that appears, scroll down to find the name you want. Hopefully, you'll see several websites.

MATTHEWS	Mary Love's Genealogy Page
	Matthews & Patton Family Photo Tree Web Page
	Family Ties & Other Twigs & Branches
	Renesch, O'Brien, Meckler, Matthews & Ferone Family Photos
	OurPage: Stanley -Matthews Family
	Barry's Place
	Ancestors of Roger George BLINKO
	Healey and Brown Family Genealogy

5. Click a website to explore it. You'll find all sorts of fascinating pages, as shown in Figure 8-12.

QUICKSTEPS

CONSIDERING THE ROOTS-L MAILING LIST *(Continued)*

- Send an email message to roots-d-request@rootsweb.com with the single word "subscribe" (without the quotation marks) in the message to receive a digest of messages in place of the individual messages. You can still respond to messages and send your own messages.

When you first sign up, you will be sent a confirmation request with a link for you to click to confirm you want to subscribe to the Roots-L mailing list. Clicking the link will open a webpage where you can change your name and other options. You can then click **Subscribe To List Roots**, if that is what you want to do, or click **Cancel My Subscription Request**, if that is your wish.

If you subscribe, you will then get the first of four welcoming e-mails with the following subjects:

- **Roots-L.Welcome** Overview and guidelines
- **Roots-L.Welcome1** Surname lists, netiquette issues, and getting started
- **Roots-L.Welcome2** SmartList commands and searching the archives
- **Roots-L.Welcome3** Frequently asked questions (FAQ) and other files to search

Continued . . .

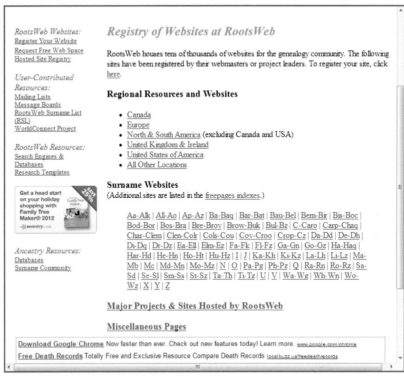

Figure 8-10: **The RootsWeb Registry of Websites provides a hierarchical structure for searching for a particular website starting with either a geographic region or a surname.**

Connect Using Ancestry.com

Ancestry.com provides a number of ways to connect and work with others in your genealogy research. Many of these are in the Collaborate drop-down menu in the menu bar at the top of the page. The options here are

- **Recent Member Connect Activity** Shows the actions of people that you have connected with who are researching people on your family trees (see Figure 8-13).

CONSIDERING THE ROOTS-L MAILING LIST *(Continued)*

If you don't get the last three welcome messages, you may request them by sending an email to roots-l-request@rootsweb.com, put "archive" (without the quotation marks) in the message subject, and put "get roots-l.welcome1" (without the quotation marks) in the body of the message.

Vary the "1" in "welcome1" with "2" and "3" for the other messages.

If you find that you don't want to continue to receive Roots-L messages, you can discontinue them by sending an email message to roots-l-request@rootsweb.com with the single word "unsubscribe" (without the quotation marks) in the message.

USE THE ROOTS-L MAILING LIST

Using the Roots-L mailing list is like any other email. You will receive email messages or a digest of them that you can read and reply to if you desire. You can also send messages to the mailing list, reaching many thousands of people, by using the email address roots-l@rootsweb.com.

You can send commands to Roots-L, such as "subscribe," "unsubscribe," and others for searching and other purposes (see the Welcome2 message), by using the email address roots-l-request@rootsweb.com, and the command word or words in the body of the message, which should not contain anything else. For complete instructions, see the Welcome2 message.

The messages you send out, both replies and those initiated by you, are screened by volunteers to assure that the content is appropriate for the genealogy intent of the mailing list. The general rule is to use common sense, keep the messages short, and keep them focused on genealogy. The first welcome letter puts it this way:

Continued . . .

Figure 8-11: **There are many genealogy societies throughout the United States and around the world that are potential resources for your research.**

- **Message Boards** Allows you to search over 17 million posts on 161,000 message boards as well as post your own queries on those boards.
- **Ancestry World Archives Project** Asks you to help in indexing historical records that are available online but need indexes so they can be searched. Basically what you are asked to do is read historical records on your computer and type in an index for the record you are reading. Ancestry provides free software to help you do this, and the resulting index is free for everyone to use. You give a lasting gift if you have the time to do it.

QUICKSTEPS

CONSIDERING THE ROOTS-L MAILING LIST *(Continued)*

"Mainly have fun, be nice, and help each other." A couple of other specifics to keep in mind:

- Make sure your email messages, both replies and ones you initiate, are in plain text and not HTML or any other enhanced formatting. Many, if not most, email messages today are sent with HTML formatting to allow special fonts, so you may need to instruct your email program to use plain text.

- Keep your messages under 10,000 bytes in length, roughly a maximum of 150 to 200 lines of text. Long messages not of general interest are screened out.

- Do not include copyrighted material such as that from current-day newspapers, magazines, or books, or material not belonging to you such as that in other peoples email or websites.

- Do not use the mailing list for commercial purposes such as to advertise a product. A one-time brief announcement of a product or service that is of general interest to the genealogy community may be acceptable.

- Be nice. Do not use language that some people might object to, and do not use derogatory comments about other people, their comments, writing, or products. If you need to disagree with someone, do so with kindness and humility, and generally privately.

The Roots-L mailing list is a tremendous resource that can be of great benefit to your genealogy research. It can also inundate you with email and take up a lot of time sorting the wheat from the chaff.

*Figure 8-12: **Many surname webpages can provide possible links to your ancestors and interesting insights to other branches of your family.***

- **Member Directory**   Allows you to search the Ancestry member directory for a particular person. Our experience is that this is not very useful. Very few known Ancestry users turn up in a search.

- **Public Profile**   Allows you to enter and update your own personal profile.

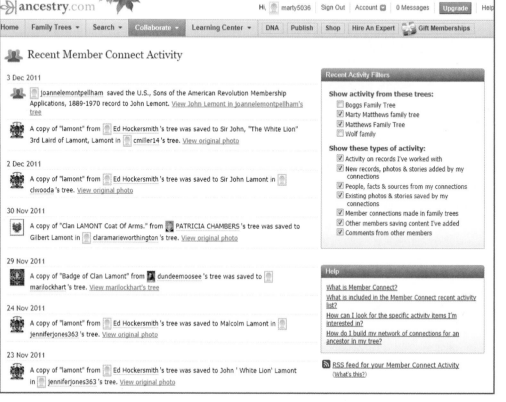

Figure 8-13: *Contact with other members starts in several ways, including hints, message board postings, and messages.*

USE MEMBER CONNECT

Ancestry's Member Connect helps you find and work with other Ancestry members who are researching the same people that you are. You can use this in three ways:

● On the Ancestry.com home page you will see a Recent Member Connect Activity box that was discussed in Chapter 5. Its purpose is to give you an up-to-date status of what others are doing and finding about your ancestors. From this page you can click

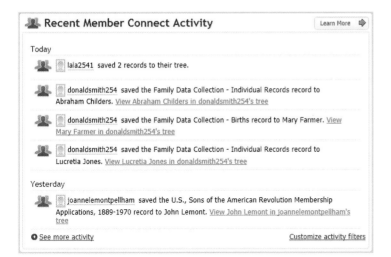

Learn More to get a better explanation of how Member Connect works (also discussed in Chapter 5).

- On the ancestor profile pages within your family tree you will see a tab entitled "Member Connect" where you can find out about others working with that ancestor, compare the information they have with yours, and anonymously (if you wish) contact that person.

- On historical records there is a section on the left of the record that shows comments from other members, allows you to leave a comment, and find others who are researching your ancestor.

As you are working with Ancestry.com you will get a message, shown in Figure 8-14, that another Ancestry member is researching the same person and giving you a way of anonymously contacting him or her. You will get a notice if and when the other person replies, and you see the messages you have sent and received by clicking **Messages** in the upper-right corner of the Ancestry page.

*Figure 8-14: **Ancestry.com does a lot in the background to try and connect members who are researching the same people, such as this notice allowing you to contact another member interested in the same person.***

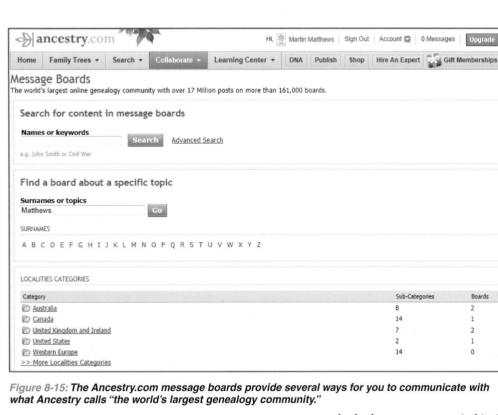

USE THE ANCESTRY MESSAGE BOARDS

The first step in using the Ancestry message boards is to find the right one; there are over 161,000 of them. As shown in Figure 8-15, you have several ways to start. You can search for

- Messages in any message board that contain names or keywords that you enter
- Message boards whose principal focus is a surname or topic that you enter
- Message boards whose principal focus is a surname or a group of surnames beginning with a letter of the alphabet that you have entered
- Message boards whose principal focus is a regional locality or country that you have selected

Figure 8-15: The Ancestry.com message boards provide several ways for you to communicate with what Ancestry calls "the world's largest genealogy community."

An example of how this works would be to try and find information about Marty's great-grandfather W.R. (Riley) Matthews who he knows was married in 1855 in Moore County, North Carolina, to Lydia Catherine Riddle based on North Carolina marriage records. In the 1860 Census Lydia Riddle is grouped with her mother and sisters (known from the 1850 Census), and was referred to as "Lydia Mathis," along with Marty's grandfather (Burrel Jones Matthews, born 1860), referred to as "Burwell J. Mathis, age 1." Marty has yet to find Riley's parents or date and place of his birth and death. The word of mouth from Marty's parents and grandparents was that Riley died in the Civil War. The process of trying to find information about Riley in the Ancestry message boards might go as follows:

1. Assuming you have an active Ancestry account, open Ancestry.com.

2. From Ancestry's home page, hover over **Collaborate** in the menu bar at the top of the page and click **Message Boards**.

Advanced Search

Tip: Visit the Board FAQ for tips on how to make your searches more effective.

Name or Keyword	Riley Matthews
Subject of Message	
Author of Message	
Last Name (surname)	Matthews ☑ Use Soundex
Message Classification	All
Posted Within	Anytime

Search

3. Under Search For Content, click in the **Names Or Keywords** text box, type W.R. Matthews / Mathis, and click **Search**. The result was 48 messages, many just finding a "W." or "R.," none having any obvious relationship to Marty's great-grandfather.

4. The next attempt was also in the Search For Content area, where Marty this time clicked **Advance Search**, typed Riley Matthews / Mathis in the Name Or Keyword text box, typed Matthews in the Last Name text box, clicked **Use Soundex**, and clicked **Search**. The result was 356 messages, many with references to just "Riley" or just "Matthews." There was one referencing a "William Riley Matthews."

5. To open a message that looks promising so you can read more, click the message header on the upper left of a message. In this case, while interesting, the person mentioned was not Marty's great-grandfather.

William Smitherman r/o Andrew Lucinda ?   Posted on: 21 Nov 2000, by ◉ JanetSmitherm...
  Surnames > Smitherman

...In 1854 they had a son named William Alexander Smitherman, then in 1858 Mary was married to William Riley Matthews. We do not know what happened to William Smitherman. I have been unable to find a record of death ...

6. The third attempt was to search for an appropriate surname message board by clicking in the **Surname Or Topic** text box, typing Matthews, clicking **Go**, and clicking the **Matthews** board.

7. In the Matthews message board that opens, click in the **Name Or Keywords** textbox, type W.R. Matthews, click the **Matthews** only search option, and click **Search**. Only one message appeared and it was not relevant. Going to the Matthews message board using the alphabet did not help.

8. The final attempt was to use geographic categories by clicking **United States**, clicking **States**, clicking **North Carolina**, clicking **Counties**, clicking **Chatham** (as a place to start), clicking in the **Name Or Keywords** textbox, typing W.R. Matthews / Mathis, clicking the **Chatham** only search option, and clicking **Search**, with the same results as described in step 3.

9. Marty repeated step 8, changing the name to just Matthews, and then changing the counties to first Cumberland, then Moore, and finally Lee, which are all in the same area. As a last resort, Marty tried "North Carolina – Unknown." There were a number of interesting messages for him to follow up on, but none that was obviously related to his great-grandfather.

POSTING A QUERY ON THE ANCESTRY MESSAGE BOARD

When you have searched the message boards and not found any messages that relate to what you want to find out, the next step is to post your message on the board and see if anybody answers your query. To do this:

1. Use the steps in "Use the Ancestry Message Boards" to open the message board on which you want to post.

2. Beneath the title of the message board (the North Carolina county in Marty's case), click **Begin New Thread**.

3. In the Post New Thread dialog box that opens, click in the **Subject** text box, type a short, succinct subject, press **TAB**, type your query, make sure the **Send Me An Alert** box is checked, type any related surnames, click **Preview** to see how your query will look, click **Edit** to make any needed corrections, and, when ready, click **Post**.

The most common classification is "Query," but there are a number of others for you to choose. In many cases—for example, if you are posting to a county—unless you are very sure you are in the correct county, post the same message to neighboring counties or related surnames.

The rules for posting on the Ancestry message boards are the same as described earlier in this chapter in the QuickFacts "Considering the Roots-L Mailing List."

Participate in a Facebook Group

Over the years working with genealogy, we've seen a lot of changes. One of the most amazing is how the Internet has changed how we do many things—and one of the Internet tools most visible today is Facebook. From inspiring an Oscar-nominated movie, enabling revolution in the streets, and scrambling governments to shut Facebook down to stifle the flow of information, to less dramatic actions of grandmothers showing their friends online photos of a new grandchild, Facebook is a versatile and dynamic Internet tool changing our vision of what our world may be. Genealogists are right there in increasing numbers, making use of Facebook to communicate and track what is going on with friends and family as well as to participate in interesting genealogy groups.

Groups are specialized pages created to support people who share a common interest. Examples include people organizing a class reunion, an investing club, or a group interested in genealogy. Groups enable members to communicate with each other, post photos or videos, chat, and edit shared documents—ideal

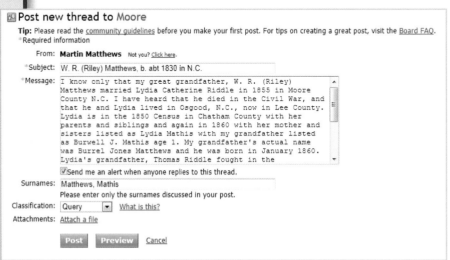

for informally sharing family trees with family or ideas about genealogy with
similarly motivated people.

For the remainder of this chapter we'll discuss how you can find and join an
existing group and what you can do in one.

Work with an Existing Group

Hundreds, perhaps thousands, of genealogy groups already exist within
Facebook. Facebook Groups support both groups that meet physically, such
as clubs, and those that only meet online. You may want to find one of these
existing genealogy groups rather than create a new one.

Find a Group

There are several ways to find groups. If you know what group you want
to join, you can just search for the name. You can accept an invitation from
a friend, or you can ask friends and/or family members for the names of
genealogy groups they belong to.

SEARCH FOR GROUPS

The most common way to find groups is to search for them.
Searching for groups is a bit tricky. You search by keyword,
unless you know the exact name of the group. When you
get a list of matches, you'll need to filter it for groups. Then
you find the group you want to join. If the group is open,
you can immediately join it, or if the group is closed, you
can request to join. Figure 8-16 shows an example of a
keyword search narrowed to groups.

1. Click in the **Search** text box, and type the keyword describing
   the groups you want to join, in this case, <u>genealogy</u>. You'll see a
   list matching your keyword.

2. When you get the initial search result, scroll down the list, and
   at the bottom click **See More Results For** keyword to see

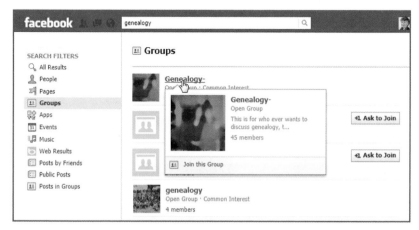

Figure 8-16: **You can find groups by searching for a name or by using keywords.**

See more results for genealogy ▸
Displaying top 7 results

additional results. Facebook often displays a regular search result instead of a list of possibilities, and you want a list—asking for more results allows you to take the next step in accomplishing this.

3. Click **Groups** in the leftmost column to filter the list so that only groups are available, as was done in Figure 8-16.

4. As you scroll through the list, hover your mouse over the group name to see certain information for the group, giving you a sense of what it is about and who its members are.

5. If the group is open, you can click the name to see posts for a group.

USE FRIENDS OR FAMILY TO FIND GROUPS

Searches work well if you have an idea what you're looking for, and if the group privacy setting allows it to be seen by the public ("closed" or "open" will be found by searches; "secret" will not be found). But if there is a specific group you'd like to join, you're better off finding someone already in the group who can invite you to join, or ask the admin to invite you.

Join a Group

Groups can be open, closed, or secret. If they are open, or public, anyone can join. If they are closed, you'll need an invitation. If they are secret, you'll never know about them unless an existing member invites you. The first step is to find a group you want to join and open the group site, as described earlier. Then you simply either join or ask to join:

- Click **Join** or **Join This Group** to become a member immediately—this can be done if the group is open.

- Click **Ask To Join Group** if the group is closed and you must be approved for membership. Your confirmation will come to you via email and a Facebook Messages notice.

When a group has decided to have you join them, you will receive an email invitation and you can immediately go and participate in the group.

CAUTION

If you get an invitation via an email to join a group with which you're unacquainted, check out the site before you confirm your interest. Do not click the email link, but go to the group site on Facebook. Links can contain hidden viruses.

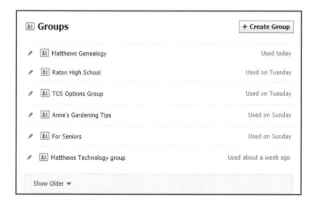

Figure 8-17: *From your home page you can view your Groups page showing recent activity.*

View Group Requests and Memberships

Facebook makes it easy to keep track of your existing memberships and outstanding requests:

- On your home page, in the leftmost column, click **Groups** to see your group activity. If you do not see Groups, click **More** to expand the list.

- If you belong to more than one group, you'll see a list of groups beneath the Groups label. As you hover your cursor over the Groups label, you'll see "More." Click **More** to see all your group requests and memberships. Click the group name to see its activity.

- If you have older groups that are not being displayed, click **Show Older** to see other inactive groups.

Figure 8-17 shows an example of a Groups page with outstanding groups.

Have Fun with a Group

Using a group is similar to using a regular Facebook page, except that you'll find some of the instructions in a different place.

Add Friends to a Group

If members of a group are permitted to add other members, you can add friends to a group. If you don't see the command to add friends, you'll know that you don't have permission. In this case, you request that the admin add a person to the group.

1. Click a group with which you have become a member and want to participate.

2. On the Group page, click in the **Add Friends To Group** text box on the rightmost column, under the thumbnails of current members. The Add Friends To Group dialog box is displayed. If you do not have permission to add a friend, you will see a message showing that your admin will need to approve her or him.

3. Begin typing a name, and a list will be displayed as you type. Click the person you want to include. They will be immediately added to your group.

4. You can always come back to this process and resume adding new friends later. If your admin needs to invite the person, he or she will add the person to the group when the invitee's acceptance is received.

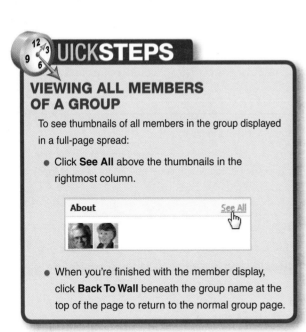

Chat with the Group

A chat including all members of a group can be scheduled. One idea is ask the admin to send an email to all members announcing a time and date for the chat. Then at that time, each member must begin the chat in order to be included.

1. At the top of the rightmost column, click the gear icon, and click **Chat With Group**. A chat window will open.

2. Click in the text box at the bottom of the chat window, and type your message.

3. When you are ready, press **ENTER**. All chat responses from the group will be reflected in the larger text box above.

4. When the chat is over, click **X** to remove the chat from the page.

Create a Document

If your group is working together to create a document, or if you want to create a document for the group to read:

1. On the top of the center column, beneath the group name, click **Docs**. The document page will open, as seen in Figure 8-18.

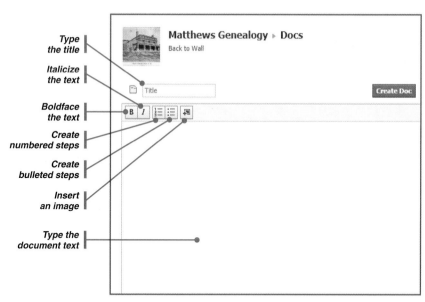

Type the title

Italicize the text

Boldface the text

Create numbered steps

Create bulleted steps

Insert an image

Type the document text

Figure 8-18: *You can create a document in Facebook to be shared or worked on together.*

2. Click in the **Title** text box, and type a title for the document.

3. Click in the main text box, and type your document. Figure 8-18 shows the formatting options available to you as you create the document.

4. When your document is ready for others to view, click **Create Doc**.

5. Click **Back To Wall** to return to the main Group page.

Post a Link

Posting a link requires that you copy and paste the URL to the Status Update text box. Information from the website will be displayed automatically. To post a link suggesting to your group that they view another website or page:

1. Find and copy the URL of the website you want to include for the group.

2. Click **Write Post**, click in the **Write Something** text box, and then paste the URL of the website. A thumbnail image of the page will display.

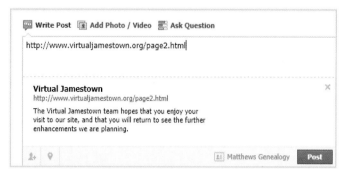

3. Click **Post** to post it for others.

TIP

To share links with others outside the group, click **Share** beneath the posting for a menu of options for where to share the link. Click the location you want, such as **On Your Own Wall**, and then click **Share Link** in the resulting dialog box. The link will be posted to your chosen location so that more of your friends can see it.

Carole Matthews
Does your research lead you to think that Reilly Matthews was from England or France?

☐ From France

☑ **From England**

+ Add an option...

👥 Like · Comment · Unfollow Post · about an hour ago

Figure 8-19: **You can poll the members for their opinions about various concerns of the group.**

Create an Event

To create an event for your group members:

> ✓ Notifications ▾ ⚙ ▾
> Chat with Group
> **Create Event**
> Edit Group
> Report Group
> Leave Group

1. In the top of the rightmost column, click the gear icon, and click **Create Event** on the menu. A Create Event page is displayed, as shown as a completed form in Figure 8-20.

2. Set the parameters of the event:

   ● Click in the **Event Name** text box, and type the title of the event.

   ● Click the **Date And Time** calendar, and find the date you want. Click the **Time** down arrow, and set the time.

   ● Click **Add End Time** to be able to set a date and time that the event will end.

   ● Click in the **Location** text box to set the location or other identifying information (optionally, you may enter an address).

   ● Click in the **Details** text box to describe the event in more detail.

   ● Click **Select Guests** to choose your guests. Click the checkboxes of the individuals in the group you want to invite, and then click **Save And Close**.

   ● In the options at the bottom, click a checkbox to remove the checkmark, thereby deselecting one or more of the three qualifications of who is automatically invited, if the public can view and RSVP, and whether the guest list is displayed on the Event page.

3. Click **Create Event** to make it final.

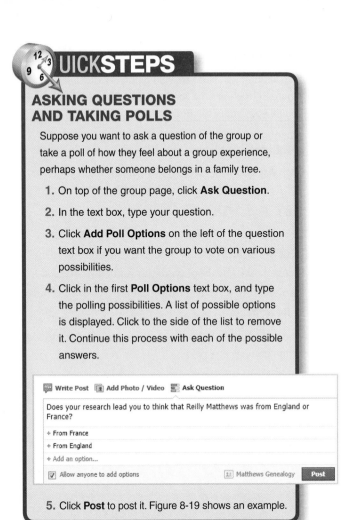

QUICKSTEPS

ASKING QUESTIONS AND TAKING POLLS

Suppose you want to ask a question of the group or take a poll of how they feel about a group experience, perhaps whether someone belongs in a family tree.

1. On top of the group page, click **Ask Question**.

2. In the text box, type your question.

3. Click **Add Poll Options** on the left of the question text box if you want the group to vote on various possibilities.

4. Click in the first **Poll Options** text box, and type the polling possibilities. A list of possible options is displayed. Click to the side of the list to remove it. Continue this process with each of the possible answers.

> 📝 Write Post   📷 Add Photo / Video   ☰ Ask Question
>
> Does your research lead you to think that Reilly Matthews was from England or France?
>
> + From France
> + From England
> + Add an option...
>
> ☑ Allow anyone to add options   👥 Matthews Genealogy   **Post**

5. Click **Post** to post it. Figure 8-19 shows an example.

Figure 8-20: *Setting up an event for a group is easy and can help support group programs or meetings.*

Figure 8-21: *You can invite listed group friends, search for non-group friends, or send an email to non-Facebook friends.*

INVITE FRIENDS TO AN EVENT

To invite additional friends to an event:

1. Click **Events** beneath your name and picture on the home page to view the events. If you have more than one, click the event you want to view.

2. If you have joined the event, you can invite others by clicking **Invite Friends** in the menu bar at the top of the rightmost column. The Invite Friends dialog box is displayed, as seen in Figure 8-21.

3. You can use these three methods to find friends to invite:

   ● Click the names of the friends you want to invite.

   ● Click in the **Search** text box and type the name of a non-group friend. Select the correct friend.

   ● Click in the **Invite By Email Address** text box, and type email addresses of non-Facebook friends you want to invite.

4. Click **Submit**. You'll see a Security Check dialog box. Type the coded text into the text box. If you can't read the text, click **Try Different Words** to display another code. If you can't read it at all, click **An Audio Captcha** to hear it. To figure out what the security check is all about, click **What's This?**.

Invite by E-mail Address: Use commas to separate e-mails

someone@isp.com ×

Hi, We are planning a Matthews family reunion next September. It won't be complete without you!

Submit   Cancel

● Click **Submit**. You'll see a message that the invitations have been sent.

RESPOND TO AN EVENT INVITATION

To respond to an event invitation:

In your home page, click **Events** to view your events. Click **Join** for the event you want to participate in, or click **Decline** for those that you don't. The RSVP To This Event dialog box will open.

View Group Photos

Photos can be wonderful for a group. They can reveal good times together, recapture old memories, and combine family collections of photos. To see photos for a group:

1. Click the name of the group on the leftmost column of the home page.

2. Click **Photos** below the group name.

Matthews Genealogy
🔒 Closed Group
👥 2 Members 📷 Photos 📄 Docs

3. To see the contents of an album, click the top picture on a page.

4. To see the photos in full view, click the photo.

Share a Comment

Comments are how communications are enabled among the group. The quality and frequency of the communications are what vitalize and stimulate group spirit. No comments, no group.

You can either share an original comment or respond to someone else's comment.

September 2012

Family Reunion At Old Homestead
Thursday, September 27, 2012 at 10:30pm
Carole Matthews invited you · 1 guest

Join · Decline

QUICKSTEPS

LEAVING OR DELETING A GROUP

You may find yourself in a group that simply doesn't interest you. Or perhaps the group simply serves no purpose for you any longer. You can leave a group you no longer are attached to, and you can delete a group.

LEAVE A GROUP

Be aware that if you choose to leave a group, you'll have to display the group page again and click **Ask To Join Group** if you ever change your mind. Note that if you are the admin of the group, someone else will be asked to act as admin for the group.

1. Click the group name on the leftmost column of the home page to display the group page.

2. Click **See All** on the rightmost column, above the member thumbnails.

Continued . . .

LEAVING OR DELETING A GROUP

(Continued)

3. Find your own thumbnail and click **Remove X** to the right of the thumbnail. The Leave *groupname* dialog box is displayed.

Leave Sports Club

Are you sure you want to give up your administrator privileges and leave this group? The administrator position will be offered to other people who are currently in the group. This will also prevent members from re-adding you.

If you ever want to rejoin, visit the group and click Ask to Join Group.

Leave Group   **Cancel**

4. Click **Leave Group**.

DELETE A GROUP

Facebook automatically gets rid of groups with no remaining members. So to get rid of a group, all members must be deleted. Remember, however, that in order to delete members, you have to be the admin with the most tenure—the originating admin, or at least the one remaining the longest. To delete members:

1. Click the group name on the home page.

2. Click **See All** in the rightmost column above the members' thumbnails.

3. Click the **X** next to each member to delete them from the group.

START A DISCUSSION

To share an original comment or start a new discussion with the members of a group:

1. Display the group page by clicking its name on the home page.

2. Click in the **Write Something** text box, and type your comment.

💬 Write Post   📷 Add Photo / Video   ▤ Ask Question

Be sure and respond to the family reunion invitation so we will know who is planning on attending. |

👤+   📍   📋 Matthews Genealogy   **Post**

3. Click **Post**.

RESPOND TO SOMEONE ELSE

To respond to someone else's comment:

1. Display the group page by clicking its name on the home page. Find the comment to which you want to respond.

2. Click **Comment** beneath the post, click in the text box, and type your comment.

👍 Like · Comment · Unfollow Post · Share · about an hour ago

Write a comment...

3. Press **ENTER** or click **Reply**.

John Peters Wolf, 58, Seattle, WA

OVERVIEW

My mother's paternal line currently can be followed back eight generations to Thomas Rodgers, born in England in 1665. Her maternal line is currently known only back to my grandmother, Sarah Moyer Hay, born in New Jersey in 1886. My father's paternal line can be traced back four generations to Velvel Margolis, born in 1847 in Russia, while I've followed his maternal line back three generations to Benjamin Cohen, born in Latvia on an unknown date. In my genealogy work I have used FamilySearch.com and ArlingtonCemetery.net websites, among others, as well as the Personal Ancestral File (PAF) software.

STORY

From my earliest days my brothers and I have been surrounded by family history—portraits of stern, formally dressed old men and elegant ladies from the 1700s and 1800s stared down upon us from their perch on the wall. We sat on uncomfortable chairs that we were told had a connection with Abe Lincoln. From time to time a box of matched dueling pistols was brought out to show guests. And then there were the old letters.

My dad says he found them one day when he was asked to clean out my mother's aunt's garage. While loading things for the trip to the dump he noticed what looked like old stamps. An avid stamp collector, he set the box aside. What he eventually discovered was a collection of 54 letters and related communications between Commodore John Rodgers, USN, and key individuals of the time, such as Presidents John Quincy Adams, James Monroe, and James Madison, plus historic figures such as General Lafayette, James Lawrence ("Don't give up the ship"), and Stephen Decatur ("My country, right or wrong"). Some of the letters are 200 years old and yet make the past and our family history come alive in the present (see Figure 8-22). And there are more.

As my dad moved into retirement he pulled out additional boxes of letters from my mother's family—letters from the Wyoming Territory, from sons on warships in Cuba, from ranches in Texas, and from schools back east. Only fragile threads of oral history connected these objects, letters, and people. Since my mother died young and we were not often in touch with the last members of her family, my father became the repository of my mother's family lineage. He took great pride in telling us our connection to Commodore Rodgers, the Hays of Nutley, New Jersey, or to privateers who sailed the waters off Barbados. The trouble was none of us could remember the names and keep it all straight in our heads the way he could. Even when he wrote it out it wasn't easy to follow. I tried to make a family tree, but was unable to develop a clear picture. It was even more challenging when I tried to grasp my father's family tree—what little information he had was based on hearsay, lacked dates, or even spelling of names. When my father became very ill there was an urgent need to document what we had before it passed beyond reach.

PULLING IT TOGETHER

That is when I started looking for tools to make sense of this hodgepodge of history I had inherited and discovered the free genealogy program Personal Ancestral File (PAF). I started plugging information into the appropriate blanks. In a short time, I made sense of the jumble of stories, people, and dates and was able to draw solid lines connecting one family member to the next. The charts showed me the ancestors linking me to my seafaring great, great, great grandfather Commodore Rodgers and the letters to him concerning matters on board ships long gone. From sites like Wikipedia.org I read about his exploits and history, and found pictures of him and his ships (see Figure 8-23), and on FindAGrave.com there is a picture of his pyramid grave marker (see Figure 8-24).

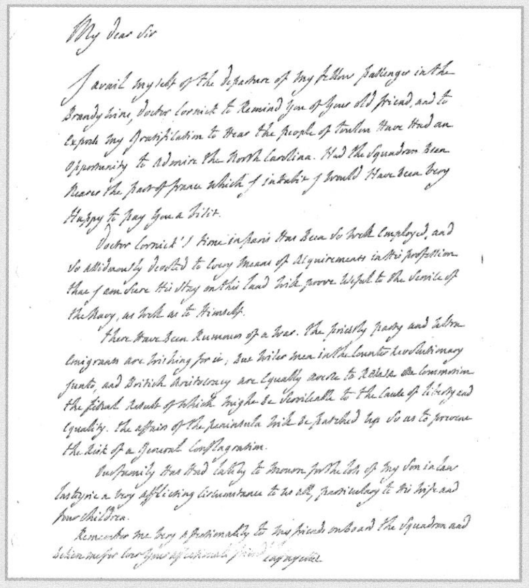

The handwritten letters and images in the top row are part of Figure 8-22. The right-hand typed text reads:

COMMODORE JOHN RODGERS CORRESPONDENCE

The collection includes letters from Lafayette, Presidents John Quincy Adams, James Monroe and James Madison, United States Navy officers James Lawrence ("Don't give up the ship"), Isaac Hull, Stephen Decatur ("My country right or wrong"), other naval officers and personnel, Henry Clay and others, all written between 1805 and 1838.

The Navy men, with Rodgers, were the heroes of "The Old Navy". Rodgers's own career covered our wars with France (1798-1801), with the Barbary States, (1801-1806 and 1815), and the War of 1812. He was Senior Officer in the Navy for 17 of his 40 Navy years, president of the Board of Navy Commissioners for 19 years, and interim Secretary of the Navy, turning down the Secretaryship twice. He served as Lieutenant on "The Constellation", Captain on the "Maryland", Commander on the "John Adams", the "New York", the "Congress", the "Constitution" and the "President", and was Commander-in-Chief of the Mediterranean Squadron aboard the flag-ship "North Carolina".

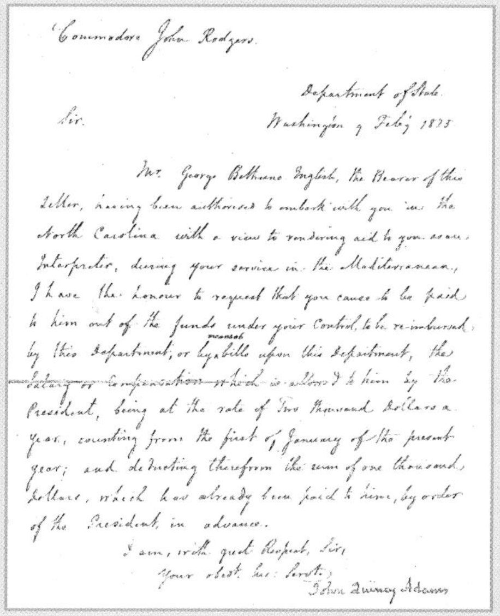

Except where indicated all the described letters are addressed to Commodore John Rodgers.

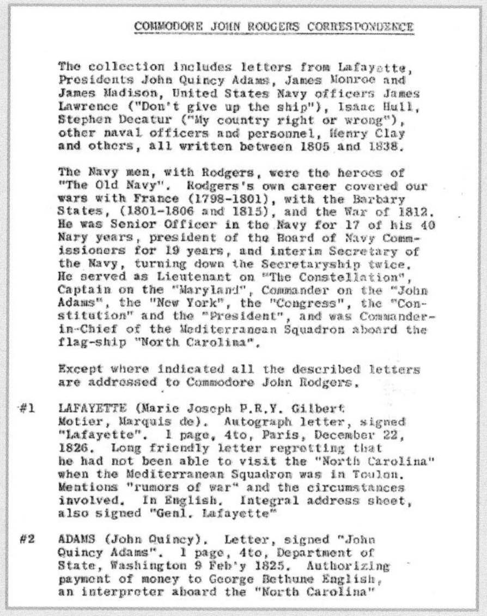

#1 LAFAYETTE (Marie Joseph P.R.Y. Gilbert Motier, Marquis de). Autograph letter, signed "Lafayette". 1 page, 4to, Paris, December 22, 1826. Long friendly letter regretting that he had not been able to visit the "North Carolina" when the Mediterranean Squadron was in Toulon. Mentions "rumors of war" and the circumstances involved. In English, integral address sheet, also signed "Genl. Lafayette"

#2 ADAMS (John Quincy). Letter, signed "John Quincy Adams". 1 page, 4to, Department of State, Washington 9 Feb'y 1825. Authorizing payment of money to George Bethune English, an interpreter aboard the "North Carolina"

Figure 8-22: *Here are two of the letters my father found written to my ancestor Commodore John Rodgers, the first from Lafayette of Revolutionary War fame, and the second from John Quincy Adams, then secretary of state, and the future president, along with the beginning of the appraisal letter.*

Figure 8-23: *There are photos of Commodore Rodgers and his ships on several web sites. Here are two from Wikipedia.*

Figure 8-24: *FindaGrave.com provided several pictures of Commodore Rodgers' grave.*

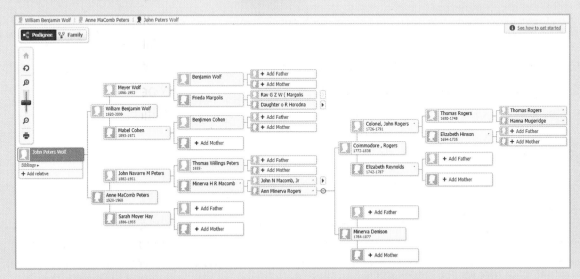

John Navarre Macomb, Jr.

Colonel, United States Army

John Navarre of New York
Appointed from New York, Cadet, United States Military Academy, 1 September 1828 (14)
Brevet Second Lieutenant, 4th United States Artillery, 1 July 1832
Second Lieutenant, 30 September 1833
First Lieutenant, 15 October 1836
First Lieutenant, Topographical Engineers, 7 July 1838
Captain, 4 August 1851
Major, 6 August 1861
Lieutenant Colonel And Assistant Aide-de-Camp, 28 September 1861
Colonel And Additional Aide-de-Camp, 15 May 1862
Honorably mustered out of the U.S. VOlunteers, 31 May 1866
Lieutenant Colonel, Engineers, 3 March 1863
Colonel, 7 March 1867
Retired 30 June 1882
Breveted Colonel, 13 March 1865, for faithful and meritorious services during the war.
Died 16 March 1889

J. N. Macomb, Jr. was a great grandson of Philip Livingston, signer of the Declaration of Independence.

John Navarre Macomb: Died 16 March 1889. Section 1, Grave 75 (right next to Rucker's site). His card says, "Future interment of his daughter Nanny R. Macomb." She was subsequently buried in this grave in 1952.

*Figure 8-25: **The unofficial Arlington Cemetery website proved to be much easier to search than the official site at arlingtoncemetery.mil and provided a lot of information.***

While it is fascinating and fun to research a famous ancestor like Commodore Rodgers, I was also interested in my other ancestors. To that end I looked on the *unofficial* Arlington National Cemetery website (arlingtoncemetery.net) and was able to find my great-great-grandfather Colonel John N. Macomb, Jr., and a lot of information about him and his wife, Ann Rodgers, the daughter of the Commodore, as you see in Figure 8-25.

Aided by search engines, such as FamilySearch.org, I was also able to research my father's family and build a family tree based on his stories and remembrances. See the family tree in Figure 8-26. This was a great surprise to him and a very happy moment before he passed on. Having a way to capture information in a form that is easy to use, save, share, and build upon is a wonderful relief and a lot of fun.

*Figure 8-26: **This family tree brought together all the stories my father had told us, as well as the letters and other items from our ancestors.***

Chapter 9

Getting Around Roadblocks

At some point in your research, you will find you have reached what appears to be a dead end. Perhaps your great-great-grandmother's father is missing, or the courthouse that stored your family's vital records burned down. Whatever the case, these stumbling blocks happen to all family historians. This chapter offers some suggestions to help you regain your "research" footing.

Place Your Ancestors in Context

You may know that your great-great-grandfather was from Ireland or that an ancestor of your mother arrived in Virginia in the 1640s but don't know when or how they arrived or where they were born. Understanding what happened in their birthplace that would cause them to leave their homes to travel across the ocean or join a wagon train to cross the American continent may help solve some of the brick walls you face in your research.

For example, Marty has hit a dead end trying to find one of his great-great-grandfathers. He knows that Riley Matthews (his great-grandfather) was born in about 1830, married Catherine Riddle in 1855, fought in the Civil War, and died in about 1864. However, he cannot find any other records about Riley, including the name of his parents and actual birth and death dates. Considering what was happening in the United States during Riley's lifetime, such as the railroad and telegraph crossing North America, wagon trains carrying settlers "out west," gold discovered in California, and the rift between the states resulting in the Civil War, any of these events, and many local ones, could be the cause of the lack of records for Riley. To circumvent this brick wall, Marty is reviewing possible ancestors of Riley's to "back into" Riley's information. For example, Catherine Riddle's grandfather fought in the Revolutionary War under a Captain Matthews. Riddle and Matthews became friends and moved from Virginia to North Carolina together. Could Captain Matthews be an ancestor of Riley Matthews? So far Marty has not been able to prove it, but it is a possible path for research.

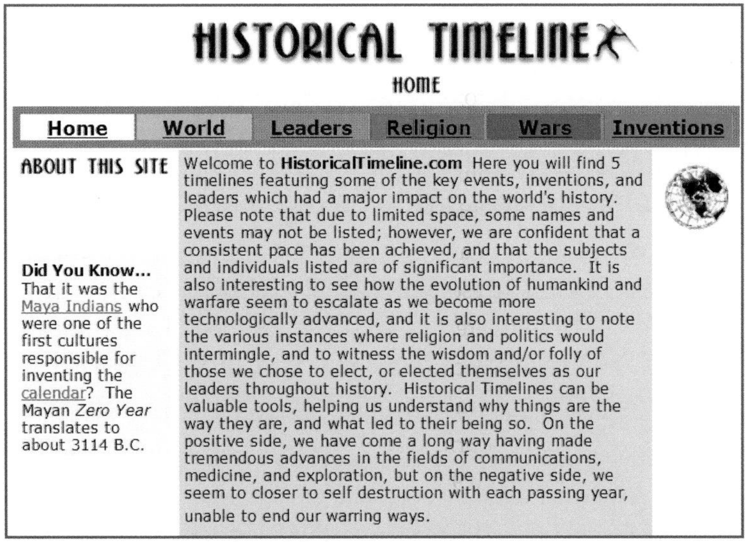

One of the many websites that discuss history, the Historical Timeline (historicaltimeline.com, seen in Figure 9-1), offers some interesting facts and links. Use a search engine to search for other timelines and the historical events that relate to your ancestors.

Once you encounter an obstacle in your research, the first step may be to step back. For what information are you looking? Just where is the roadblock? What are you trying to ascertain? What information have you already gathered? What do you know about the time in which your ancestor lived? Start with each ancestor's file and consider their lifestyle, the times, and places in which they lived. What was their family dynamic? What religious affiliations did the family have?

HISTORICAL TIMELINE
HOME

| Home | World | Leaders | Religion | Wars | Inventions |

ABOUT THIS SITE

Did You Know...
That it was the Maya Indians who were one of the first cultures responsible for inventing the calendar? The Mayan *Zero Year* translates to about 3114 B.C.

Welcome to **HistoricalTimeline.com** Here you will find 5 timelines featuring some of the key events, inventions, and leaders which had a major impact on the world's history. Please note that due to limited space, some names and events may not be listed; however, we are confident that a consistent pace has been achieved, and that the subjects and individuals listed are of significant importance. It is also interesting to see how the evolution of humankind and warfare seem to escalate as we become more technologically advanced, and it is also interesting to note the various instances where religion and politics would intermingle, and to witness the wisdom and/or folly of those we chose to elect, or elected themselves as our leaders throughout history. Historical Timelines can be valuable tools, helping us understand why things are the way they are, and what led to their being so. On the positive side, we have come a long way having made tremendous advances in the fields of communications, medicine, and exploration, but on the negative side, we seem to closer to self destruction with each passing year, unable to end our warring ways.

Figure 9-1: Historical facts can often lead to hints about your ancestors' movements.

9

Recognize Historical and Geographical Context

Many know of the devastation and resulting emigration caused by the mid-19th–century potato famine in Ireland, but did you know that conflict impacted all of the British Isles in the mid-17th century as well? (There is a great website giving an overview of the latter: british-civil-wars.co.uk.) Throughout the 17th, 18th, and 19th centuries, people from many countries came to the "new world" to escape wars, natural disasters, political, and religious persecution. Take the time to study what was occurring in your ancestor's location that may have prompted their decision to come to America. An interesting website that outlines the influx of immigration from the 1500s through modern times can be found at unc.edu/~perreira/198timeline.html, as seen next. Another overview of peoples in the Americas can be found at thesocialcontract.com/artman2/publish/tsc1404/article_1248.shtml.

Immigration Timeline	
The Colonial Era (1565-1775)	The Open Door Era (1776-1881)
The Era of Regulation (1882-1916)	The Era of Restriction (1917-1964)
The Era of Liberalization (1965 – 2000)	The Immigrant Security Era (2001 +)

If you have lost the trail of an ancestor that you suspect came from England, Ireland, or Scotland, consider that they may have been "transports," or indentured servants. Until the Revolutionary War in 1776, many British convicts were punished by transportation to the colonies under the Transportation Act of 1717. Several thousand of our ancestors arrived in this manner. If you suspect your ancestor was one of these "unfortunates," you may start a search at nationalarchives.gov.uk/records/research-guides/transportation-australia.htm. This site references Australia because after the Revolutionary War, the convicts were sent primarily to Australia. Another interesting site is found at yorkcastleprison.org.uk. Limited information about those who were transported is found at that site, as seen in Figure 9-2.

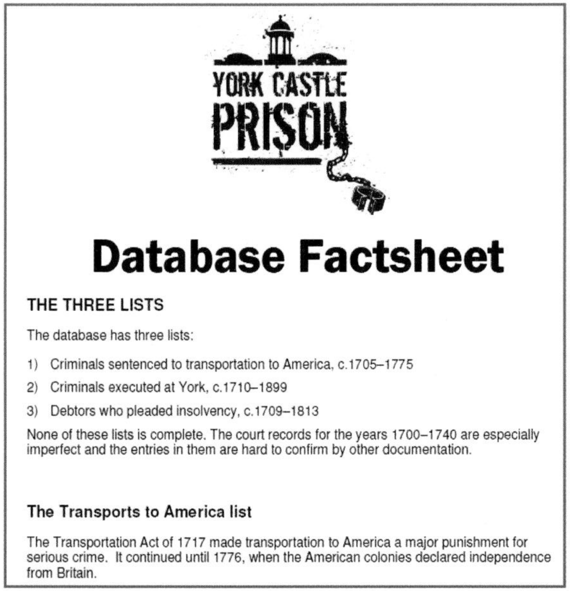

YORK CASTLE PRISON

Database Factsheet

THE THREE LISTS

The database has three lists:

1) Criminals sentenced to transportation to America, c.1705–1775
2) Criminals executed at York, c.1710–1899
3) Debtors who pleaded insolvency, c.1709–1813

None of these lists is complete. The court records for the years 1700–1740 are especially imperfect and the entries in them are hard to confirm by other documentation.

The Transports to America list

The Transportation Act of 1717 made transportation to America a major punishment for serious crime. It continued until 1776, when the American colonies declared independence from Britain.

Figure 9-2: *Many early immigrants did not come of their own volition.*

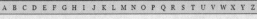

A B C D E F G H I J K L M N O P Q R S T U V W X Y Z

Individual Record

Name
Surname: Inglebold
Given Name: Anna Maria
Soundex Code: I524

Birth, Christening and Other Information
Gender: Female
Orphan: Unknown
Position in Parent's Family: Unknown
Landowner: Unknown
Literate: Unknown
Convict: Unknown

Port of Departure
Town: Rotterdam
County: Zuid-Holland
Nation: Netherlands

Length of Indenture
Year of Indenture: 1773

Place of Indenture
Town: Philadelphia
County: Philadelphia
Colony: Pennsylvania

Agent
Surname: Wallace
Given name: James

Master
Surname: Clark
Given name: Daniel
Title: of Maxfield

Learn More

■ *Find out more* about this immigrant.

■ *Share information* about this immigrant.

■ The *Immigrant Servants Database* is sponsored by **Price and Associates**.

Especially during the 17th and 18th centuries, many English, Irish, German, and Scottish immigrants to North America, were *indentured servants.* Young people would promise to work for a family in the new world for a specific length of time. In turn the family would provide funds for the servants' passage to America and a promise to feed and clothe them until the term of servitude was completed. A great number of websites discuss this practice. Several are listed here:

- academicamerican.com/colonial/topics/colonialintro.html
- history.com/topics/colonial-culture
- www.let.rug.nl/usa/ (www is required)
- immigrantservants.com/search/simple.php

The last site in the list is sponsored by Price and Associates, a professional genealogy firm, and has a list of more than 23,000 names of indentured servants. Access names on that list by entering a name or clicking a letter of the alphabet and clicking **Search**. From the list that appears, select a name to learn more about that person. You may see such information as the ship on which the person arrived, the year they started their indentured service, and the county and colony in which that person lived, as seen next.

LOOK AT GEOGRAPHY'S EFFECT ON EMIGRATION

It was not only political or religious unrest that compelled a move from traditional homelands. Geography impelled emigration as our ancestors learned more information about the Americas. Forsaking crop failures for jobs in newly industrialized cities or leaving snow-piled regions for land in more temperate climates, there were perhaps as many geographical reasons for emigration as there were political. People came to the Americas from nearly every European country, including many Scandinavian countries. These emigrants traveled overland to various European ports to board sailing ships for the long voyage to better land, fertile fields, and a new chance. As seen next, emigration routes varied by country and region, and ships sailed to many American ports.

NOTE

Immigrantservants.com's Learn More link, seen to the right of the name of the individual record, leads to the home site of Price and Associates and offers additional professional research help.

The Journey from Finland to America

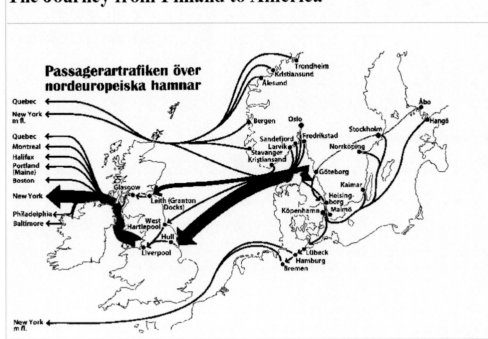

Passagerartrafiken över nordeuropeiska hamnar

As you search for information about your ancestors, perhaps through ships' manifests or other immigration documents, look for names that sound similar to those of your ancestors. As seen in Anne's story later in this chapter, there were many spelling changes, both on the part of the newly arrived immigrant and the hearing or spelling capabilities of those keeping records.

If you find information on a census record, as seen in Figure 9-3, that indicates your ancestor was born in another country and cannot find additional information, consider starting with the outline found at net.lib.byu.edu/ fslab/researchoutlines/NonGeographic/ TracingImmigrantOrigins.pdf. This site provides a step-by-step guide for tracing your immigrant ancestors. It includes suggestions for your search as well as articles, suggestions, links, and other methods of obtaining information about your relatives that were born outside the United States.

CONSIDER THE EFFECT OF THE INDUSTRIAL REVOLUTION

As the Industrial Revolution of the 1800s took firm hold in America, many people immigrated to the United States and Canada for a chance at a better economic life. As foreign immigrants arrived, earlier settlers started moving west for a chance at more land. Land grants and other government programs encouraged this practice. As the United States expanded, the westward-bound wagons carried the knowledge of the new technology with them. Especially after the California Gold Rush in 1849, and railroads and steam engines

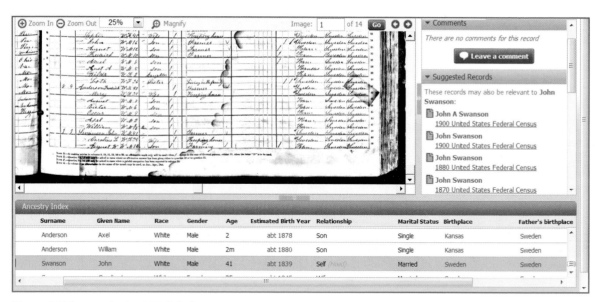

Figure 9-3: *As seen in the 1880 U.S. Census, Bobbi's maternal great-grandfather was born in Sweden.*

became prominent before and after the Civil War, there was a need for people to help build the rails themselves, as well as man the businesses that supported the growth of towns.

On the west coast of what is now the United States, many immigrants from Asia, the Pacific nations, and Russia arrived through Angel Island in San Francisco. While the records are not as complete as found on the Ellis Island website, you can start searching at aiisf.org/history.

Study the Culture Then and Now

From the wealthy Catholic planters that settled Maryland in the 1600s, the Quakers in Pennsylvania, to the English immigrants to New England, a wide variety of cultures and attitudes have prevailed in the "new world." By understanding the cultures and habits of the early settlers you may be able to eliminate some

QUICK**FACTS**

UNDERSTANDING U.S. PASSENGER AND IMMIGRATION LISTS

Many sailing ships that arrived in North America did not maintain consistent passenger or crew lists until a U.S. law was passed in 1819. From that time on ships were required to carry and supply lists of all their passengers. The U.S. Passenger Lists contained each passenger's name, age, gender, occupation, country of origin, country of destination, and whether the passenger survived the journey. Usually, family groups were listed together on the lists. While the National Archives lists are not available online, a list is available on microfilm and CD-ROM for genealogists. Also, Ancestry.com has very extensive passenger lists for Boston, New York, Philadelphia, and New Orleans from 1820 to 1943/5 that can be searched by name or browsed by date and ship name, as shown next.

In addition to the National Archives offices in Washington, D.C., these and other immigration records may be found at National Archives Regional Facilities, LDS Family History Centers, and some public libraries. You can find additional information about these records at archives.gov/research/immigration/passenger-arrival .html. Another useful resource about these records can be found at archives.com/experts/richard-l-diane/how-to-find-immigration-records-passenger-lists-1.html.

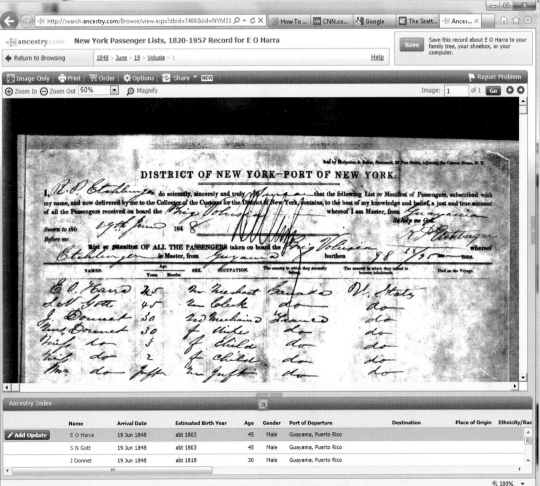

brick walls. For example, when a first husband died and his widow remarried, she would sometimes change the surname of her children to that of her new husband. If you seem to have lost an ancestor in their childhood, consider checking for marriage records of the widow.

QUICKFACTS

TRANSLATING DOCUMENTS

In your research you may find old letters, certificates, legal documents, and even newspaper clippings written in another language. Even documents for English-speaking ancestors, such as birth, marriage, and death records, may have used Latin words. As a first step, consult the Internet. There are websites that provide free translation tools to help decipher a few words, as well as links to professional translators for long letters or legal documents. Several are shown here. And, if you have Microsoft Word on your computer, you have a built-in translation tool.

- In Word 2010, click **Review** and **Translate** as shown.

- In Word 2007, click **Review**, and select **Translate** from the Proofing group.

- In Word 2003, from the menu bar, click **Tools**. Click **Language** and **Translate**.

Free translation tools are also available online. Most limit the number of words that may be entered:

- babelfish.yahoo.com/
- freetranslation.com/
- e-transcriptum.net/

DEAL WITH COMMON TRANSLATION ISSUES

You may encounter some issues when translating from other languages (or even old English) that make translation difficult. For example:

- Abbreviations. As seen in some U.S. Census records and other documents, abbreviations and shortcuts are used in all languages.

- Word meanings that have changed over time. An example is "manufacture," which in earlier times meant made by hand, usually by a craftsman.

Continued . . .

Study old family pictures for clues to celebrations, holy days, and holidays. As many extended families stayed together in the new world, look for old diaries, journals, or family Bibles for mentions of important events.

From your local library, check out books about the ethnicity of your ancestor and study them to find items that coincide with family legends or traditions. How does your family celebrate special events today? Perhaps you may find the tradition dates to similar traditions in another country.

Use the Internet to find sites that may provide information about the ethnic heritage for which you are searching. For example, Bobbi found a resource to help in her search for her maternal great-grandparents at augustana.edu/x13856 .xml. This is a site that maintains information about Swedish immigration as shown next.

TRANSLATING DOCUMENTS (Continued)

- Slang, obscure, archaic, or obsolete terms that have no current counterpart.

- Documents written with poor spelling or no punctuation.

- Illegible handwriting.

Once again, use the Internet as a start in your word search. Look at medievalgenealogy.org.uk/guide/hand.shtml for some useful links.

LOCATE TRANSLATION TOOLS ONLINE

Whether you need to translate just a few words or locate a professional translator, you may want to start online. Listed here are a few websites we found when searching for translation assistance. Most of these links are sponsored by professional fee-based services.

- genealogy.about.com/od/translation

- genealogyblog.com/?p=14956

- genealogysearch.org/free/translation.html

- angelfire.com/ok3/pearlsofwisdom/italian-latin-genealogywords.html

- academic-genealogy.com/foreignlanguagestranslations.htm

- swedenroots.com/

- genealogypro.com/directories/translators.html

Review What You Have Gathered

Review each item you've accumulated. Validate your entries and ensure you haven't made a transposition in dates or entered a relative into the wrong branch of the family. Take the time to carefully re-examine each source you have cited and compare what you found or knew at the time you found the source to what you have learned in the meantime.

Consider creating a timeline for each ancestor's file. Create a form, such as the one seen in Figure 9-4, that includes each event you have discovered for each ancestor. You can include where you obtained the information and any other pertinent comments.

BESSIE (AKA BETSY) JANE WALLACE					
EVENT	DATE	OTHERS NAMES INVOLVED IN SOURCE	RELATIONSHIP TO **BESSIE**	SOURCE	COMMENTS/OTHER
Birth	10 SEP 1849			Birth Certificate photocopy	
Marriage		John Absalom Cornelius	husband		
Census	1866	William Ruthinda	father mother	Census 1870	shown as "Betsy"
Moved	1867	J A Cornelius	husband	Land deed	Homesteaded Pleasant Ridge, Whatcom County (Now Skagit County)
Child	08 AUG 1869	Arthur E. Cornelius	child	Census 1870	no birth certificate found
Child	1870	Nellie Mary Cornelius	child	letter to Ruthinda 1871	
Widowhood	15 FEB 1880			Puget Sound Mail 1880	
Marriage	15 JUL 1882	John Oscar Rudene	husband #2	Puget Sound Mail 1882	
Death	1940			Family journal	

NOTES: Mother = Ruthinda Mounts Wallace
              Father = William Wallace

              Maternal Uncle = James Mounts

*Figure 9-4: **Creating a form for each ancestor can sometimes help identify an ancestor.***

Check Your Sources

What documentation do you have in each ancestor's file? Are the dates of birth, marriage, and death verifiable? Consider the following when reviewing your sources:

- Are they original documents? That is, was the information on the record created at the time of the event (or near the actual time)? Marriage certificates and birth and death certificates that have been created by governmental agencies are usually the best resource. However, if there are no such records available, consider using church records and even family Bibles.

- Are the details reliable? From whom or where did you find the information? Was the document or resource created by someone who witnessed the event or by someone who was told about the event at a later time? If the resource was created by a third party, can a primary source be obtained or viewed?

- When was the information recorded? If the document was created near the event, it may be more accurate than something created months or years later. Our memories do tend to "remember creatively" from time to time.

Most family historians include identification of their sources in their files for future research. See Chapter 6 of this book for more information on how to effectively cite your information. Review the source material to ensure you have not transcribed incorrect information or confused a grandfather with his grandson who bore the same name.

Find Collaborative Information

Collaborative communication is a traditional way of obtaining information. Genealogists often gain much information from working with others. Talk to your family members to see if they know of anyone else within the family who is researching. With the advances in today's communication technology, the world is now available for collaboration. (For information on using groups and social networking for genealogy collaboration, see Chapter 8.)

As you connect with other researchers, determine if their information can verify what you have discovered. They may have found that elusive birth certificate that verifies the date for which you have been searching. You may have a copy of the marriage document they need for their records. As with all resources, original records or certified copies of original records are the best validation.

In addition to message boards, blogs, wikis, online family trees, and other useful tools as discussed in Chapter 8, online genealogy collaboration sites are now available. One of these sites can be found at histopolis.com.

Identify Conflicting Information

Time and distance create genealogy conflicts. One source may show an ancestor's birthplace as "Bigtown," while another source shows that person was born in "Village." Nearly every family historian has encountered this issue. Confusion can arise from the spelling of a family surname or even a given name. Birth dates may differ on baptismal records and a birth certificate issued after the fact. In their records, many family historians note both dates and indicate the source from which both bits of information were obtained.

Some records do not state the exact date (or even year) in which someone was born. For example, records may indicate an approximate date, such as "abt. 1840" for "about 1840" or "c. 1744" for "circa 1744." Other records may simply show a span of time in which an event took place. These records might show information such as "bet. 15 April 1838 and 31 July 1840" indicating that this person was born sometime between April 15, 1838, and July 31, 1840. If you have a baptismal record for that person showing a birth date of 31 August 1839 as well as a birth certificate (issued after the fact) that shows a birth date of 1 August, 1838, you may want to include both sources in your research file.

Information gained from *primary sources* is usually more accurate than data from *secondary sources.* Different documents may be considered both primary and secondary sources, as seen in Table 9-1. Primary sources are those created by *eyewitnesses* to the event at the *time the event occurred.* Family historians should strive to personally view primary sources and record as much information about the source as possible. Secondary sources are records created at a later date, often by a third party who may not know the correct information.

NOTE

Be aware that calendars have changed over the centuries. For example, in 1582 the Julian calendar was changed to the Gregorian calendar by order of Pope Gregory XIII. However, the new calendar dates were not formally adopted by Britain until 1752 or by China until 1949.

DOCUMENT	PRIMARY	SECONDARY
Government-Issued Birth Certificate	Birth date and parents' names	Parents' information as to age or birthplace
Government-Issued Marriage Certificate or License	Marriage date and witness names	Birth dates of husband and/or wife and residence locations
Government-Issued Death Certificate	Death date and location	Age, parent, or spouse information; birthplace of deceased
Tax Roll or Certificate	Land ownership	Residence location
Land Deeds or Documents	Land ownership and, in some localities, proof of residence	Residence location
Church Birth or Baptismal Records	Event date and place, names of parents	
Church Marriage or Death Records	Event date and place, names	Dates of birth, parent information, and prior residence locations
Wills and Probate Records	Evidence of family relationships	
Census Records	Residence and occupation at a specific time and existence of children and others	Birth dates, correct spelling of names
Military Records	Military service information	Dates of birth and residence
Newspaper Notices of Marriage, Birth, or Death (Including Obituaries)	Good for date and place of event	Data other than the event information
Naturalization Record	Event date and place	Dates and location of birth
Information Found Online	Never a primary source	This data simply gives the researcher a starting place to find primary sources.

Table 9-1: *Primary and Secondary Genealogy Source Examples*

Look at Additional Sources

If the record for which you are searching has been destroyed, consider other ways of finding the information. If the birth records in the county courthouse were destroyed in a flood in 1882, for example, consider contacting the parish or church that was in existence at the time to search for a baptismal or confirmation record. Check with local newspapers to see if there were indexes created listing the records that were lost.

If you are looking for a specific name in the United States, check both federal and state census records. Census records usually show the names (although they may be misspelled) of all persons living at that location at the time of the census. If you can find the name of the person you seek but no other information, look for neighbors' names. Then, check the next census for the same information. While it may be that your ancestor had moved (or died), it may also be that the region was renamed and you can find that information in another set of records. Check newspaper and library archives around the time of that census to see if a restructuring occurred.

Look for voting records, land purchases and sales, and probate records to discern additional information. If you are searching for someone in another country, consider reviewing emigration records or ships' manifests. These are usually published in the country's native tongue and will need to be translated. See the QuickFacts "Translating Documents" earlier in this chapter for translation information.

If you know where your ancestor lived and died, consider contacting the cemeteries in the area for information. Most keep records and may have the data you seek. Look for reproductions of old newspapers, such as the one Bobbi found that records the death of her maternal great-grandfather in 1880 seen in Figure 9-5.

Try Alternative Locations

As our ancestors moved about, especially in the United States, records were lost or never created, and we may "lose" a relative as a result. Consider looking in other locations around the last known residence. For example, as our country grew, territories were granted statehood, boundaries were changed, and other such political events affected recordkeeping. In one document she

NOTE

The PERiodical Source Index, or "PERSI," available through the Allen County Public Library in Fort Wayne, Indiana, contains more than 6,000 genealogy and history publications. Part of your family's history may already have been published by another historian. This resource is available on CD-ROM and through many public libraries.

Puget Sound Mail

Successor to The Bellingham Bay Mail

La Conner, Washington Territory

Death of John A. CORNELIUS.

On last Saturday morning (Feb. 15, 1880) John A. CORNELIUS, one of the most worthy and respected citizens of Whatcom County, departed this life after a painful and lingering illness, at his home at Pleasant Ridge, which he located and established some thirteen years ago. His funeral took place on Tuesday, and his remains were followed to the little cemetery on the Ridge by a host of friends and neighbors . . . Deceased was about forty years of age, a native of Oregon, and leaves a wife and three children to mourn his sad demise.

Figure 9-5: *Use newspaper archives as stepping stones to locating ancestor information.*

USING DNA TO SOLVE THE MYSTERY

The genome project begun in the 1970s and 1980s has become part of our culture. DNA testing, shown on nearly every crime show on television, is now being used to determine kinship by genealogists. Since DNA is passed through generations, relationship can be established in certain cases.

There are two types of tests currently being performed for this purpose: the Y-line test, which establishes family ties between males, and the mtDNA test, which matches both males and females. Since the mtDNA (mitochondrial DNA) is passed by one's mother, a match can mean that at one point in time, the testees had a common maternal ancestor.

DNA cannot help you with the names of your ancestors, but it can

- Prove the research you've done on your family tree
- Provide information about your ethnic origin
- Determine if you are related to others with the same last name
- Determine if two testees are related or descended from a common ancestor

found, Bobbi's great-grandfather is shown to be born in Oregon, although other documents show his birthplace as Washington Territory. Since what is now the state of Washington was originally part of Oregon Territory, that is not surprising. Finding the birth certificate for this man has been a challenge for her, as his exact date and place of birth are not known.

Look at old maps and gazetteers for names and boundary lines of towns and villages. Look for alternative spellings or names. For example, New York City was called "Mannahatta" by the Native Americans, and then named "New Amsterdam" by the Dutch settlers. The name was changed to "New York" in 1664 when the Duke of York established ownership of the territory.

Consult the libraries and archives in the region where you lost track of your ancestor to see if there were natural disasters or political changes that changed the topography or place names. For example, when the Shasta Dam was built in California in 1937, the small town of Kennett was flooded. Another example is the destruction of Valdez, Alaska, during the earthquake of 1964 and resulting tsunami. While the town was rebuilt nearby and renamed "New Valdez," the original town was abandoned.

Consider Alternative Ancestors

If your search for one ancestor has created a roadblock, considering researching another ancestor, such as the ancestor's brother or cousin. This trail may be the link that leads back to the ancestor you've "lost." Contact other family members to see if they have information on this "alternative" ancestor or if they know of others who have researched that person.

Try Alternative Times

If you are unable to locate a specific ancestor in a specific time period, consider looking at different times. For example, in Becky's story in Chapter 7 of this book, she discussed her research on a relative that she thought fought in the Civil War. After doing more research, she discovered the relative had actually fought in the War of 1812, 50 years earlier than what she had believed.

Items

World War I Draft Registration Card

The information included on each World War I Draft Registration Card (WWI) can differ somewhat but the general information shown includes order and serial numbers (assigned by the Selective Service System), full name, date and place of birth, race, citizenship, occupation, personal description, and signature. It is important to note that not all of the men who registered for the draft actually served in the military and not all men who served in the military registered for the draft.

Fee (includes shipping & handling): $5.00

FAQs   ◀ **1 - 5 of 5** ▶

What are WWI Draft Registration Cards?

Who would have registered?

What information is included on the cards?

What formats are reproductions available in?

What if I don't have all the information requested?

If you do have a military ancestor, the National Archives has draft records for Civil War Union soldiers, as well as extensive records for World War I. You can even order copies of the World War I draft registration cards online, as seen next. While there was no draft for either the War of 1812 or the Spanish American War in 1898, you can find military records for both conflicts in the National Archives.

USE PHOTOGRAPHS TO DETERMINE THE TIME PERIOD

Another method of determining time is by using old photographs. The clothes and hairstyles of the people in the photograph, as well as the photograph type itself, can help determine the time period in which the picture was taken. Until about the 1920s, photographs were expensive and considered quite solemn occasions, which may be why so many formal photographs from earlier times show such serious expressions.

- **Daguerreotypes**   Invented in 1839 by Louis Daguerre, these images were featured on a highly polished silver foil sheet backed by a copper sheet that made the image look like a mirror.

- **Ambrotypes**   Often found in leather holders, these were taken from 1856 to about 1860. These were images affixed to glass.

- **Tintypes**   Also known as ferrotypes, tintypes came into vogue during the Civil War. Often pictures taken during the war were decorated with patriotic symbols, such as flags. These images were printed on tin rather than the glass of the earlier ambrotypes.

- **Brown tintypes**   These came into being in 1870 when a process was developed that added the sepia or brown tone to the finished photograph. At about this same time, some photographers were adding scenic backgrounds that would display behind the subjects.

- **Cabinet cards**   These items were popular from about 1866 to 1890. These photos were mounted on a piece of cardstock and often contained the name of the photographer at the bottom of the portrait.

For more information about types of photographs and the time periods in which they were popular, go to the following websites:

- genealogy.com/73_taylor.html

- familychronicle.com/dating.html

- vintagephoto.com/reference/dating.html

VIEW FASHIONS TO DATE A PHOTOGRAPH

It is not just within the 21st century that fashion changes rapidly. If you look at family photos, you can often tell the time period by what people are wearing, their expressions, and even the background of the photograph. For example, Figure 9-6 is a picture of Bobbi's maternal grandmother taken in about 1899 on the steps of what is now Stanford University. Of the many sites online that give information about fashion, here are several that discuss dating photographs by the clothes being worn:

- uvm.edu/landscape/dating/clothing_and_hair/index.php
- photosmadeperfect.com/Photo Dating Page Top pg/AAPhoto Dating Fashion History.htm
- webyfl.com/researchingoldphotographs.aspx

Try Alternative Spellings

Perhaps more than any other issue, different spellings can lead to genealogy stone walls. There are many reasons for different spellings:

- **Simplification**   Many immigrants to the United States changed their names to make the name easier to spell or pronounce in English.
- **Mispronunciation**   If the owner of a name pronounced it with a strong accent or the hearer did not hear the name correctly, it would often be recorded incorrectly in the records.
- **Fear of retaliation or discrimination**   If the surname was connected to an enemy or a group subject to discrimination, names were often changed to conceal this fact.
- **Illiteracy**   Many people coming to a new country could not read, write, or spell their names. Many officials hearing the name would write it down phonetically.
- **Different alphabets**   Immigrants, especially those coming to North America, often came from countries that used different alphabets. Names were Anglicized based on the pronunciation rather than the original spelling.

To find other possible spellings, consider the following workarounds:

- Say the name out loud. By pronouncing the name, you may "hear" it differently. In the 1860 Census Marty's great-grandmother and great-grandfather's surname, Matthews, was listed as "Mathis."

Figure 9-6: **You can often date a photograph by the clothes being worn.**

- Try spelling the name phonetically. Children are especially good at this, and they'll love you for asking their help!

- Add or subtract a letter. MacGregor, McGregor, and MackGreger are all possibilities for the same name. Often names have silent letters; try subtracting that "silent Y" or changing the "Y" to an "I."

- Consider the difference if letters were transposed. Whether writing or typing, mistakes happen. Sometimes the "ei" of a name was actually "ie."

- Add or subtract an "s." One of Bobbi's lines has the surname of Mounts. She has found a number of records that indicate the last name is singular—"Mount"—rather than the plural "Mounts."

- The handwriting on many old records in any language is often difficult to discern. Try using a "G" instead of a "C" or "W" for a "V" or a "U."

- Your ancestor may have changed his name deliberately. Consider reviewing all of your researched relatives for that line to see if there are any similar-sounding names.

Review Biographies

An often over-looked resource for scaling genealogy brick walls is biographies of others who lived at the time of your ancestor. Many biographies contain historical and geographical information as well as names of other people who were part of the subject's life. There is a website found at geneabios.com in which you can search for a surname to see if there are any matches. Bobbi found an ancestor who died in 1816 on this site as shown here.

Biography of

William Wallace of Pawlet, VT

Pawlet (VT) One Hundred Years
Hiel Hollister
1867
J. Munsell, Albany

WALLACE, WILLIAM, married a sister of Deacon Penfield, and settled near the base of the hill north of the village. We have often heard him highly spoken of. He died in 1816, aged 46; his wife in 1835, aged 59. His family have all left town.

With your Ancestry.com subscription, you have access to the American Genealogical-Biographical Index. Access this site at search.ancestry.com/search/db.aspx?dbid=3599. Also, on Ancestry.com you can search the Biography & Genealogy Master Index at search.ancestry.com/search/db.aspx?dbid=4394. Your local library may also provide access to these and other biographical databases and indexes to aid you in your search.

USING GENEALOGY NUMBERING SYSTEMS

Consider using a numbering system so that you don't confuse generations. For example, in many families, descendants named their children after their own mother or father. Say the father Joseph (b 1829) had two sons, Joseph, Jr.(b 1853) and Thomas (b 1855). Thomas and his wife Helen named their first son Joseph (b 1878). When Joseph, Jr. and his wife Sally had their first son in 1880, they also named him Joseph. Unless you have solid documentation about the births and marriages, it might be very easy to confuse all the Josephs. See Chapter 1 of this book for more information on verifying your sources.

There are many genealogy numbering systems in use today. Most use a combination of numbers and/or letters to indicate generations and birth order. Some systems start with you, the subject, and work backward. This type of system is known as the *ascending* method. *Descending* systems start with the oldest known ancestor and work forward. You can learn each method from the following links:

- eogen.com/_Search?q=numbering+systems
- genealogyandfamilyhistory.com/?p=58
- acorn.net/gen/numbering.html
- wikia.com/wiki/Genealogical_numbering_systems

Consult or Hire Professional Genealogists

Much of the excitement and fun of researching your family's history is in finding that elusive bit of information that "grafts" a branch of your family tree. However, there may be times that, try as you might, you cannot find the uncle who moved "out West" in 1830 or the great-great-aunt who was mentioned in several of your grandmother's letters to her sister. Fortunately, for those times, there are professionals whom you can hire to help get past the roadblocks.

There are a number of professional organizations within the United States and throughout the world by which a genealogist may be certified. Before you contact a professional, consider the following:

- What specific information do you want the researcher to find?
- What information can you give the researcher that you already have verified?
- What is your monetary limit?
- What is the ultimate goal in seeking the help of the professional?

COMPARE CERTIFIED GENEALOGIST CRITERIA

As mentioned, there are professional organizations from which you can contact a professional researcher. Each group has slightly different requirements for their members.

- **Association of Professional Genealogists** You may access their website at apgen .org. While they have no testing process, each member must adhere to a professional genealogist's code.

- **Board for Certification of Genealogists** This group screens, tests, and certifies genealogists in the United States, the British Isles, Canada, and Europe. There are six certification categories provided by this group. After passing the tests, researchers must renew their application every five years and agree to adhere to the Genealogists Code of Ethics. See bcgcertification.org. Click **Find A Genealogist** to search for a certified researcher, as seen in Figure 9-7.

- **The International Commission for the Accreditation of Professional Genealogists** Go to icapgen.org to access this group, recommended by Family Search.org. This group's stringent four-part certification process includes testing, screening, and credential renewal every five years.

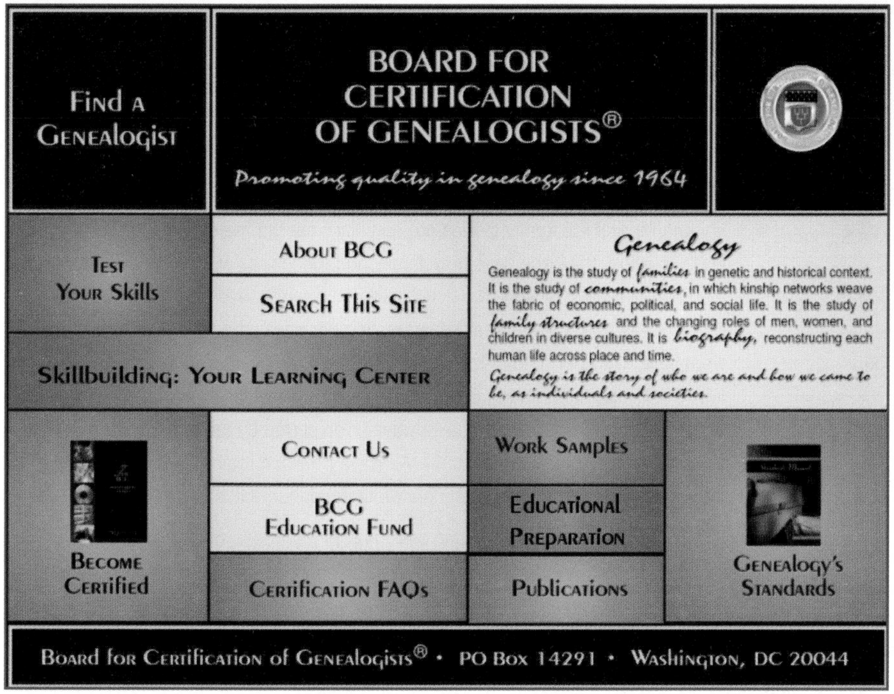

*Figure 9-7: **Professional genealogists can help clear researching "brick walls."***

WORK WITH A PROFESSIONAL

After you have identified the information you want and contacted a professional, ensure that both parties understand what is sought. Ask for a written proposal from the professional that outlines estimated hours; costs per hour; and any additional costs, such as mileage, travel, lodging, photocopying, and/or transcription or translation fees. Ask for at least three references and a copy of a sample final report that is similar in scope to the services you want performed.

Email or call the professional with any questions or concerns. Once you have both agreed on the job, get a written contract that states all of the information you have both agreed upon. If the job requires specific steps, ensure that those achievements are referenced in the contract. Specifically ask for weekly or monthly status reports that include what has been accomplished, what has been achieved, and what is left to conclude the arrangement.

When the job is done, carefully review the report submitted by the professional. Ensure that each of the findings are well documented and are cited in proper form. Write down any questions and plan a final meeting with the researcher. During this final meeting, you may find that there are leads generated by the research that were not a part of the final report that may help you in further research.

Anne Colligan, 68, Coupeville, WA

OVERVIEW

I have made the most progress in my mother's ancestry. The Schürch line, my mother's paternal line, has been researched back 14 generations to the birth of Hans Schürch in Switzerland. The Burnham branch, my mother's maternal line, goes back 13 generations to the birth of John Burnham in 1617 in Norwich, Norfolk County, England. At the current time, I've only been able to go back three generations in my father's (Nichols) family. The Schürch family has periodic reunions, and there is a Schürch family newsletter that continues to update all of us on newer research. To date, I've not used genealogy software, as I have so much information on paper.

STORY

It seems like all of my life I've heard stories about our family. The Schürch family (and its many Anglicized spellings) originally came to America from Switzerland, and at last count (as my mother said) there were 43 ways to spell our name. From Shirk to Sherrick and from Schörg to Sherch, all of these names have been part of my history. When I was young, the mere numbers fascinated me. At a family reunion in 1986, a relation created the graphic seen in Figure 9-8 that included all of the variations of our family name.

*Figure 9-8: **There are at least 43 ways to spell our family name, and each branch has a wealth of stories.***

I was born Pricilla Anne Nichols in Reedsburg, Wisconsin. My mother, Dorothy Shirk (the 11th-generation Schürch) was born in New Preston, Connecticut, 29 Mar 1909. My father, Milton Elmer Nichols, a pharmacist, was born 17 Mar 1902 in Oconto, Wisconsin.

My mother and the family stories are actually what got me started in genealogy. Hearing about the early days from family and friends, as well as the pictures and mementos, made me feel so much a part of the family, even the ones I'd never met. I guess that one of the most interesting parts was the thought that my family went back five or six centuries. My mother had a family tree about the Schürch family in Switzerland dating to the first known ancestor, Hans Schürch, who was born in 1550. My imagination has always been stirred by the thought of belonging to such a large, international family. We have now documented our family for 14 generations. The first page of the generational document is shown in Figure 9-9.

One of the family stories has long been part of my treasures. As Mennonites, many of the Schürch family started immigrating to America in the 1700s. Among one of the first Schürch children born in the United States was Joseph Shirk (Schürch). He was born in 1820 and died in 1902. With only a few years of formal education he became a well-recognized scientist and surveyor, creating his own precision instruments. Figure 9-10 is part of a story that was transcribed by my mother describing one of his inventions being used in both France and India. His story is even found on the Internet at gameo.org/encyclopedia/contents/shirk_joseph_s._1820_1902.

GETTING STARTED

It seems that there really was no "getting started place" for me, just a continuation. My mother's family was very well documented on both her maternal and paternal lines. My maternal grandmother was Laura Patterson Burnham who was born in Gotham, Wisconsin, in 1874. My maternal grandfather was Michael Martin Shirk, born 12 Jun 1875 in Dixon, Illinois. I never knew my Grandfather Shirk, as he died in 1940, before I was born. My maternal grandmother, whose picture is shown on the next page, had a much different life than that of her siblings. She was one of six children whose mother died when Laura was about 12. Because my grandmother's name was the same as his mother's name, Laura's uncle, Walter Burnham, selected her to live with him in New Preston, Connecticut.

Descendants of Hans Schurch

Generation No. 1

1. HANS[1] SCHURCH was born Bet. 1550 - 1570 in Switzerland. He married VERENA SCHNEIDER.

More About HANS SCHURCH:
Residence: Bef. 1610, Moved from Sumiswald to Walterwil, Switzerland

Child of HANS SCHURCH and VERENA SCHNEIDER is:
2.   i.   CASPER[2] SCHURCH, b. Bet. 1570 - 1590.

Generation No. 2

2. CASPER[2] SCHURCH (*HANS[1]*) was born Bet. 1570 - 1590. He married MARGARET TRUSSEL Abt. 1610.

Child of CASPER SCHURCH and MARGARET TRUSSEL is:
3.   i.   ULRICH[3] SCHURCH, b. June 19, 1614.

Generation No. 3

3. ULRICH[3] SCHURCH (*CASPER[2], HANS[1]*) was born June 19, 1614. He married BARBARA KUPFERSCHMID Abt. 1635. She was born February 06, 1613/14.

Child of ULRICH SCHURCH and BARBARA KUPFERSCHMID is:
4.   i.   PETER[4] SCHURCH, b. October 16, 1639.

Generation No. 4

4. PETER[4] SCHURCH (*ULRICH[3], CASPER[2], HANS[1]*) was born October 16, 1639. He married (1) ANNA REINHARD. He married (2) VERENA EGGIMAN.

Child of PETER SCHURCH and ANNA REINHARD is:
5.   i.   JACOB[5] SCHURCH, b. May 20, 1660.

Generation No. 5

5. JACOB[5] SCHURCH (*PETER[4], ULRICH[3], CASPER[2], HANS[1]*) was born May 20, 1660. He married (1) ?. He married (2) ?. He married (3) BARBARA BRAND.

Child of JACOB SCHURCH and BARBARA BRAND is:
6.   i.   ULRICH[6] SCHURCH, b. July 22, 1703.

Generation No. 6

6. ULRICH[6] SCHURCH (*JACOB[5], PETER[4], ULRICH[3], CASPER[2], HANS[1]*) was born July 22, 1703. He married MARIA GRUNDBACH November 19, 1730.

More About ULRICH SCHURCH:
Immigration: 1752, Sumiswald-Bern Canton-Switzerland

Child of ULRICH SCHURCH and MARIA GRUNDBACH is:

1

Figure 9-9: **Fourteen generations of the Schürch family are now known.**

Uncle Walter was very well-to-do and sent her to finishing school in true Victorian fashion. After she married my grandfather, the uncle left all of his fine Victorian furniture to her. I grew up with the furniture, and while all of the pieces are

The Shirk cradles were so balanced that one could give them the necessary swing from right to left, holding the snath in the left hand and the nib with one finger of the right hand without the point of the scythe seeking contact with the ground, the sawed ash fingers retaining perfect alignment under all conditions.

In European countries the grain cradle is still standard equipment. An interesting story was brought back from France by a member of the A. E. F., a native of Lancaster County. When quartered in Flanders, he saw hanging among the farming equipment, where he was stopping, a grain cradle which to him, seemed like meeting an old friend from home, for on the pole were branded the familiar words, "Joseph Shirk, Spring Grove, Pa. U.S.A."

A missionary from faraway India, on returning to his field of labor after a visit to his native Pennsylvania, took with him a Shirk cradle and introduced it to the rice-growing districts there. The natives were greatly astonished at it but, to their regret, had to discard it because the rice in that district ripened very unevenly and the cradle failed to discriminate between the grain already ripe and that still green—a condition handled successfully only by tediously sorting it out in little bunches and cutting it with a sickle.

The invention of the cradle by increasing man power at harvesttime gave a great impetus to grain growing and paved the way for mass production of all kinds of small grain, and great and mighty feats of harvesting were recorded, the greatest of which was made by Michael Cromer[1] of near Mercersburg, who cradled in two hours, between sunrise and sunset, twelve and a half acres of wheat.

Although Joseph Shirk gave to humanity a number of inventions, any one of

Figure 9-10: **My ancestor, Joseph Shirk, became well known as an innovator and inventor.**

special, a wide, low chair covered in petit-point is one of my favorites. I still have that chair, and Figure 9-11 shows my brother and me sitting for a formal "portrait" in our finest clothes. You can tell the child on the right is me because of the hair ribbon mother always kept in my hair.

One of my treasured heirlooms is a hand-woven sheet made from flax. My maternal great-great-grandmother, Laura Patterson Burnham, grew the flax on their farm and prepared, spun, and wove the flax into the sheet shown in Figure 9-12. It is now more than 100 years old and is still strong and soft.

Figure 9-13 is a picture of Laura Patterson Burnham and Daniel Burnham's tombstone. Another one of my treasures (which did not scan in very well) is a

Figure 9-11: *Anne and Andy sat in Grandma Burnham Shirk's chair for their first formal portrait.*

Figure 9-12: *I can only imagine the time it took to create this sheet from the flax grown by my great-great-grandmother.*

poem written by my great-great-uncle (another) Walter Burnham in 1853 while he was courting his wife, Edna. The life led by my ancestors has always seemed more gentle and kind than what is in my life today. I have leather-bound books of pictures and stories, as shown next, that seem to reflect a quieter and more peaceful time. Perhaps the lack of electricity and its accompanying noise are what draws me to thinking their lives were more peaceful.

Figure 9-13: *Laura and Daniel Burnham's tombstone includes information on one of their daughters as well as their own information.*

However, now that I think about it, it is just that electrical capability that has ensured an even deeper connection for me to my relatives now passed on. My parents had been taking family movies for as long as anyone could remember. On them, I can see my Grandfather Shirk and other relatives I never got to meet. The way these pictures connect me to my family is amazing! For example, how many children got to see their own christening or their own first birthdays before the age of video cams and cell phones?

Then, around 1940, my great-uncle, Charlie Burnham, who worked for a newspaper, had access to equipment that could record sound onto 78 rpm vinyl disks. One recording that is particularly poignant for me was taped during my brother Robert's seventh birthday party. The recording was done in June before my twin brother, Andy and I were born in October, at the height of World War II. On it, I hear my brother and cousins sing patriotic songs such as "America the Beautiful" and "This Is the Army, Mr. Jones." Hearing them, even now, makes my heart so happy. My other brother, John, was not quite three years old and sang "Christmas Is Coming." I've never really understood the significance of a Christmas song being sung in the middle of June, but it still makes me smile.

Being able to see and hear my family members, I feel connected in a way that still photographs and words on a page can only imitate. My brother has now transferred these audio tapes and movies onto CD-ROMs and distributed them to all the family.

CHALLENGES

My next challenge, as time permits, is finding out information about the Nichols family. My father's father died when he was two, and his mother remarried. According to what my father reluctantly shared later, life with his stepfather and stepsiblings was difficult. I do have a picture of my father in his mother's arms, as seen in Figure 9-14. This must have been taken shortly before his father died.

Figure 9-14: Anne Nichols, holding Milton Elmer Nichols, taken in 1902.

OBJECTIVES

My objectives are learning more about the family, especially my father's line. My brother continues to be the keeper of the genealogy records for the family as I work on other projects. My long-term goal is to preserve the information and stories and share them with nieces, nephews, grandnieces, and grandnephews so they, too, can know the feeling of being part of a warm and loving family. That sense of connection is much too valuable to release.

An example of this connection is a cookbook compiled by a distant relation. On one of the pages she included a word portrait, shown next, about the Schürch grandmothers all over the world. While it focused on the Schürch family, it could be the story of all grandmothers and great-grandmothers throughout the world.

Grandma Sherk——A Portrait
by
Ron and Mary Lou Sherk

Grandma Sherk (Shirk, Schurch, Sherrick, or any one of the other forty-plus spellings) probably had a Swiss Mennonite maiden name. She may well have been an Eby, Stauffer, Wenger, Meyers, Brand, Berg, Strickler, Hershey, Tschantz, Schnaebel, Brake, Martin, Kauffman, Hunsicker, or Musser before she married.

Her great (or great great) grandmother undoubtedly grew up in a small Swiss village in Canton (province) Bern. It could have been Heimiswil, Burgdorf, or Sumiswald——in the Emmental region, which is renowned for its Swiss cheese and chocolate.

Those same meticulously maintained villages survive today surrounded by small farms where houses are built in the same architectural style as three hundred years ago. Today in Canton Bern, although there are no Mennonites left, one finds farms owned by Schürchs for centuries.

How to...

- *Review Your Progress*
- *Assure Sources*
- *Sourcing Your Genealogy*
- *Prepare and Back Up Your Information*
- *Publish Your Information*
- *Printing in Family Tree Maker*
- *Create a Home Page on Genealogy.com*
- *Use Web Space on RootsWeb.com*

Chapter 10

Pulling It All Together

For many people, a major reason for studying genealogy is to leave a family history for their children and descendants. This can take many forms, from hardcover books to notes, and computer files and websites to email. In the genealogy story in this chapter, Harriet De Wolfe talks about writing and publishing a book on one part of her ancestry. Whatever form yours takes, you probably want it to be as complete and accurate as your time and budget allow. In this chapter we'll look at how to review what you have and determine if it is at the point where you want to at least preserve and possibly publish it. Then we'll look at the options you have for both preserving and publishing, and finally how to create a simple website for your family history.

Evaluate What You Have

Throughout the process of researching your ancestry you should be constantly reviewing both how to extend your ancestry backward and how to assure that it is accurate and has adequate source citations.

Review Your Progress

How much is enough? When do you stop? There is, of course, no one answer to those questions for everybody. Some people have been able to follow their ancestors back before the start of the Christian era. Others have put together a fascinating ancestral story in the last hundred years, or even more recent times. The key is your objectives; what would you like to accomplish? Also, how much time and money do you want to spend on it, and when do you want to at least pause, if not quit altogether? In this chapter's genealogy story, Harriet De Wolfe has spent over 30 years researching her family with many trips and much time spent in libraries and other historical facilities, and has chosen to write about a 50-year period of one part of her family in the early 1800s—a fascinating story.

For you to determine what is enough, you have to answer the following questions:

- What is your objective? What is it that you want to find out about your ancestors?
- How much time, both overall and in any one period, do you want to dedicate to your research?
- Can you travel to libraries and other historical repositories and to your ancestral locations and/or hire others to give you advice and/or do research for you?
- How many dead ends and unknowns or questionable links are you willing to accept?
- How much detail and background around your ancestors' lives do you want to add?
- Do you have or can you get others to help you in your research, and what are their objectives?
- What is it that you want to produce: a simple pedigree chart, a detailed genealogy, a family narrative, or a detailed family history?

REVIEW YOUR OBJECTIVES

Write down each of your objectives in clear simple terms, and then for each objective answer the following:

- Have you accomplished the objective, and are you satisfied with it?
- How far have you gotten in accomplishing your objective? Is it far enough?
- If you have not fully accomplished your objective, do you want to continue to work on it?
- How likely is it that you can overcome any roadblocks in the near term?
- How realistic is the objective now that you have worked for some time on it? Do you want to change it? How does that affect the objective's accomplishment?
- How important is the objective? Prioritize your objectives and note where each objective is in the priority list.

Summarize this analysis of your objectives and answer whether you have accomplished enough of your objectives to at least pause and consider publishing your results.

CONSIDER YOUR RESOURCES

Everybody has some limitations on the resources that they have available to them in their genealogy research. You need to evaluate the time, money, travel, and colleague help against the needs required for further research, and determine whether you can continue or need to stop.

EVALUATE ROADBLOCKS AND DEAD ENDS

Look at each of the places in your ancestry where you cannot go further, either because you cannot locate a person's parents or a previous ancestor's children. Look at what you have done to locate those missing links. What more could possibly be done? For example:

- Are there living relatives you could contact who might have information?
- Are there websites you haven't searched?
- Have you tried a DNA search?
- Are there libraries, courthouses, and/or cemeteries that you might search?

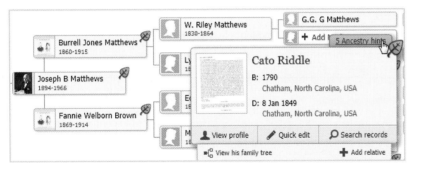

- Are there local genealogy societies and clubs you could contact?
- Have you considered contacting a genealogy volunteer or hiring a professional genealogist?

If you are using Ancestry.com, make sure you have looked at all the hints that the site provides.

1. In your family tree on Ancestry.com, hover over a person with a hint (a leaf in the upper-right corner) and click the **Ancestry Hints** in the upper-right area of the expanded detail that appears.

2. In the list of hints that opens (see Figure 10-1), click **Review Hint** for each one. Consider the hints that are displayed, select the ones that you want to use, and click **Review Selected Hints**.

3. Compare the people and events that are displayed, select the ones you want to add to your tree, and click **Save To Your Tree**.

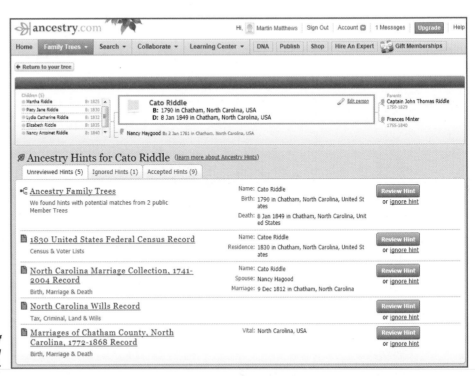

Figure 10-1: Ancestry provides a number of hints for adding to your family tree, but you have to be selective in what you actually add.

DETERMINE IF YOU ARE AT A BREAK POINT

One can always doggedly go on. There is always another ancestor to research or the possibility that another website, library, book, club, or professional genealogist can provide the clue you need to extend an ancestral line. You need to determine how likely it is you will find another clue, how valuable it would be, and what the resource cost would be. Based on that, determine if you want to break and publish what you have or continue on.

Assure Sources

Once you have decided that you have gotten all the ancestors you want at a point in time, you need to go over what you have on each ancestor and make sure it is as accurate as possible. The best way to assure yourself that the information is accurate is to have two or more corroborating sources of information for each person and each event (birth, marriage, military service, residence, and death) and each linkage, parent to child *and* that the sources are themselves solid and verifiable (see the "Sourcing Your Genealogy" QuickSteps in this chapter). Granted, this may be very difficult, if not impossible, but that should be your goal.

There are many sources of information, including

- Census data
- Government birth, death, and marriage records
- Church birth, death, and marriage records
- Family Bibles
- Military records
- Property grants, sales, and deeds
- Tax records
- Wills

- Other legal documents
- Tombstones and cemetery records
- Court transcripts
- Newspapers, magazines, and newsletters
- Drawings, paintings, and photographs
- Written family history, including letters, notes, pamphlets, and books
- Recorded oral family history

Of course, not all of these sources are of equal credibility, but don't totally discount any of them either. If nothing else, they provide clues. Census data, on which so much of genealogy is dependent, is notorious for problems and inaccuracies, yet it is invaluable.

Ancestry.com and other genealogy websites provide some source information as you locate events for your ancestors. On Ancestry:

1. Hover over a person on your family tree, and click **View Profile** to open the detailed information for that person as shown in Figure 10-2.

2. Under the Timeline are listed the events for that person. Opposite each event is listed the number of source citations. Click that number to see the specific source.

3. Click a specific source to open its detailed information, as you see in Figure 10-3.

Figure 10-2: Ancestry will add the relevant source information to your tree when you add an event you locate on Ancestry.

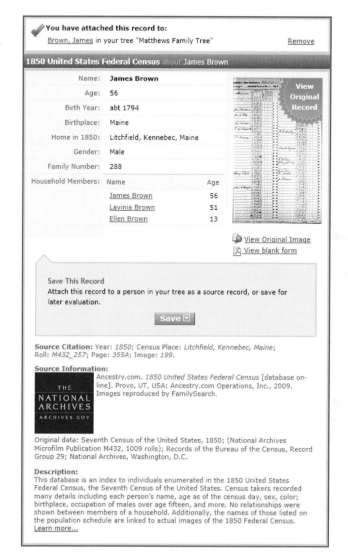

UICKSTEPS

SOURCING YOUR GENEALOGY

As you are researching your ancestry you will come across records that help you verify and even pinpoint events in your ancestor's life. These records are the *sources* of your information and become important to prove to yourself and to others that the events actually happened. Keeping track of your sources, known as *source citations,* are as important as keeping track of the event itself. Often, while researching, you'll find conflicts in the information you turn up that will make you and others studying your work want to know the source. Having source citations provides that information. They also allow you and others to easily return to the source to possibly find additional information.

When you get event information (such as for birth, marriage, immigration, or death) from Ancestry and some other sites, you will often get source information with it. But as you go beyond the genealogy websites to books, libraries, cemeteries, and museums for your information, you will need to add your own sourcing. Within Ancestry .com, Family Tree Maker, Legacy, and other websites and programs, templates are displayed for creating a source and the source citation. In documentation outside of an established program, the best practice is to use the standard source citation format.

CREATE A SOURCE CITATION IN ANCESTRY

To add an event, its source, and the source citation to Ancestry:

1. In your family tree, hover over the person to whom you want to add an event and a source, and click **View Profile**.

Continued . . .

Figure 10-3: The source information is very detailed for information found on Ancestry.

SOURCING YOUR GENEALOGY

(Continued)

2. At the bottom of the Timeline, click **+Add A Fact**, click the **Add A New Fact Or Event** down arrow, and click the event.

3. Fill in the information on the event, and click **Submit**.

4. Back in the Timeline, click the event, click **Source Citations**, and click **+Add A Source Citation**. The Create Source Citation page will open, as you can see in Figure 10-4.

5. Click the **Select A Source** down arrow, and see if your source is on the list (if it is, it likely will be added automatically); otherwise, click **Create A New Source** to open that page, shown in Figure 10-5.

6. Fill in the information for the source, and click **Save Source**. Then fill in the information for the source citation, and click **Save Source Citation**.

CREATE A SOURCE CITATION ON YOUR OWN

If you want to add a source citation for another document that does not have a template for that purpose, the best procedure is to use the same fields that are in the Ancestry templates and shown in Figures 10-4 and 10-5. There is an excellent discussion on Genealogy.com entitled "How To Cite Sources" by John Wylie. Go to genealogy.com/19_wylie.html. Also, see the section in Chapter 6 on citing your sources.

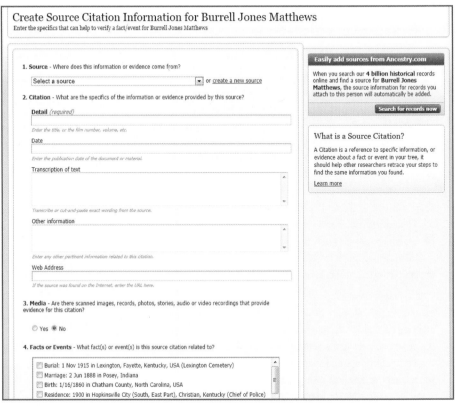

Figure 10-4: *A source is a document, index, book, person, or other material that gives you information related to a fact or event in your family tree (from Ancestry.com).*

Determine What to Do with It

Once you have decided that you are going to at least pause in researching and collecting information about your genealogy, you need to then decide what you want to do with the information that you have collected. The first step, of course, is to prepare it and back it up so that you or someone else can carry it forward in the future. You can then look at if, how, and where you want to publish what you have.

Create a New Source

Describe the source record you are citing(e.g., book, source record, census index, etc.).

Title *(required)*

Enter the full name of the book, source record, census index, etc.

Author

Enter the person, persons, or organization from where the source originated from

Publisher

Enter the entity responsible for making the source available, i.e., a publishing house, university department, etc.

Publisher Location

Enter the location of the publisher

Publisher Date

Enter the publication date

Call Number

Enter the full library call number.

Note

Enter any other pertinent information related to this source.

REFN

Enter the full REFN.

Repository

Select a repository ▾   create a new repository

Enter the library or other location where the source was found.

Save Source   or Cancel

Figure 10-5: A source citation is a reference to specific information, or evidence about a fact or event in your family tree (from Ancestry.com).

NOTE

It may seem like overkill to make copies of your genealogy files on a CD/DVD, store them on both your computer and on the Internet, and keep a copy in your safety deposit box. The message is that you, your relatives, and your descendants do not want you to lose them. You have to decide what you have to do to assure that.

Prepare and Back Up Your Information

When you decide to pause or stop further work on your genealogy, it is very important that you leave your work in such a condition that it can be easily picked up and continued without having to redo the work you did. Perform these tasks to accomplish that:

1. If you haven't already, create one or more folders on your computer to store your computer-based genealogy work. Also create one or more paper folders and a file system to store your paper-based genealogy work.

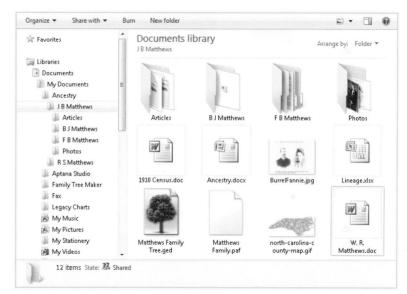

2. If you have both an online family tree—for example, in Ancestry .com—and one on your computer—for example, in Family Tree Maker— synch the two trees so that they are alike. Family Tree Maker does this automatically with Ancestry.

3. Create a GEDCOM file of your final (at least for the moment) family tree, either online or on a program on your computer, whichever holds the final family tree.

4. Store your GEDCOM file in the appropriate folder on your computer.

5. If you have paper photos and other genealogy-related paper documents and notes, scan them into your computer if that is possible. Also store the paper documents in the paper file system you created.

6. If you have photos and other documents that you have scanned into your computer or downloaded from online sources, place them in the appropriate genealogy folders you have created on your computer.

7. Copy your online genealogy folders to writable CDs or DVDs. You might also copy the online genealogy folders to an external hard drive or a second computer if either of those is available.

8. Copy your online genealogy folders to a cloud (Internet)–based online storage such as Microsoft's free SkyDrive, shown in Figure 10-6 (see the discussion in Chapter 3 on backing up your genealogy information).

9. Give copies of the CD/DVD that you made to close relatives that you hope will carry on your work. Additionally, or alternatively, give those relatives access to your cloud-based online storage account.

10. Store your paper files and a copy of your CD/DVD in a fireproof safe or in a bank safety deposit box.

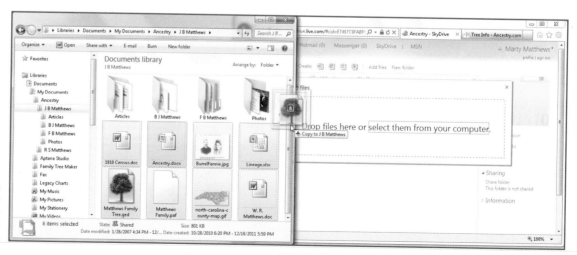

Figure 10-6: Storing your genealogy information on the Internet not only gives you a safer place to store your information, but it can also make transferring it to others easy.

Publish Your Information

After you have made sure your genealogy work has been saved and properly protected, you next should turn to how you want to distribute it to others. There are a number of possibilities:

- Share your family tree on Ancestry or other genealogy website.
- Print one or more of the reports in the program or online service you are using for genealogy information.
- Write articles, papers, pamphlets, and books on your ancestry supported by information in your family tree.
- Build a website around your family tree.

There is a significant difference in the level of activity in these four possible ways of publishing your family tree. The first two are relatively straightforward, and we'll look at them here. The fourth we'll briefly look at in the next section. Writing a document is so broad-based that it is outside the scope of this book, except for Harriet De Wolfe's experience in the genealogy story in this chapter.

SHARE YOUR FAMILY TREE

Ancestry.com provides several levels at which you can share your family tree.

1. In Ancestry display the family tree you want to share. Click **Tree Pages** and then click **Share Your Tree**. The Invite To dialog box will open.

2. Click the mail system you want to use for the invitation, for example, click **Email**.

3. Type the email address of the person you want to invite to share your family tree.

4. Click the down arrow under **Role** and select the role you want to use from those shown here.

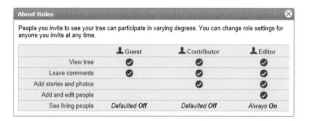

	Guest	Contributor	Editor
View tree	✓	✓	✓
Leave comments	✓	✓	✓
Add stories and photos		✓	✓
Add and edit people			✓
See living people	Defaulted Off	Defaulted Off	Always On

5. Add a personal message if you wish, and click **+Add Another Email** to add another person with whom you want to share your family tree.

6. When you have added all the email addresses that you want with their attendant roles and messages, click **Send Invites**. The invitation will be sent as you see here.

7. If you want to change or otherwise manage your invitees, display the family tree you want to share, click **Tree Pages**, click **Tree Settings**, and click **Sharing**. The Manage Invitees page will open.

8. You can change the nickname, revise the role, remove the person, and re-invite them. When you are ready, click **Save Changes**.

CAUTION

If your tree is linked to Family Tree Maker, you are reminded that if you let people edit your online family tree, that will also change the family tree in Family Tree Maker on your computer.

⚠ **This tree is linked to Family Tree Maker**

- Remember that anyone with the role of "Editor" will be able to edit your online tree and its linked tree in Family Tree Maker.
- When invitees make a change to this online tree, those changes are automatically copied to the linked tree in Family Tree Maker.

QUICKSTEPS

PRINTING IN FAMILY TREE MAKER

In the Ancestry.com family of products, printing of your family tree and associated information is handled with Family Tree Maker, which offers over 35 reports from which you can choose (see Figure 10-8). If you have both Ancestry and Family Tree Maker, Family Tree Maker will automatically import your family tree so you can work with it and print it. You can also export a GEDCOM file (see Chapter 3) from a number of programs and websites, and import it into Family Tree Maker (see Chapter 5). To print a report in Family Tree Maker:

1. Start Family Tree Maker, and once it is open click **Publish** in the menu bar. Initially you should see the charts displayed with the Collection tab, as shown in Figure 10-8.

Continued . . .

PRINT REPORTS

Printing in Ancestry.com is very limited. To get a full selection of reports, you need to use Family Tree Maker (see the "Printing in Family Tree Maker" QuickSteps in this chapter). In Ancestry you can print five generations at a time of your family tree in either Pedigree or Family view, and you can print an individual's profile.

1. In Ancestry, display the family tree you want to print and click either **Pedigree** or **Family** for the view you want.

2. Click the **Printer Friendly** icon in the controls on the left of the family tree. In the Printer Friendly page that opens, click **Print** in the upper-left corner of the page to open the Print dialog box.

3. Make any needed changes in the Print dialog box, and click **Print**. After printing you'll be taken back to your family tree.

4. To print additional generations, hover over the person in your family tree you want to start your next set of five generations (you can only print five at a time) and in the dialog box that opens, click **View Her/His Family Tree**, and then repeat steps 2 and 3.

5. To print a person's profile, hover over the person in your family tree whose profile you want to print, and click **View Profile**.

6. In the profile that opens, hover over **Print** above the tabs, click **Printer Friendly**, and then click **Print This Page**, as you can see in Figure 10-7.

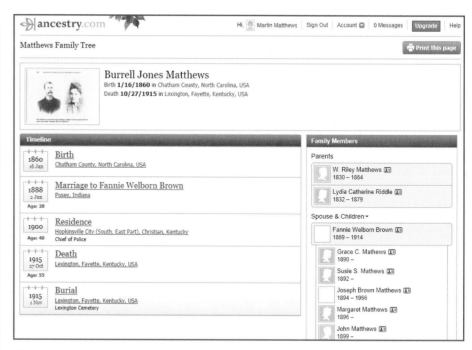

PRINTING IN FAMILY TREE MAKER

(Continued)

2. Click a chart that you are interested in looking at, and then click **Create Chart** in the left column. The chart will appear as you see in Figure 10-9.

3. In the left column you can customize the chart by clicking the icons at the top, by changing the chart title, by clicking **Advanced** to change the horizontal and vertical spacing, by changing the number of generations, and so on.

4. When you are ready, click **Print** near the upper-right corner, make any necessary changes in the Print dialog box, and click **OK**. You can also click **Share** to export as either a PDF or a JPG file.

5. Click the **Collection** tab and then click the various report types. Click several reports, and click **Create Reports** for each of them to see them in detail.

6. When you are ready, close Family Tree Maker.

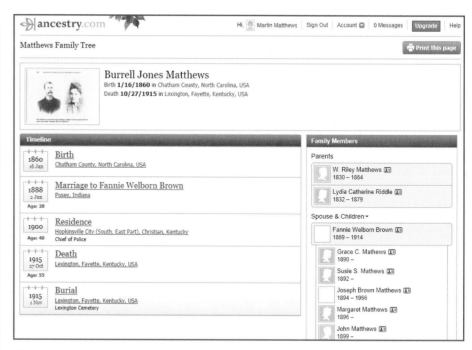

Figure 10-7: If you want a detailed paper backup of the people in your family tree, you can print out individual profile pages.

Put Your Ancestry Online

If you use Ancestry.com and leave your family tree public, which it is by default, some part of your ancestry is already online and available to others, unless you have blocked it. Ancestry searches for people on your family tree will find your tree and display the contents for others to use. As you saw earlier in this chapter, you can also invite people to view and, optionally, work on your family tree.

There are a number of other ways to put your genealogy information online, including the following:

● Create a home page on Genealogy.com that others can find and view.

● Request free space on RootsWeb.com and place a webpage there.

● Create your own website, host it where you want, and register it on RootsWeb.

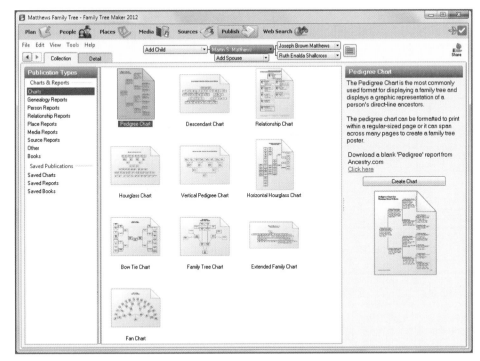

Figure 10-8: *Family Tree Maker provides an extensive set of charts and reports that can be printed from any family tree built in or imported into the program.*

We'll briefly talk about doing the first two ways and how to register the third.

Create a Home Page on Genealogy.com

Genealogy.com lets you create a free home page, basically a one-page website. Genealogy.com starts out by having you create a very basic home page. You can then come back and add to and/or change it.

1. Open Genealogy.com. Hover on **My Genealogy** in the menu bar, and click **My Home Page: Genealogy.com**. The Create Your Own Home Page page will open, as you see in Figure 10-10.

2. Type the title that you want at the top of your home page, then type a brief description of your family research, and click **Create Home Page Now**.

3. You are shown your home page. Click **Edit Your Home Page** to make any desired changes.

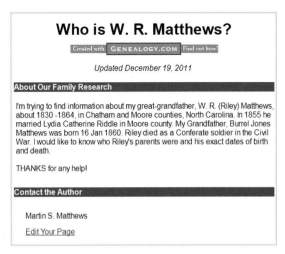

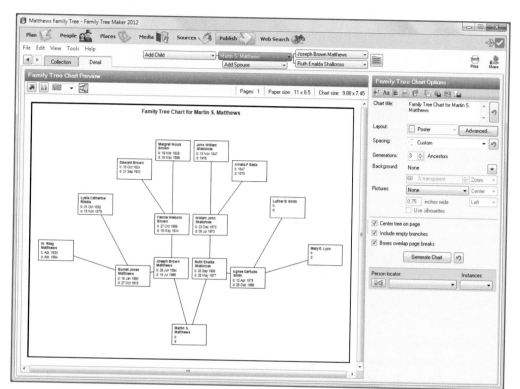

Figure 10-9: *You can do a significant amount of chart and report customization with the options available in Family Tree Maker.*

Use Web Space on RootsWeb.com

RootsWeb.com displays and provides access to a large collection of websites, as you can see in Figure 10-11. You can place a web presence on RootsWeb in three ways:

- Register a website you created and have hosted somewhere else.
- Request free web space for content you create.
- Host and register a website you create.

REGISTER A WEBSITE

If you have a website that you have created and have hosted outside of RootsWeb, you can register it in RootsWeb so people searching there can find it.

1. Open RootsWeb.com. In the home page that opens, click **Websites At RootsWeb** in the right column under Websites.

2. Click **Register Your Website** at the top of the left column.

3. In the Registering And Promoting Your Website page, clink **RootsLink** at the bottom of the page to open the registry page shown in Figure 10-12.

4. Enter the title of the website, its URL, and your email address. Select one category the site will be placed under, enter a short description, type the word displayed, and click **Submit URL**.

REQUEST FREE WEB SPACE

If you would like some free web space on RootsWeb, you can request it.

1. In the RootsWeb home page, click **Websites At RootsWeb** in the right column under Websites.

2. Click **Request Free Web Space** in the left column. In the page that opens, click **Freepages Accounts**.

Create Your Own Home Page

Now fill out the form below to choose what sort of information is on your home page. You will be able to change this information as often as you like after you create your page. You will also be able to add reports, photos, and family trees.

Step 1: Enter a Title and Text for Your Home Page

Title:
What do you want to appear at the top of your home page? You may want to include a name and location in your title, as in this example: "The Robert D. Johnsons of Nashville, TN."

(required)

About Your Family Research: *(required)*
Use this box to briefly (about 900 words or less) describe your family research, reunions, or other family news.

Step 2: Click to Finish

Create Home Page Now

Figure 10-10: Often, to find genealogy information you have to find the one person who has it. Having a home page just might be the way to find that person.

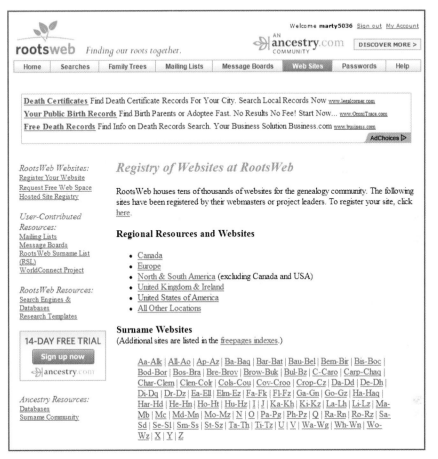

Figure 10-11: Through RootsWeb you can access other people's genealogy webpages by either surname or regional area.

3. Read the RootsWeb Agreement, and click **I Agree** at the bottom.

4. Read and fill in the request form, and click **Submit**.

A Request Submitted page will open and repeat the information you submitted.

One of the best pieces of advice in this book is in Harriet De Wolfe's genealogy story in this chapter. We'd like to repeat it here for reinforcement:

"A lot of success in genealogy research depends upon pure persistence. A person doesn't (most often) open a book and have her whole ancestry, or even the answer to part of an objective, fall in her lap. It takes opening many books, rolling through many microfilms, checking information from many websites, listening to many ideas, and on top of that, *serendipity*, to get most answers. The good thing is that the mystery and the hunt are large parts of the fun of genealogy."

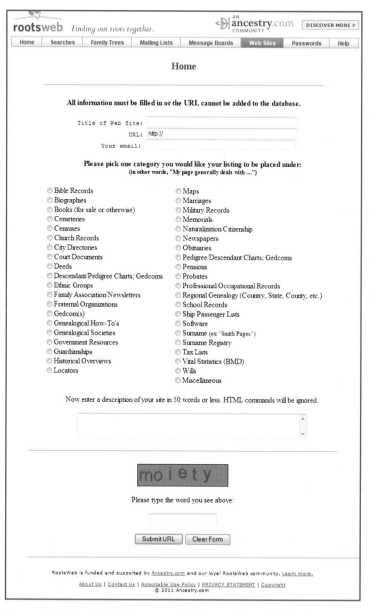

Figure 10-12: By registering your website, people can find it through RootsWeb.com

Harriet (Wahlstrand) De Wolfe, 72, Whidbey Island, WA

OVERVIEW

I have worked on genealogy for over 30 years and have been fascinated with it for a lot longer. I have visited The Church of Jesus Christ of Latter-Day Saints (LDS) Family History Center in Salt Lake City many times, often every year, and have visited homesteads, libraries, museums, cemeteries, battlegrounds, courthouses (one where my great-grandfather was hung), and historical societies where my relatives have lived, including Sweden, Canada, and several places within the United States. The culmination of all of this is a well-documented, over 200-page book entitled *One Corner of the World* about a fascinating segment of my ancestry, the story of Thomas and Elizabeth Allen Corner and their family during and after the War of 1812 (a 52-year period from 1806 to 1858) in northwestern New York state and southern Ontario (called "Upper Canada" at the time), Canada. I plan on distributing copies of this book to historical museums and libraries in Canada. I have also prepared and distributed notebooks of information and pictures to my immediate family members and shared various aspects of my genealogy work, especially work in Canada, with my local genealogy society.

In my work I have principally used Legacy software, although I have tried several others, and have spent extensive time on all the major websites, most of the secondary sites, and many of the niche sites. I do indexing every morning for FamilySearch.org as a payback for all they have done for family historians. I also believe strongly in local genealogy societies and clubs. They provide for the sharing of information and a strong base from which to learn from others how to do genealogy research.

STORY

When I was young I was sitting in my grandmother's kitchen listening to my mother and grandmother argue about our ancestors. Finally my grandmother went off and came back with a well-worn letter from which she read facts to convince my mother that my grandmother had been correct in their argument. My mother said she wanted a copy of that letter, but my grandmother wouldn't even let her look at a page of it and threatened to burn it. The letter remained a

source of friction until my grandmother said she had burned it. After a number of years when both my mother and grandmother had passed away, my aunt found the letter while cleaning out my grandmother's place and passed it on to my cousin. She casually mentioned it in a conversation and promised to send it to me. Figure 10-13 shows the first page of the letter, which is on various pieces of stationery from a defunct business.

The letter turned out to be pages and pages of disorganized family history, and at first blush, except for some alcoholism, there didn't seem to be any reason for my grandmother not sharing it. I began to try to organize it and found many holes that needed filling. I sent a copy of the letter to a cousin who works at the LDS Family History Center in Salt Lake City (my grandmother would *not* have been pleased to have that letter shared with anyone!). He sent me back a small newspaper clipping with the note "This is your family:"

> CORNER, Mrs. Thomas – Last Tues. evening, in Nelson, near Hannahsville, a man named Thomas Corner, having 2 wives living with him, came home intoxicated, when an altercation took place between him and one of the women; the other came to her rescue, and Corner discharged a pistol at her. He then beat his first victim with a boot-jack. Corner was lodged in jail Wed. He has already served 5 years for shooting his daughter. One of the women has since died, and the physician has lost hope of the other's recovery.

I was dumbfounded! Two wives! A double-murder! Poor Grandmother—afraid somehow the letter would lead to this part of the story—it was obvious why she was hiding it.

The Corner book I have written is in part about this infamous ancestor (he was the one hung outside the courthouse I visited). But to a larger extent, it is the story of his immigrant parents, Thomas and Elizabeth (Allen) Corner, early pioneers of Nelson Township, Upper Canada, and sadly forgotten in local histories. The tale encompasses what is known about their lives, the lives of their children, and the events that tore the fabric of the family apart.

SUBSTANTIATING THE LETTER

I finally got my copy of my grandmother's letter in the early 1980s, marking the beginning of my genealogy search. The original letter had been written by my grandmother's sister, Elsie Corner Cooper (shown in a late-1890s photo in Figure 10-14), who had obviously done a lot of research on our family. The letter provided many connections that got me started, but it also left a great deal for me to figure out.

[illegible] my aunt Elsie Cooper of Hoquiam, [illegible]

HOQUIAM MANUFACTURING CO.

GENERAL MILL WORK

GLASS

SIMPSON AVENUE AT ELEVENTH

HOQUIAM, WASH.

The first record we have of our forebears dates from 1688 or 1689, when our great, great, great-Grand father (probably) one of 3 brothers, went from Holland with Wm & Mary (an English Princess) when they were called to the throne of England, probably as soldiers in the army.

Two of the 3 brothers remained in England, but the third, Thomas (spelled Cornor in our old bible), settled in Ireland, married there, and in 1778, a descendant of his, another Thomas (and our Great Grand father) migrated to [illegible], when our grandfather (also Thomas) was only 4 years old, the youngest of 5 children.

The record states that Ontario, at that time [illegible] country, not having been settled [illegible] after the Revolutionary war, & our Great Grand father, and a few other venturesome souls were given [illegible] grant in the new [illegible].

The above information I gathered from an old diary of our Uncle Rev Charles Potts Corner (long dead) which is a treasured possession of another great granddaughter, [illegible] Corner Edwards of Long Island N.Y. [illegible] her father was a Methodist minister for most of [illegible] I sifted this all out when we [illegible] visited [illegible] in [illegible] — Elsie Corner Cooper June 27/52

Figure 10-13: **My grandmother refused to share a letter about our ancestry sent to her by her sister.**

Over the next 20 years I substantiated much of what was in the letter and filled many if not most of the holes. I did this through learning all I could about the practice of genealogy; taking annual trips to the Family History Library in Salt Lake City; taking trips to Ontario, Canada, and New York state; using the services of professional genealogists; and getting the help of other family members as interested as I in the family history.

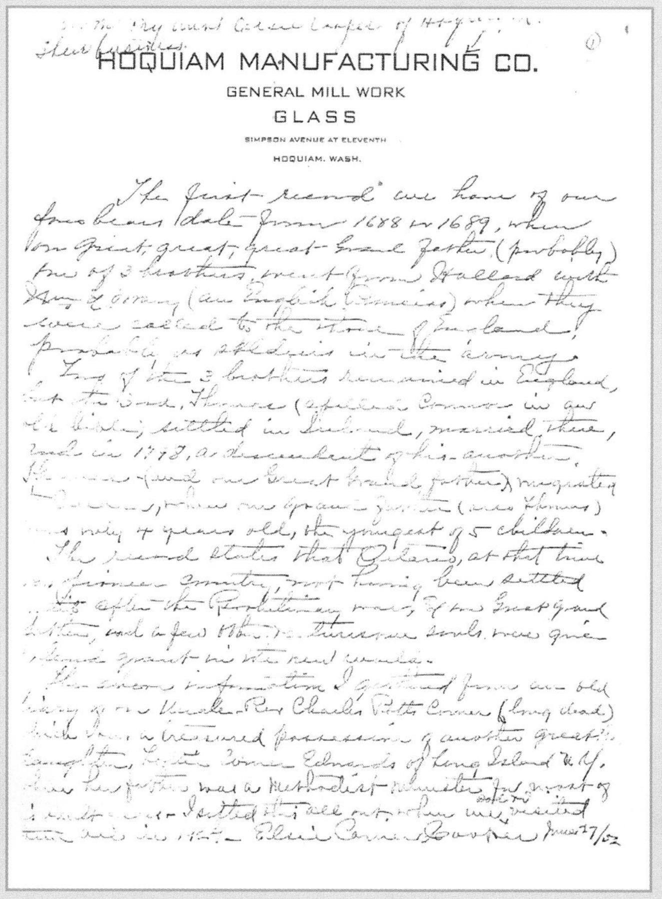

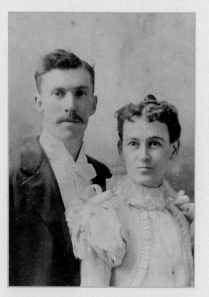

Figure 10-14: **Corner family historian Elsie Corner Cooper with her husband Cornelius, circa late 1890s**

My learning about the practice of genealogy took many forms, including reading a number of books, joining and actively participating in genealogy organizations, and the kind direction and advice of many individuals. Also, I learned much from my own problems and road blocks in 20 years of researching my family. The fundamental lesson was that a lot of genealogy research depends upon pure persistence. A person doesn't (most often) open a book and have her whole ancestry, or even the answer to part of an objective, fall in her lap. It takes opening many books, rolling through many microfilms, checking information from many websites, listening to many ideas, and on top of that, serendipity, to get most answers. The good thing is that the mystery and the hunt are large parts of the fun of genealogy.

The Family History Library, run by The LDS Church, is the largest genealogy library in the world (see Figure 10-15). It was invaluable to my research in three ways: I got direct information about my family, I got leads that helped me find information elsewhere, and I met professional genealogists that proved most helpful.

Figure 10-15: The LDS Family History Library in Salt Lake City © Intellectual Reserve, Inc. Used by Permission.

Before going to the Family History Library each year, I establish clear objectives for what I want to accomplish during that visit, such as "establish a documented connection between two ancestors." I then go through the library's online catalog and find everything I can about each objective. The catalog will list the books that I need to look at while I am at the library. These books include family histories that have been contributed to the library and are by surname and locations (for example, "Corners of New York State"). There are also thousands of rolls of microfilmed documents covering subjects such as court records, government records, military records, church records, and many, many other subjects. I was able to find linkages among family members and a number of relatives in a few family history narratives where I sometimes got the name and address of the person who contributed the information. This sometimes led to communicating with people who gave me other leads and introduced me to more family members.

On occasion, while at the Family History Library, I will hire Gordon Remington, a professional genealogist who is a specialist on New York state genealogy, to give me ideas of where to search and which books in the library to look at.

This is an invaluable time-saver and can get me looking at references I would not have otherwise found. Gordon is a ProGenealogist on Ancestry.com (see progenealogists.com/gremington.htm), has published two books on New York state genealogy, and has received numerous awards and accolades from his peers.

There is nothing like seeing and being in the area where your ancestors lived to have a closer understanding of their lives. I have made several trips to Ontario, Canada (see the photo in Figure 10-16 of the Corner home farm) and New York state for that reason and to visit libraries, courthouses, and archives to search for ancestral records. From these sources I have found substantial information and numerous documents.

While the trips are fun and rewarding, most of the documents that I have acquired have come from writing to the institution holding the sources I needed, such as Archives Canada, and sometimes from hiring genealogists in the area to search in archives or libraries when that service was not provided by the institution. It was through a by-mail source chase that I got Thomas Corner's

Figure 10-16: Corner home farm in Nelson Township, Ontario, as it was in 2006. It has remained rural for 200 years in spite of the threat of urban encroachment.

Crown Patent (similar to a U.S. Land Grant), shown in Figure 10-17, that he received in 1806 for 200 acres of land in what is now Nelson Township, Ontario, where he and his family became one of the earliest settlers.

260

PROVINCE OF UPPER-CANADA.

GEORGE the THIRD by the grace of GOD of the United Kingdom of Great-Britain and Ireland, King, Defender of the Faith.

To all to whom these Presents shall come,—GREETING.

Know Ye, that we of our special grace, certain knowledge, and mere motion have Given and Granted, and by these presents DO GIVE and GRANT unto

heirs and assigns for ever: ALL that parcel or tract of land situate In the Township of Nelson in the County of York in the Home District

in our said Province, containing by admeasurement

Two Hundred Acres

be the same more or less; being Lot Number

together with all the Woods and Waters thereon lying and being, under the reservations, limitations and conditions herein after expressed: which said Two Hundred Acres of Land are

butted and bounded, or may be otherwise known as follows; that is to say

TO HAVE AND TO HOLD the said parcel and tract of land hereby given and granted to him the said Thomas Corner his heirs and assigns for ever; saving nevertheless to us, our heirs and successors, all mines of Gold, Silver, Copper, Tin, Lead, Iron and Coal that shall or may be hereafter found on any part of the said parcel or tract of land hereby given and granted as aforesaid; and saving and reserving to us, our heirs and successors, all white Pine Trees that shall, or may now, or hereafter grow or be growing, on any part of the said parcel or tract of land hereby granted as aforesaid.

Provided always, that no part of the parcel or tract of land hereby given and granted to the said Thomas Corner and his heirs, be within any reservation heretofore made, and marked for us, our heirs and successors, by our Surveyor.

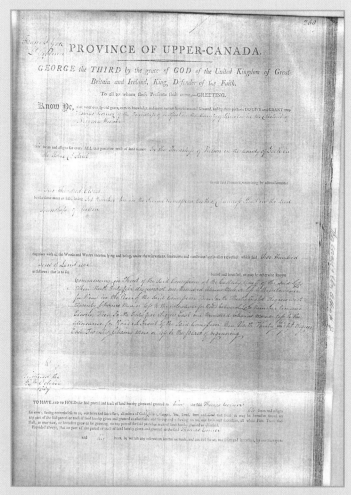

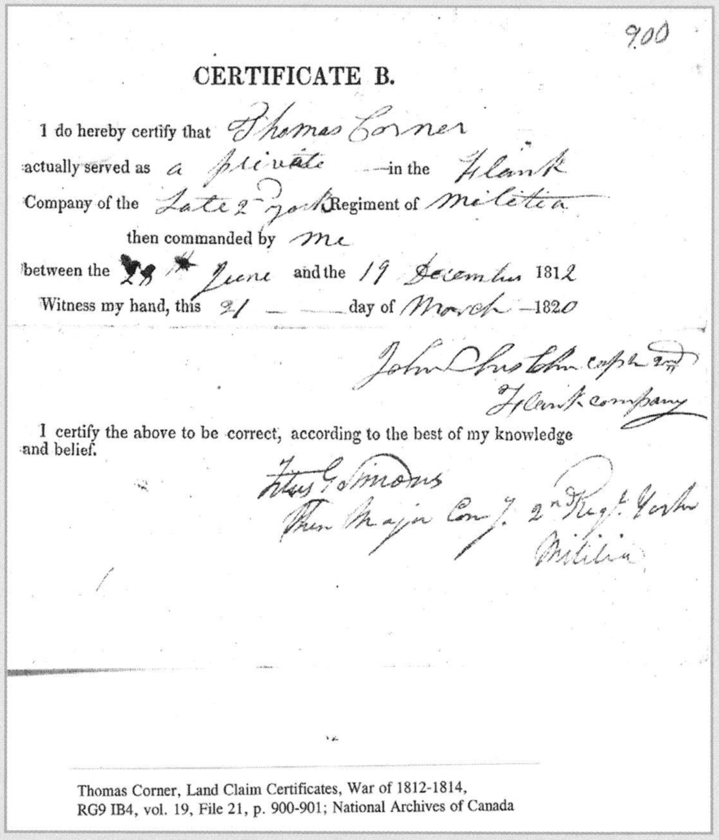

Figure 10-17: Portion of Thomas Corner's Crown Land Patent from the Crown Land Registry in Peterborough, Ontario.

In 2006, on the 200th anniversary of Thomas Corner getting his Crown Patent, I met with about 30 other of his descendants in Nelson Township, Ontario, and visited the family property, the places where the family had lived, and the local battlefields where he and his sons had fought in the War of 1812 (see Thomas Corner's certificate of service in Figure 10-18). It was a very poignant time for us and something that most probably Thomas and Elizabeth Corner would

900

CERTIFICATE B.

I do hereby certify that Thomas Corner actually served as a private in the Flank Company of the Late 2nd York Regiment of Militia then commanded by me between the 28th June and the 19 December 1812

Witness my hand, this 21 day of March 1820

John Chisholm Capt 2nd Flank company

I certify the above to be correct, according to the best of my knowledge and belief.

Titus G. Simons
Then Major Com. 2nd Regt. York Militia

Thomas Corner, Land Claim Certificates, War of 1812-1814, RG9 IB4, vol. 19, File 21, p. 900-901; National Archives of Canada

Figure 10-18: Thomas Corner's certificate of service for the War of 1812. The certificate allowed Thomas to acquire free land in exchange for his military service.

have appreciated, to have so many of their descendants gathered on their land 200 years after they petitioned for and received it.

The 2006 gathering of Corner descendants also indicated the level of interest in the family history, and a number of them have worked on their own and with me to build it. Several of us, spread across the United States and Canada, continue to keep in relatively close contact, work on separate areas and events in the family, and then pool the results. I could not have gotten where I am in this story without these people.

Another group of people that have been very helpful to me are amateur genealogists who volunteer in a program called Random Acts of Genealogical Kindness (RAOGK). It is a lightly knit web-based group who volunteer to help other amateur genealogists do research in the volunteer's local area. For example, when I needed some information from a courthouse or cemetery in New York state, I contacted a RAOGK volunteer and asked if they could possibly do what I needed. I almost always get what I want, often with "Okay, what else do you need?" It was a wonderful service. Unfortunately, in October 2011 the website (raogk.org) that was coordinating it had to shut down due to equipment problems and the passing of the administrator. The administrator's husband has promised to restart it in the future, but with no promised date. In the meantime there is a Facebook group (facebook.com/groups/33868082803/) where some of the volunteers can be contacted (the original site had 4,000 volunteers worldwide associated with it).

WRITING AND PUBLISHING THE STORY

By 2006 I had between 90 and 95 percent of the information about the original immigrant Corner family well confirmed and was starting to think about putting what I had found in a document with the comprehensive sourcing I had established. I had read enough family histories to know that I wanted to put my family history in the context of the time and location.

As a result, I felt I needed to learn more about the history of the early 1800s, the War of 1812, and about life in southern Ontario and northwestern New York at that time. I had read some, but wanted more.

I then learned of a year-long evening continuing education program at the University of Washington in genealogy and family history that combined history with family history and was taught by two instructors, one for each subject (see Figure 10-19). The intent of the course was to learn how to both unearth new

Figure 10-19: A University of Washington program helped me add history to my family history.

facts about one's ancestors, as well as view that information within the political, economic, and social context of the time. This program is actually three classes taught in the fall, winter, and spring quarters, beginning with learning about research techniques and sources for research, and ending with a presentation of findings and the submittal of a completed family history project. Two friends and I decided to take the class and dedicate a full day of library research every week to it. We arrived at the university at 8:30 or so in the morning, spent the day in the library reading and doing research, and attended the class from 6 to 8:30 in the evening—a very intense 12-hour day (add to this, I live on an island in Puget Sound and had a two-hour commute each way). It was for this program that I wrote what became the over 200-page book of the Thomas and Elizabeth Corner line of my family. The program gave me the ability to put my ancestral research into a historically correct social, economic, geographical, and military context.

criminal actions, 165

divorce and separate maintenance, 165

formats, 166

guardianship, 165

naturalization, 165

probate, 165

property lines, 165

real property disputes, 165

searching, 148, 166

wills, 165

cousins, relationship of, 26

CPU requirements, considering, 38

criminal action records, accessing, 165

culture, studying past and present, 216–218

CyndisList.com, 6

described, 87

ships' passenger lists, 152, 172

using, 145–146

D

daguerrotypes, described, 225

DAR (Daughters of the American Revolution), 163

DAR file for Wilder family, 179

"Dartmouth papers," 100

databases, using, 159

Davis, Elizabeth, 178

Davis, Jefferson, 177–178

De Wolfe, Harriet, 253–258

death certificates

information on, 22

primary versus secondary sources, 222

death records, searching, 145, 148. *See also* cemetery sites; graves; obituaries

denominations, searching, 152–153

Dewey Decimal system, 161

digital camera, system requirements for, 39

display requirements, considering, 38

divorce and separate maintenance records, accessing, 165

DNA family projects, 127–128

DNA tests

mfDNA, 224

Y-line, 224

documenting findings, 7

documenting personal stories

ancestors, 20–21

milestones, 20

relatives, 20–21

documents

accuracy, 25

analyzing, 23

Bibles, 24

collecting, 21–22

getting from Fold3.com, 143–144

organizing, 23

system requirements, 39

translating, 218–219

Donation Land Claims (D.L.C.), 7–8

double-quotes ("), using with search terms, 78

DVDs, copying folders to, 244

E

ecclesiastical records, searching, 168

ecclesiastical sites, searching, 152–153

EllisIsland.org, searching, 146

England, researching ancestors from, 213–214

ethnic heritage, getting information about, 218

ethnic records, searching, 170–171

European ancestry, searching, 171

F

Facebook groups, 196–199

adding friends to, 201

asking questions, 203–204

chatting with, 202

comments, 206–207

creating documents, 202–203

creating events, 204–206

deleting, 207

discussions, 207

event invitations, 206

finding, 199–200

Invite Friends option, 205

joining, 200

leaving, 206–207

memberships, 201

polling members, 203–204

posting links, 203

requests, 201

responding to comments, 207

searching for, 199–200

sharing comments, 206–207

sharing links, 204

taking polls, 203–204

viewing members of, 202

viewing photos, 206

family accomplishments, considering, 7–8

family history

organizing, 147

researching, 147

Family History Library, 161–162, 254–255. *See also* libraries
family information, collecting, 102–103
family medical history, creating, 169–170
family pictures, going through, 9, 218. *See also* photographs
family relationships, 26
Family Search Center, 166
family sites, investigating, 96
Family Tree Builder, downloading, 141–142
Family Tree Maker software
    creating family trees, 49
    downloading from Ancestry.com, 50
    entering people into, 47–48
    .ged files, 49
    importing files, 49
    installing, 45–47
    linking family trees, 50
    purchasing, 45–47
    requirements, 38
family trees. *See also* "world family tree"
    Family Tree Maker software, 49
    getting information from, 33
    Legacy software, 52
    merging, 148
    protecting, 83
    relationships in, 26
    sharing, 245–246
    starting, 102
FamilySearch.org, 84–86
    account setup, 115–116
    census records, 118–119
    copying information, 118, 122
    Exact checkbox, 117
    improving searches, 138
    learning resources, 136–137

pasting information, 118, 122
searching, 122, 136–137
searching for family trees, 119–122, 124
searching for individuals, 116–119
sorting search results, 118
FamilyTreeSearcher.com, 87
fashions, viewing to date photos, 226
federal sites
    Bureau of Land Management, 90–92
    Library of Congress, 90
    National Archives, 90
female names, searching in United States, 135
ferrotypes, described, 225
Find utility, opening, 78
findagrave.com, searching, 147
Fold3.com, 3
    getting documents from, 143–144
    searching, 143–144
Foote, Becky, 177–182
Foote, John, 178
Foote, Margaret (Leitch), 178
foreign records, searching, 170–171
forms, creating for ancestors, 219

G

Gabelein, Arthur Frederic, 155
Gabelein, Minna Juliana (Kramer), 155
Gabelein family, 154
gazetteer, contents of, 158
GB (gigabyte), explained, 39
Gbps (gigabits per second), explained, 40
GEDCOM file format
    explained, 40–41, 84
    exporting from Ancestry.com, 51–52

importing into Ancestry.com, 111–112
    Legacy software, 54–55
    using, 49, 243
    viewing data, 55–56
genealogical societies, 190, 192
genealogist criteria, comparing, 228
genealogy
    communities, 96
    groups, 96
    origin, 1
    sourcing, 241–242
genealogy information
    asking for, 132
    backing up, 243
    collaborating, 220–221
    conflicting, 221
    preparing, 243
    publishing, 245–247
    putting online, 248–252
    reviewing, 219
    storing on Internet, 244
genealogy libraries, working with, 94. *See also* libraries
genealogy numbering systems, using, 228
genealogy resources
    1900 Census, 14
    blogs, 14–15
    cemetery records, 13–14
    communities, 14–15
    forums, 14–15
    government information, 14
    headstones, 13–14
    memory and documents, 11–12
    online sites, 14–15
    querying relatives, 12
    searching library collections, 13

indexes
    American Genealogical-
        Biographical, 227
    using, 132–133, 138, 159
indexing projects, volunteering for, 166
Industrial Revolution, impact of, 215–216
information
    asking for, 132
    backing up, 243
    collaborating, 220–221
    conflicting, 221
    preparing, 243
    publishing, 245–247
    putting online, 248–252
    reviewing, 219
    storing on Internet, 244
Inglis, Ruth, 21
Inglis, Sidney Arthur, 22
international records, finding, 170–171. *See
   also* immigration sites
Internet, 39. *See also* searching
    adware, 59
    antivirus programs, 59–60
    controlling security, 61–62
    safety, 58
    security programs, 59–60
    spyware, 59
    threats, 58–59
    Trojan horses, 59
    viruses, 59
    worms, 59
Internet browser requirements,
   considering, 38
Internet connection requirements,
   considering, 38

Internet Explorer
    controlling content, 62
    InPrivate Browsing, 62
    security settings, 61
interviewing relatives, 27
IPL (Internet Public Library), 161–162
Ireland, researching ancestors from,
   213–214
Irish potato famine, 213
Island County, Washington, 7–8
Islands in the Ocean of Memory, 17

J

Jenanne's story, 70–73
    challenges, 71–72
    getting started, 70–71
    objectives, 72–73

K

Kaspersky Internet Security, 60
KB (kilobyte), explained, 39
Kbps (kilobits per second), explained, 40
kindredtraits.com, 87

L

Laing, Jenny, 98
Lamont, Allister, 32
Lamont, Godfrey, 32
Lamont, Hugh, 32
land deeds, primary versus secondary
   sources, 222
land grants, researching, 91

LDS church, Tracing Immigrant Origins
   guide, 170
LDS Family History Library, 161–162,
   254–255. *See also* libraries
Legacy software
    downloading, 51–53
    entering events, 57–58
    entering people into, 55–57
    family trees, 52
    GEDCOM file format, 54–55
    importing information, 54–55
    purchasing, 51–53
    requirements, 38
    setting up family trees, 53–54
    setting up folders, 51
Legge, George, 99–100
Legge, Patricia Anne, 98
Leitch, Olive, 180–181
Lemont, Thomas, 30–32
libraries. *See also* Family History Library;
   genealogy libraries; local libraries
    Allen County Public, 164
    DAR (Daughters of the American
        Revolution), 163
    Family History Library, 161–162
    New England Historic, 164
    New York Public, 164
    Newberry, 163–164
    regional, 164
    state, 164
Library of Congress, 90
    classification system, 162
    online catalog, 159
    purpose, 162–163
    using, 163
Like A USB Flash Drive option, 66

local libraries. *See also* libraries; online
 libraries
  catalogs, 159, 161–162
  databases, 159
  Dewey Decimal system, 161
  indexes, 159
  microfiche, 159
  microfilm, 159
  resources, 158
locations, trying alternatives, 223–224
locking computers, 68–69
Lyon, Waldo, 28

M

Macomb, John N., 210
magazine articles, finding, 96
marriage certificates, primary versus
 secondary sources, 222
marriage licenses, information on, 23
marriage records, searching, 148
marriages, adding second, 136
Marty's story, 29–33
  ancestry by J B Matthews, 1938, 30
  challenges, 30–31
  family tree, 29
  father's maternal line, 32
  getting started, 29–30
  objectives, 31–33
  overview, 29
  searching process, 30
  substantiating ancestry, 30
Matthews, Burrel Jones, 105–109
Matthews forum, 185
Matthews, Joseph B., 24, 27, 160
Matthews, Martin S., 27

Matthews, Riley, 212
Matthews, W. R., 122
Matthews, W. Riley, 120
MB (megabyte), explained, 39
Mbps (megabits per second), explained, 40
medical facility records, using, 169–170
medical history, creating, 169
Mellroth, Dora Norene, 154
memory requirements, considering, 38
memory size, explained, 39
mfDNA testing, 224
MHz (mega Hertz), explained, 40
microfiche, using, 159
microfilm, using, 159
Microsoft Office 2010 requirements, 38
Microsoft Security Essentials, 60
Microsoft Word, translation tool in, 218
milestones, documenting, 20
military information, finding, 3
military records
  information in, 27, 225
  primary versus secondary sources, 222
  searching, 148
  searching for, 91
military sites, searching, 152
Mounts, Eli Polk, 17
Mounts, James, 7–8
mouse requirements, considering, 38
Moyer Hay, Sarah, 208
'Mr. Bellevue', 25
The Munger Book, 125
Murphy, Barbara, 71, 73
Murphy, Jenanne, 70–73
Murphy, John W., 70
Murphy, Michael, 70–73

MyFamily.com, building websites at,
 142–143
MyHeritage.com, 85–87
  Family Tree Builder, 141–142
  searching, 141–142

N

names. *See also* surnames
  searching in United States, 222–223
  varied spellings, 105
National Archives, 90, 151
national archives, accessing, 174
The National Personnel Records Center, 3
Native Americans
  genealogy database, 145
  researching ancestry, 190
naturalization records
  accessing, 165
  primary versus secondary sources, 222
nephews, relationship of, 26
New England Historic Genealogical
 Society, 164
New York Public Library, 164
Newberry Library, 163–164
newspaper resources
  information in, 25
  primary versus secondary sources, 222
  using, 95
Nichols, Anne, 233
Nichols, Milton Elmer, 230, 233
Nichols, Pricilla Anne, 230
nieces, relationship of, 26
Norton Internet Security, 60
NOT search term, using, 76

roadblocks. *See also* searching
  analyzing, 212
  evaluating, 237–238
Rodgers, John, 208–210
Rodgers, Thomas, 208
Roots Magic software, requirements, 38
Roots-L mailing list, considering, 190–193
RootsWeb.com, 6, 84
  Baptist Roots page, 153
  email archive, 188–189
  links, 188
  mailing lists, 139–140, 188–189
  message boards, 140
  registering websites, 250, 252
  requesting web space, 250–251
  searching, 138–139
  website links, 190–191
  WorldConnect Project, 139
royalty, finding members of, 32

S

Sandberg, Bobbi, 16–18
scanning documents, 39
Schûrch, Hans, 230
Schûrch family generations, 231
Scotland, researching ancestors from, 213–214
search directories, using, 80
search sites
  Bing tips, 79–80
  Google hints, 78–79
  using, 76
search techniques, 80
search terms
  AND, 76
  NOT, 76

OR, 76
  using double-quotes (") with, 78
  WITH, 76–77
searches, narrowing down, 80
SearchForAncestors.com, using, 171
searching. *See also* Internet; obstacles to research
  AccessGenealogy.com, 145
  AncestorHunt.com, 145
  Ancestry.com, 133–135
  birth records, 148
  cemeteries, 167–168
  census data, 149–151
  census records, 148
  church records, 152–153
  compilations, 132–133
  courthouse records, 148, 166
  death records, 145, 148
  ecclesiastical sites, 152–153
  EllisIsland.org, 146
  ethnic records, 170–171
  European ancestry, 171
  FamilySearch.org, 136–137
  findagrave.com, 147
  Fold3.com, 143–144
  foreign records, 170–171
  genealogylinks.net, 171
  genealogytoday.com, 147
  GeneaSearch.com, 147
  gengateway.com, 147
  gensource.com, 148
  immigration sites, 151–152
  indexes, 132–133
  international records, 170–171
  marriage records, 148
  military records, 148
  military sites, 152

MyHeritage.com, 141–142
names in United States, 222–223
National Archives, 151
OneGreatFamily.com, 148
RootsWeb.com, 138–140
ship passenger lists, 152
state indexes, 145
vital records, 148–149
WorldVitalRecords.com, 148
searching Internet, stating queries, 132
secondary versus primary sources, 221–222
security programs, using, 59–60
Selective Service documents, information in, 27
serial numbers, use in military, 3
Shallcross, Edward, 20, 24
Shallcross, John William, 20
Shallcross, William "Bill," 25
Shallcross, William John, 20, 27
Shell, John, 155
Shell, Marguerite, 155
Shell family, 156
ship passenger lists, searching, 152
Shirk, Dorothy, 230
Shirk, Joseph, 230–231
Shirk, Michael Martin, 230
siblings, relationship of, 26
Sires, Miron William, 155
Sires, Pamela Sue, 154
Sires family, 156
sites. *See* genealogy sites; websites
SkyDrive page, opening, 67
Smith, Luther B., 20
software
  alternatives, 42–44
  choosing, 44

software (*cont.*)
    comparing, 42–43
    Find the Best site, 43
    requirements, 38
    reviewing needs for, 41–42
    running, 37–38
    Top Ten Reviews, 42
Soundex utility, using with Ancestry,
    134–135
source citation, creating, 241–243
sources
    assuring, 239–240
    checking, 220
    citing, 132–133
    expanding, 222–223
    finding, 120–122
    primary versus secondary, 221–222
spellings, trying alternatives, 226–227
spouses, adding second, 136
spyware, definition and solution, 59
state government sites, locating, 92–93, 97
state indexes, searching, 145
state websites, accessing, 77
stories. *See* genealogy stories
success in genealogy, basis of, 252, 254
surnames, finding, 147, 193. *See also* names
Swedish immigration site, 218

T

tasks, identifying, 36–37
tax rolls, primary versus secondary
    sources, 222
TB (terabyte), explained, 39
time periods
    determining, 225
    expanding, 224–226

tintypes, described, 225
tombstone rubbings, considering, 168
Tom's story, 125–129
    1860 Census, 127
    1910 Census, 125–126
    challenges, 127–128
    getting started, 125–126
    objectives, 129
    overview, 125
Tracing Immigrant Origins guide, 170
translation tools, 218–219
transmission speeds, explained, 40
Transportation act of 1717, 213
Trevor's story, 98–100
    challenges, 100
    getting started, 98–99
    objectives, 100
    overview, 98
Trojan horses, definition and solution, 59

U

uncles, relationship of, 26
universities
    archives, 94–95
    special collections, 94–95
University of Idaho online resource, 164. *See also* online libraries
University of Washington program,
    257–258
U.S. Citizenship and Immigration
    Services, 151
U.S. military information, finding, 3
U.S. Passenger Lists, information in, 217
USGenWeb.com genealogy site, 6

V

verifying relationships, 7
viruses, definition and solution, 59
vital records, searching, 148–149
voice, recording, 9

W

Wahlstrand De Wolfe, Harriet, 253–258
Wakefield Wilder, Mary, 178
Wallace, Leander, 5
Wallace, Ruthinda, 7–8
Wallace, William, 7–8
Washington, Martha (Dandridge), 178
web directories, using, 80
websites. *See also* genealogy sites
    archives, 94
    categorizing, 61
    church records, 94
    Family Search Center, 166
    fashions for dating photos, 226
    finding, 77
    genealogists, 228
    genealogy libraries, 94
    genealogy numbering systems, 228
    Historical Timeline, 212
    immigration, 213, 215
    immigration lists, 217
    indentured servants, 214
    Library of Congress, 162
    newspaper resources, 95
    passenger lists, 217
    photos and time periods, 225
    professional genealogists, 228
    RAOGK (Random Acts of Genealogical
        Kindness), 257